THE LIFE AND LETTERS
OF
MARY WOLLSTONECRAFT SHELLEY

VOLUME I

PREFACE

The following biography was undertaken at the request of Sir Percy and Lady Shelley, and has been compiled from the MS. journals and letters in their possession, which were entrusted to me, without reserve, for this purpose.

The earlier portions of the journal having been placed also at Professor Dowden's disposal for his *Life of Shelley*, it will be found that in my first volume many passages indispensable to a life of Mary Shelley have already appeared, in one form or another, in Professor Dowden's pages. This fact I have had to ignore, having indeed settled on the quotations necessary to my narrative before the *Life of Shelley* appeared. They are given without comment or dilution, just as they occur; where omissions are made it is in order to avoid repetition, or because the everyday entries refer to trivial circumstances uninteresting to the general reader.

[Pg vi]Letters which have previously been published are shortened when they are only of moderate interest; unpublished letters are given complete wherever possible.

Those who hope to find in these pages much new circumstantial evidence on the vexed subject of Shelley's separation from his first wife will be disappointed. No contemporary document now exists which puts the case beyond the reach of argument. Collateral evidence is not wanting, but even were this not beyond the scope of the present work it would be wrong on the strength of it to assert more than that Shelley himself felt certain of his wife's unfaithfulness. Of that there is no doubt, nor of the fact that all such evidence as did afterwards transpire went to prove him more likely to have been right than wrong in his belief.

My first thanks are due to Sir Percy and Lady Shelley for the use of their invaluable documents,—for the photographs of original pictures which form the basis of the illustrations,—and last, not least, for their kindly help and sympathy during the fulfilment of my task.

I wish especially to express my gratitude to Mrs. Charles Call for her kind permission to me[Pg vii] to print the letters of her father, Mr. Trelawny, which are among the most interesting of my unpublished materials.

I have to thank Miss Stuart, from whom I obtained important letters from Mr. Baxter and Godwin; and Mr. A. C. Haden, through whom I made the acquaintance of Miss Christy Baxter.

To Professor Dowden, and, above all, to Mr. Garnett, I am indebted for much valuable help, I may say, of all kinds.

FLORENCE A. MARSHALL.

CHAPTER I

They say that thou wert lovely from thy birth,
Of glorious parents, thou aspiring Child.
I wonder not, for one then left the earth
Whose life was like a setting planet mild,
Which clothed thee in the radiance undefiled
Of its departing glory: still her fame
Shines on thee thro' the tempest dark and wild
Which shakes these latter days; and thou canst claim
The shelter, from thy Sire, of an immortal name.
SHELLEY.

"So you really have seen Godwin, and had little Mary in your arms! the only offspring of a union that will certainly be matchless in the present generation." So, in 1798, wrote Sir Henry Taylor's mother to her husband, who had travelled from Durham to London for the purpose of making acquaintance with the famous author of *Political Justice*.

[Pg 2]This "little Mary," the daughter of William and Mary Wollstonecraft Godwin, was destined herself to form a union the memory of which will live even longer than that of her illustrious parents. She is remembered as *Mary Shelley*, wife of the poet. In any complete account of his life she plays, next to his, the most important part. Young as she was during the few years they passed together, her character and her intellect were strong enough to affect, to modify, in some degree to mould his. That he became what he did is in great measure due to her. This, if nothing more were known of her, would be sufficient to stamp her as a remarkable woman, of rare ability and moral excellence, well deserving of a niche in the almost universal biographical series of the present day. But, besides this, she would have been eminent among her sex at any time, in any circumstances, and would, it cannot be doubted, have achieved greater personal fame than she actually did but for the fact that she became, at a very early age, the wife of Shelley. Not only has his name overshadowed her, but the circumstances of her association with him were such as to check to a considerable extent her own sources of invention and activity. Had that freedom been her lot in which her mother's destiny shaped itself, her talents must have asserted themselves as not inferior, as in some respects superior, to[Pg 3] those of Mary Wollstonecraft. This is the answer to the question, sometimes asked,—as if, in becoming Shelley's wife, she had forfeited all claim to individual consideration,—why any separate Life of her should be written at all. Even as a completion of Shelley's own story, Mary's Life is necessary. There remains the fact that her husband's biographers have been busy with her name. It is impossible now to pass it over in silence and indifference. She has been variously misunderstood. It has been her lot to be idealised as one who gave up all for love, and to be condemned and anathematised for the very same reason. She has been extolled for perfections she did not possess, and decried for the absence of those she possessed in the highest degree. She has been lauded as a genius, and depreciated as one overrated, whose talent would never have been heard of at all but for the name of Shelley. To her husband she has been esteemed alternately a blessing and the reverse.

As a fact, it is probable that no woman of like endowments and promise ever abdicated her own individuality in favour of another so transcendently greater. To consider Mary altogether apart from Shelley is, indeed, not possible, but the study of the effect, on life and character, of this memorable union is unique of its kind. From Shelley's point[Pg 4] of view it has been variously considered; from Mary's, as yet, not at all.

Mary Wollstonecraft Godwin was born on the 30th of August 1797.

Her father, the philosopher and philosophical novelist, William Godwin, began his career as a Dissenting minister in Norfolk, and something of the preacher's character adhered to him all his life. Not the apostolic preacher. No enthusiasm of faith or devotion, no constraining fervour, eliciting the like in others, were his, but a calm, earnest, philosophic spirit, with an irresistible impulse to guide and advise others.

This same calm rationalism got the better, in no long time, of his religious creed, which he seems to have abandoned slowly, gradually, and deliberately, without painful struggle. His religion, of the head alone, was easily replaced by other views for which intellectual qualities were all-sufficient. Of a cool, unemotional temperament, safe from any snares of passion or imagination, he became the very type of a town philosopher. Abstractions of the intellect and the philosophy of politics were his world. He had a true townsman's love of the theatre, but external nature for the most part left him unaffected, as it found him. With the most exalted opinion of his own genius and merit, he was nervously susceptible to the[Pg 5] criticism of others, yet always ready to combat any judgment unfavourable to himself. Never weary of argument, he thought that by its means, conducted on lines of reason, all questions might be finally settled, all problems satisfactorily and speedily solved. Hence the fascination he possessed for those in doubt and distress of mind. Cool rather than cold-hearted, he had a certain benignity of nature which, joined to intellectual exaltation, passed as warmth and fervour. His kindness was very great to young men at the "storm and stress" period of their lives. They for their part thought that, as he was delighted to enter into, discuss and analyse their difficulties, he must, himself, have felt all these difficulties and have overcome them; and, whether they followed his proffered advice or not, they never failed to look up to him as an oracle.

Friendships Godwin had, but of love he seems to have kept absolutely clear until at the age of forty-three he met Mary Wollstonecraft. He had not much believed in love as a disturbing element, and had openly avowed in his writings that he thought it usurped far too large a place in the ordinary plan of human life. He did not think it needful to reckon with passion or emotion as factors in the sum of existence, and in his ideal programme they played no part at all.

Mary Wollstonecraft was in all respects his[Pg 6] opposite. Her ardent, impulsive, Irish nature had stood the test of an early life of much unhappiness. Her childhood's home had been a wretched one; suffering and hardship were her earliest companions. She had had not only to maintain herself, but to be the support of others weaker than herself, and many of these had proved unworthy of her devotion. But her rare nature had risen superior to these trials, which, far from crushing her, elicited her finest qualities.

The indignation aroused in her by injustice and oppression, her revolt against the consecrated tyranny of conventionality, impelled her to raise her voice in behalf of the weak and unfortunate. The book which made her name famous, *A Vindication of the Rights of Women*, won for her then, as it has done since, an admiration from half of mankind only equalled by the reprobation of the other half. Yet most of its theories, then considered so dangerously extreme, would to-day be contested by few, although the frankness of expression thought so shocking now attracted no special notice then, and indicated no coarseness of feeling, but only the habit of calling things by their names.

In 1792, desiring to become better acquainted with the French language, and also to follow on the spot the development of France's efforts in[Pg 7] the cause of freedom, she went to Paris, where, in a short time, owing to the unforeseen progress of the Revolution, she was virtually imprisoned, in the sense of being unable to return to England. Here she met Captain Gilbert Imlay, an American, between whom and herself an attachment sprang up, and whose wife, in all but the legal and religious ceremony, she became. This step she took in full conscientiousness. Had she married Imlay she must have openly declared her true position as a British subject, an act which would have been fraught with the most dangerous, perhaps fatal consequences to them both. A woman of strong religious feeling, she had upheld the sanctity of marriage in her writings, yet not on religious grounds. The heart of marriage, and reason for it, with her, was love. She regarded herself as Imlay's lawful wife, and had perfect faith in his constancy. It wore out, however, and after causing her much suspense, anxiety, and affliction, he finally left her with a little girl some eighteen months old. Her grief was excessive, and for a time threatened to affect her reason. But her healthy temperament prevailed, and the powerful tie of maternal love saved her from the consequences of despair. It was well for her that she had to work hard at her literary occupations to support herself and her little daughter.

It was at this juncture that she became[Pg 8] acquainted with William Godwin. They had already met once, before Mary's sojourn in France, but at this first interview neither was impressed by the other. Since her return to London he had shunned her because she was too much talked about in society. Imagining her to be obtrusively "strong-minded" and deficient in delicacy, he was too strongly prejudiced against her even to read her books. But by degrees he was won over. He saw her warmth of heart, her generous temper, her vigour of intellect; he saw too that she had suffered. Such susceptibility as he had was fanned into warmth. His critical acumen could not but detect her rare quality and worth, although the keen sense of humour and Irish charm which fascinated others may, with him, have told against her for a time. But the nervous vanity which formed his closest link with ordinary human nature must have been flattered by the growing preference of one so widely admired, and whom he discovered to be even more deserving of admiration and esteem than the world knew. As to her, accustomed as she was to homage, she may have felt that for the first time she was justly appreciated, and to her wounded and smarting susceptibilities this balm of appreciation must have been immeasurable. Her first freshness of feeling had been wasted on a love which proved to have been one-sided and[Pg 9] which had recoiled on itself. To love and be loved again was the beginning of a new life for her. And so it came about that the coldest of men and the warmest of women found their happiness in each other. Thus drawn together, the discipline afforded to her nature by the rudest realities of life, to his by the severities of study, had been such as to promise a growing and a lasting companionship and affection.

In the short memoir of his wife, prefixed by Godwin to his published collection of her letters, he has given his own account, a touching one, of the growth and recognition of their love.

The partiality we conceived for each other was in that mode which I have always considered as the purest and most refined style of love. It would have been impossible for the most minute observer to have said who was before and who was after. One sex did not take the priority which long-established custom has awarded it, nor the other overstep that delicacy which is so severely imposed. I am not conscious that either party can assume to have the agent or the patient, the toil spreader or the prey, in the affair. When in the course of things the disclosure came, there was nothing in a manner for either party to disclose to the other....

There was no period of throes and resolute explanation attendant on the tale. It was friendship melting into love.

They did not, however, marry at once. Godwin's opinion of marriage, looked on as indissoluble, was that it was "a law, and the worst of all laws." In accordance with this view, the[Pg 10] ceremony did not take place till their union had lasted some months, and when it did, it was regarded by Godwin in the light of a distinct concession. He expresses himself most decisively on this point in a letter to his friend, Mr. Wedgwood of Etruria (printed by Mr. Kegan Paul in his memoirs of Godwin), announcing his marriage, which had actually taken place a month before, but had been kept secret.

Some persons have found an inconsistency between my practice in this instance and my doctrines. But I cannot see it. The doctrine of my *Political Justice* is, that an attachment in some degree permanent between two persons of opposite sexes is right, but that marriage, as practised in European countries, is wrong. I still adhere to that opinion. Nothing but a regard for the happiness of the individual, which I have no right to ignore, could have induced me to submit to an institution which I wish to see abolished, and which I would recommend to my fellow-men never to practise but with the greatest caution. Having done what I thought was necessary for the peace and respectability of the individual, I hold myself no otherwise bound than I was before the ceremony took place.

It is certain that he did not repent his concession. But their wedded happiness was of short duration. On 30th August 1797 a little girl was born to them.

All seemed well at first with the mother. But during the night which followed alarming symptoms made their appearance. For a time it was hoped that these had been overcome, and a[Pg 11] deceptive rally of two days set Godwin free from anxiety. But a change for the worst supervened, and after four days of intense suffering, sweetly and patiently borne, Mary died, and Godwin was again alone.

[Pg 12]
CHAPTER II
AUGUST 1797-JUNE 1812

Alone, in the sense of absence of companionship, but not alone in the sense that he was before, for, when he lost his wife, two helpless little girl-lives were left dependent on him. One was Fanny, Mary Wollstonecraft's child by Imlay, now three and a half years old; the other the newly-born baby, named after her mother, Mary Wollstonecraft, and the subject of this memoir.

The tenderness of her mother's warm heart, her father's ripe wisdom, the rich inheritance of intellect and genius which was her birthright, all these seemed to promise her the happiest of childhoods. But these bright prospects were clouded within a few hours of her birth by that change in her mother's condition which, ten days later, ended in death.

The little infant was left to the care of a father of much theoretic wisdom but profound practical ignorance, so confirmed in his old bachelor ways by years and habit that, even when love so far conquered him as to make him quit the single[Pg 13] state, he declined family life, and carried on a double existence, taking rooms a few doors from his wife's home, and combining the joys—as yet none of the cares—of matrimony with the independence, and as much as possible of the irresponsibility, of bachelorhood. Godwin's sympathies with childhood had been first elicited by his intercourse with little Fanny Imlay, whom, from the time of his union, he treated as his own daughter, and to whom he was unvaryingly kind and indulgent.

He moved at once after his wife's death into the house, Polygon, Somers Town, where she had lived, and took up his abode there with the two children. They had a nurse, and various lady friends of the Godwins, Mrs. Reveley and others, gave occasional assistance or superintendence. An experiment was tried of a lady-housekeeper which, however, failed, as the lady in becoming devoted to the children showed a disposition to become devoted to Godwin also, construing civilities into marked attentions, resenting fancied slights, and becoming at last an insupportable thorn in the poor philosopher's side. His letters speak of his despondency and feeling of unfitness to have the care of these young creatures devolved on him, and with this sense there came also the renewed perception of the rare maternal qualities of the wife he had lost.

[Pg 14]"The poor children!" he wrote, six weeks after his bereavement. "I am myself totally unfitted to educate them. The scepticism which perhaps sometimes leads me right in matters of speculation is torment to me when I would attempt to direct the infant mind. I am the most unfit person for this office; she was the best qualified in the world. What a change! The loss of the children is less remediless than mine. You can understand the difference."

The immediate consequence of this was that he, who had passed so many years in contented bachelorhood, made, within a short time, repeated proposals of marriage to different ladies, some of them urged with a pertinacity nothing short of ludicrous, so ingenuously and argumentatively plain does he make it that he found it simply incredible any woman should refuse him to whom he had condescended to propose. His former objections to marriage are never now alluded to and seem relegated to the category of obsolete theories. Nothing testifies so strongly to his married happiness as his constant efforts to recover any part of it, and his faith in the possibility of doing so. In 1798 he proposed again and again to a Miss Lee whom he had not seen half a dozen times. In 1799 he importuned the beautiful Mrs. Reveley, who had, herself, only been a widow for a month, to marry him. He was really attached to her, and was much wounded when, not long after, she married a Mr. Gisborne.

During Godwin's preoccupations and occasional[Pg 15] absences, the kindest and most faithful friend the children had was James Marshall, who acted as Godwin's amanuensis, and was devotedly attached to him and all who belonged to him.

In 1801 Godwin married a Mrs. Clairmont, his next-door neighbour, a widow with a son, Charles, about Fanny's age, and a daughter, Jane, somewhat younger than little Mary. The new

Mrs. Godwin was a clever, bustling, second-rate woman, glib of tongue and pen, with a temper undisciplined and uncontrolled; not bad-hearted, but with a complete absence of all the finer sensibilities; possessing a fund of what is called "knowledge of the world," and a plucky, enterprising, happy-go-lucky disposition, which seemed to the philosophic and unpractical Godwin, in its way, a manifestation of genius. Besides, she was clever enough to admire Godwin, and frank enough to tell him so, points which must have been greatly in her favour.

Although her father's remarriage proved a source of lifelong unhappiness to Mary, it may not have been a bad thing for her and Fanny at the time. Instead of being left to the care of servants, with the occasional supervision of chance friends, they were looked after with solicitous, if not always the most judicious care. The three little girls were near enough of an age to be companions to each other, but Fanny was the senior by three years and a half. She bore Godwin's name, and was[Pg 16] considered and treated as the eldest daughter of the house.

Godwin's worldly circumstances were at all times most precarious, nor had he the capability or force of will to establish them permanently on a better footing. His earnings from his literary works were always forestalled long before they were due, and he was in the constant habit of applying to his friends for loans or advances of money which often could only be repaid by similar aid from some other quarter.

In the hope of mending their fortunes a little, Mrs. Godwin, in 1805, induced her husband to make a venture as a publisher. He set up a small place of business in Hanway Street, in the name of his foreman, Baldwin, deeming that his own name might operate prejudicially with the public on account of his advanced political and social opinions, and also that his own standing in the literary world might suffer did it become known that he was connected with trade. Mrs. Godwin was the chief practical manager in this business, which finally involved her husband in ruin, but for a time promised well enough. The chief feature in the enterprise was a "Magazine of Books for the use and amusement of children," published by Godwin under the name of Baldwin; books of history, mythology, and fable, all admirably written for their special purpose.[Pg 17] He used to test his juvenile works by reading them to his children and observing the effect. Their remark would be (so he says), "How easy this is! Why, we learn it by heart almost as fast as we read it." "Their suffrage," he adds, "gave me courage, and I carried on my work to the end." Mrs. Godwin translated, for the business, several childrens' books from the French. Among other works specially written, Lamb's *Tales from Shakespeare* owes its existence to "M. J. Godwin & Co.," the name under which the firm was finally established.

New and larger premises were taken in Skinner Street, Holborn, and in the autumn of 1807 the whole family, which now included five young ones, of whom Charles Clairmont was the eldest, and William, the son of Godwin and his second wife, the youngest, removed to a house next door to the publishing office. Here they remained until 1822.

No continuous record exists of the family life, and the numerous letters of Godwin and Mrs. Godwin when either was absent from home contain only occasional references to it. Both parents were too much occupied with business systematically to superintend the children's education. Mrs. Godwin, however, seems to have taken a bustling interest in ordering it, and scrupulously refers to Godwin all points of doubt or[Pg 18] discussion. From his letters one would judge that, while he gave due attention to each point, discussing *pros* and *cons* with his deliberate impartiality, his wife practically decided everything. Although they sometimes quarrelled (on one occasion to the extent of seriously proposing to separate) they always made it up again, nor is there any sign that on the subject of the children's training they ever had any real difference of opinion. Mrs. Godwin's jealous fussiness gave Godwin abundant opportunities for the exercise of philosophy, and to the inherent untruthfulness of her manner and speech he remained strangely and philosophically blind. From allusions in letters we gather that the children had a daily governess, with occasional lessons from a master, Mr. Burton. It is often asserted that Mrs. Godwin was a harsh and cruel stepmother, who made the children's home miserable. There is nothing to prove this. Later on, when moral guidance and sympathy were needed, she fell short indeed of what she might have been. But for the material wellbeing of the children she cared well enough, and was at any rate desirous that they should be happy, whether or not she always took the best means of making them so. And Godwin placed full confidence in her practical powers.

In May 1811 Mrs. Godwin and all the children except Fanny, who stayed at home to keep house[Pg 19] for Godwin, went for sea-bathing to Margate, moving afterwards to Ramsgate. This had been urged by Mr. Cline, the family doctor, for the good of little Mary, who, during some years of her otherwise healthy girlhood, suffered from a weakness in one arm. They boarded at the house of a Miss Petman, who kept a ladies' school, but had their sleeping apartments at an inn or other lodging. Mary, however, was sent to stay altogether at Miss Petman's, in order to be quiet, and in particular to be out of the way of little William, "he made so boisterous a noise when going to bed at night."

The sea-breezes soon worked the desired effect. "Mary's arm is better," writes Mrs. Godwin on the 10th of June. "She begins to move and use it." So marked and rapid was the improvement that Mrs. Godwin thought it would be as well to leave her behind for a longer stay when the rest returned to town, and wrote to consult Godwin about it. His answer is characteristic.

When I do not answer any of the lesser points in your letters, it is because I fully agree with you, and therefore do not think it necessary to draw out an answer point by point, but am content to assent by silence.... This was the case as to Mary's being left in the care of Miss Petman. It was recommended by Mr. Cline from the first that she should stay six months; to this recommendation we both assented. It shall be so, if it can, and undoubtedly I conceived you, on the spot, most competent to select the residence.

[Pg 20]Mary accordingly remained at Miss Petman's as a boarder, perhaps as a pupil also, till 19th December, when, from her father's laconic but minute and scrupulously accurate diary, we learn that she returned home. For the next five months she was in Skinner Street, participating in its busy, irregular family life, its ups and downs, its anxieties, discomforts, and amusements, its keen intellectual activity and lively interest in social and literary matters, in all of which the young people took their full share. Entries are frequent in Godwin's diary of visits to the theatre, of tea-drinkings, of guests of all sorts at home. One of these guests affords us, in his journal, some agreeable glimpses into the Godwin household.

This was the celebrated Aaron Burr, sometime Vice-President of the United States, now an exile and a wanderer in Europe.

At the time of his election he had got into disgrace with his party, and, when nominated for the Governorship of New York, he had been opposed and defeated by his former allies. The bitter contest led to a duel between him and Alexander Hamilton, in which the latter was killed. Disfranchised by the laws of New York for having fought a duel, and indicted (though acquitted) for murder in New Jersey, Burr set out on a journey through the Western States, nourishing schemes of sedition and revenge. When he[Pg 21] purchased 400,000 acres of land on the Red River, and gave his adherents to understand that the Spanish Dominions were to be conquered, his proceedings excited alarm. President Jefferson issued a proclamation against him, and he was arrested on a charge of high treason. Nothing could, however, be positively proved, and after a six months' trial he was liberated. He at once started for Europe, having planned an attack on Mexico, for which he hoped to get funds and adherents. He was disappointed, and during the four years which he passed in Europe he often lived in the greatest poverty.

On his first visit to England, in 1808, Burr met Godwin only once, but the entry in his journal, besides bearing indirect witness to the great celebrity of Mary Wollstonecraft in America, gives an idea of the kind of impression made on a stranger by the second Mrs. Godwin.

"I have seen the two daughters of Mary Wollstonecraft," he writes. "They are very fine children (the eldest no longer a child, being now fifteen), but scarcely a discernible trace of the mother. Now Godwin has been seven or eight years married to a second wife, a sensible, amiable woman."

For the next four years Burr was a wanderer in Holland and France. His journal, kept for the benefit of his daughter Theodosia, to whom[Pg 22] he also addressed a number of letters, is full of strange and stirring interest. In 1812 he came back to England, where it was not long before he drifted to Godwin's door. Burr's character was licentious and unscrupulous, but his appearance and manners were highly prepossessing; he made friends wherever he went. The Godwin household was full of hospitality for such Bohemian wanderers as he. Always itself in a precarious state of fortune, it held out the hand of fellowship to others whose existence from day to day was uncertain. A man of brains and ideas, of congenial and lively temperament, was sure of a fraternal welcome. And though many of Godwin's older friends were, in time, estranged from him through their antipathy to his wife, she was full of patronising good-nature for a man like Burr, who well knew how to ingratiate himself.

Burr's Journal, February 15, 1812.—Had only time to get to Godwin's, where we dined. In the evening William, the only son of William Godwin, a lad of about nine years old, gave his weekly lecture: having heard how Coleridge and others lectured, he would also lecture, and one of his sisters (Mary, I think) writes a lecture which he reads from a little pulpit which they have erected for him. He went through it with great gravity and decorum. The subject was "The influence of government on the character of a people." After the lecture we had tea, and the girls danced and sang an hour, and at nine came home.

Nothing can give a pleasanter picture of the family, the lively-minded children keenly interested[Pg 23] in all the subjects and ideas they heard freely discussed around them; the elders taking pleasure in encouraging the children's first essays of intellect; Mary at fourteen already showing her powers of thought and inborn vocation to write, and supplying her little brother with ideas. The reverse of the medal appears in the next entry, for the genial unconventional household was generally on the verge of ruin, and dependent on some expected loan for subsistence in the next few months. When once the sought-for assistance came they revelled in momentary relief from care.

Journal, February 18.—Have gone this evening to Godwin's. They are in trouble. Some financial affair.

It did not weigh long on their spirits.

February 24.—Called at Godwin's to leave the newspapers which I borrowed yesterday, and to get that of to-day. *Les goddesses*(so he habitually designates the three girls) kept me by acclamation to tea with *la printresse* Hopwood. I agreed to go with the girls to call on her on Friday.

February 28.—Was engaged to dine to-day at Godwin's, and to walk with the four dames. After dinner to the Hopwoods. All which was done.

March 7.—To Godwin's, where I took tea with the children in their room.

March 14.—To Godwin's. He was out. Madame and *les enfans* upstairs in the bedroom, where they received me, and I drank tea with his *enfans*.... Terribly afraid of vigils to-night, for Jane made my tea, and, I fear, too strong. It is only Fan that I can trust.

March 17.—To Godwin's, where took tea with the children, who always have it at 9. Mr. and Madame at 7.

[Pg 24]*March 22.*—On to Godwin's; found him at breakfast and joined him. Madame a-bed.

Later.—Mr. and Mrs. Godwin would not give me their account, which must be five or six pounds, a very serious sum for them. They say that when I succeed in the world they will call on me for help.

This probably means that the Godwins had lent him money. He was well-nigh penniless, and Mrs. Godwin exerted herself to get resources for him, to sell one or two books of value which he had, and to get a good price for his watch. She knew a good deal of the makeshifts of poverty, and none of the family seemed to have grudged time or trouble if they could do a good turn to this companion in difficulties. It is a question whether, when they talked of his succeeding in the world, they were aware of the particular form of success for which he was scheming; in any case they seem to have been content to take him as they found him. They were the last friends from whom he parted on the eve of sailing for America. His entry just before starting is—

Called and passed an hour with the Godwins. That family does really love me. Fanny, Mary, and Jane, also little William: you must not forget, either, Hannah Hopwood, *la printresse*.

These few months were, very likely, the brightest which Mary ever passed at home. Her rapidly growing powers of mind and observation were nourished and developed by the stimulating intellectual atmosphere around her; to the anxieties[Pg 25] and uncertainties which, like birds of ill-omen, hovered over the household and were never absent for long together, she was well accustomed, besides which she was still too young to be much affected by them. She was fond of her sisters, and devoted to her father. Mrs. Godwin's temperament can never have been congenial to hers, but occasions of collision do not appear to have been frequent, and Fanny, devoted and unselfish, only anxious for others to be happy and ready herself to serve any of them, was the link between them all. Mary's health was, however, not yet satisfactory, and before the summer an opportunity which offered itself of change of air was willingly accepted on her behalf by Mr. and Mrs. Godwin. In 1809 Godwin had made the acquaintance of Mr. William Baxter of Dundee, on the introduction of Mr. David Booth, who afterwards became Baxter's son-in-law. Baxter, a man of liberal mind, independence of thought and action, and kindly nature, shared to the full the respect entertained by most thinking men of that generation for the author of *Political Justice*. Godwin, always accessible to sympathetic strangers, was at once pleased with this new acquaintance.

"I thank you," he wrote to Booth, "for your introduction of Mr. Baxter. I dare swear he is an honest man, and he is no fool." During Baxter's[Pg 26] several visits to London they became better acquainted. Charles Clairmont too, went to Edinburgh in 1811, as a clerk in Constable's printing office, where he met and made friends with Baxter's son Robert, who, as well as his father, visited the Skinner Street household in London, and through whom the intimacy was cemented. In this way it was that Mary was invited to come on a long visit to the Baxters at their house, "The Cottage," on the banks of the Tay, just outside Dundee, on the road to Broughty Ferry. The family included several girls, near Mary's own age, and with true Scotch hospitality they pressed her to make one of their family circle for an indefinite length of time, until sea-air and sea-bathing should have completed the recovery begun the year before at Ramsgate, but which could not be maintained in the smoky air and indoor life of London. Accordingly, Mary sailed for Dundee on the 8th of June 1812.

CHAPTER III
JUNE 1812-MAY 1814
GODWIN TO BAXTER.

SKINNER STREET, LONDON.
8th June 1812.

MY DEAR SIR—I have shipped off to you by yesterday's packet, the *Osnaburgh*, Captain Wishart, my only daughter. I attended her, with her two sisters, to the wharf, and remained an hour on board, till the vessel got under way. I cannot help feeling a thousand anxieties in parting with her, for the first time, for so great a distance, and these anxieties were increased by the manner of sending her, on board a ship, with not a single face around her that she had ever seen till that morning. She is four months short of fifteen years of age. I, however, spoke to the captain, using your name; I beside gave her in charge to a lady, by name I believe Mrs. Nelson, of Great St. Helen's, London, who was going to your part of the island in attendance upon an invalid husband. She was surrounded by three daughters when I spoke to her, and she answered me very agreeably. "I shall have none of my own daughters with me, and shall therefore have the more leisure to attend to yours."

I daresay she will arrive more dead than alive, as she is extremely subject to sea-sickness, and the voyage will, not improbably, last nearly a week. Mr. Cline, the surgeon, however, decides that a sea-voyage would probably be of more service to her than anything.

I am quite confounded to think what trouble I am bringing on you and your family, and to what a degree I may be said to have taken you in when I took you at your word in your invitation upon so slight an acquaintance. The old proverb says, "He is a wise father who knows his own child," and I feel the justness of the apothegm on the present occasion.

There never can be a perfect equality between father and child, and if he has other objects and avocations to fill up the greater part of his time, the ordinary resource is for him to proclaim his wishes and commands in a way somewhat sententious and authoritative, and occasionally to utter his censures with seriousness and emphasis.

It can, therefore, seldom happen that he is the confidant of his child, or that the child does not feel some degree of awe or restraint in intercourse with him. I am not, therefore, a perfect judge of Mary's character. I believe she has nothing of what is commonly called vices, and that she has considerable talent. But I tremble for the trouble I may be bringing on you in this visit. In my last I desired that you would consider the first two or three weeks as a trial, how far you can ensure her, or, more fairly and impartially speaking, how far her habits and conceptions may be such as to put your family very unreasonably out of their way; and I expect from the frankness and ingenuousness of yours of the 29th inst. (which by the way was so ingenuous as to come without a seal) that you will not for a moment hesitate to inform me if such should be the case. When I say all this, I hope you will be aware that I do not desire that she should be treated with extraordinary attention, or that any one of your family should put themselves in the smallest degree out of their way on her account. I am anxious that she should be brought up (in this respect) like a philosopher, even like a cynic. It will add greatly to the strength and worth of her character. I should also observe that she has no love of dissipation, and will be perfectly satisfied with your woods and your mountains. I wish, too, that she should be *excited* to industry. She has occasionally great perseverance, but occasionally, too, she shows great need to be roused.

You are aware that she comes to the sea-side for the purpose of bathing. I should wish that you would inquire now and then into the regularity of that. She will want also some treatment for her arm, but she has Mr. Cline's directions completely in all these points, and will probably not require a professional man to look after her while she is with you. In all other respects except her arm she has admirable health, has an excellent appetite, and is capable of enduring fatigue. Mrs. Godwin reminds me that I ought to have said something about troubling your daughters to procure a washerwoman. But I trust that, without its being necessary to be thus minute, you will proceed on the basis of our being earnest to give you as little trouble as the nature of the case will allow.—I am, my dear sir, with great regard, yours,

WILLIAM GODWIN.

At Dundee, with the Baxters, Mary remained for five months. She was treated as a sister by the Baxter girls, one of whom, Isabella, afterwards the wife of David Booth, became her most intimate friend. An elder sister, Miss Christian Baxter, to whom the present writer is indebted for a few personal reminiscences of Mary Godwin, only died in 1886, and was probably the last survivor of those who remembered Mary in her girlhood. They were all fond of their new companion. She was agreeable, vivacious, and sparkling; very pretty, with fair hair and complexion, and clear, bright white skin. The Baxters were people of education and culture,[Pg 30] active minded, fond of reading, and alive to external impressions. The young people were well and carefully brought up. Mary shared in all their studies.

Music they did not care for, but all were fond of drawing and painting, and had good lessons. A great deal of time was spent in touring about, in long walks and drives through the moors and mountains of Forfarshire. They took pains to make Mary acquainted with all the country round, besides which it was laid on her as a duty to get as much fresh air as she could, and she must greatly have enjoyed the well-ordered yet easy life, the complete change of scene and companionship. When, on the 10th of November, she arrived again in Skinner Street, she brought Christy Baxter with her, for a long return visit to London. If Mary had enjoyed her country outing, still more keenly did the homely Scotch girl relish her first taste of London life and society. At ninety-two years old the impression of her pleasure in it, of her interest in all the notable people with whom she came in contact, was as vivid as ever.

The literary and artistic circle which still hung about the Skinner Street philosophers was to Christy a new world, of which, except from books, she had formed no idea. Books, however, had laid the foundation of keenest interest[Pg 31] in all she was to see. She was constantly in company with Lamb, Hazlitt, Coleridge, Constable, and many more, hitherto known to her only by name. Of Charles Lamb especially, of his wit, humour, and quaintness she retained the liveliest recollection, and he had evidently a great liking for her, referring jokingly to her in his letters as "Doctor Christy," and often inviting her, with the Godwin family, to tea, to meet her relatives, when up in town, or other friends.

On 11th November, the very day after the two girls arrived in London, a meeting occurred of no special interest to Christy at the time, and which she would have soon forgotten but for subsequent events. Three guests came to dinner at Godwin's. These were Percy Bysshe Shelley with his wife Harriet, and her sister, Eliza Westbrook. Christy Baxter well remembered this, but her chief recollection was of Harriet, her beauty, her brilliant complexion and lovely hair, and the elegance of her purple satin dress. Of Shelley, how he looked, what he said or did, what they all thought of him, she had observed nothing, except that he was very attentive to Harriet. The meeting was of no apparent significance and passed without remark: little indeed did any one foresee the drama soon to follow. Plenty of more important days, more interesting meetings to Christy, followed during the next few[Pg 32] months. She shared Mary's room during this time, but her memory, in old age, afforded few details of their everyday intercourse. Indeed, although they spent so much time together, these two were never very intimate. Isabella Baxter, afterwards Mrs. Booth, was Mary's especial friend and chief correspondent, and it is much to be regretted that none of their girlish letters have been preserved.

The four girls had plenty of liberty, and, what with reading and talk, with constantly varied society enjoyed in the intimate unconstrained way of those who cannot afford the *appareil* of convention, with tolerably frequent visits at friends' houses and not seldom to the theatre, when Godwin, as often happened, got a box sent him, they had plenty of amusement too. Godwin's diary keeps a wonderfully minute skeleton account of their doings. Christy enjoyed it all as only a novice can do. All her recollections of the family life were agreeable; if anything had left an unpleasing impression it had faded away in 1883, when the present writer saw her. For Godwin she entertained a warm respect and affection. They did not see very much of him, but Christy was a favourite of his, and he would sometimes take a quiet pleasure, not unmixed with amusement, in listening to their girlish talks and arguments. One such discussion she [Pg 33]distinctly remembered, on the subject of woman's vocation, as to whether it should be purely domestic, or whether they should engage in outside interests. Mary and Jane upheld the latter view, Fanny and Christy the other.

Mrs. Godwin was kind to Christy, who always saw her best side, and never would hear a word said against her. Her deficiencies were not palpable to an outsider whom she liked and chose to patronise, nor did Christy appear to have felt the inherent untruthfulness in Mrs. Godwin's character, although one famous instance of it was recorded by Isabella Baxter, and is given at length in Mr. Kegan Paul's *Life of Godwin*.

The various members of the family had more independence of habits than is common in English domestic life. This was perhaps a relic of Godwin's old idea, that much evil and weariness resulted from the supposed necessity that the members of a family should spend all or most of their time in each other's company. He always breakfasted alone. Mrs. Godwin did so also, and not till mid-day. The young folks had theirs together. Dinner was a family meal, but supper seems to have been a movable feast. Jane Clairmont, of whose education not much is known beyond the fact that she was sometimes at school, was at home for a part if not all of this time. She was lively and quick-witted, and probably[Pg 34] rather unmanageable. Fanny was more reflective, less sanguine, more alive to the prosaic obligations of life, and with a keen sense of domestic duty, early developed in her by necessity and by her position as the eldest of this somewhat anomalous family. Godwin, by nature as undemonstrative as possible, showed more affection to Fanny than to any one else. He always turned to her for any little service he might require. It seemed, said Christy, as though he would fain have guarded against the possibility of her feeling that she, an orphan, was less to him than the others. Christy was of opinion that Fanny was not made aware of her real position till her quite later years, a fact which, if true, goes far towards explaining much of her after life. It seems most likely, at any rate, that at this time she was unacquainted with the circumstances of her birth. To Godwin she had always seemed like his own eldest child, the first he had cared for or who had been fond of him, and his dependence on her was not surprising, for no daughter could have tended him with more solicitous care; besides which, she was one of those people, ready to do anything for everybody, who are always at the beck and call of others, and always in request. She filled the home, to which Mary, so constantly absent, was just now only a visitor.

[Pg 35]It must have been at about this time that Godwin received a letter from an unknown correspondent, who expressed much curiosity to know whether his children were brought up in accordance with the ideas, by some considered so revolutionary and dangerous, of Mary Wollstonecraft, and what the result was of reducing her theories to actual practice. Godwin's answer, giving his own description of her two daughters, has often been printed, but it is worth giving here.

Your inquiries relate principally to the two daughters of Mary Wollstonecraft. They are neither of them brought up with an exclusive attention to the system of their mother. I lost her in 1797, and in 1801 I married a second time. One among the motives which led me to choose this was the feeling I had in myself of an incompetence for the education of daughters. The present Mrs. Godwin has great strength and activity of mind, but is not exclusively a follower of their mother; and indeed, having formed a family establishment without having a previous provision for the support of a family, neither Mrs. Godwin nor I have leisure enough for reducing novel theories of education to practice, while we both of us honestly endeavour, as far as our opportunities will permit, to improve the minds and characters of the younger branches of the family.

Of the two persons to whom your inquiries relate, my own daughter is considerably superior in capacity to the one her mother had before. Fanny, the eldest, is of a quiet, modest, unshowy disposition, somewhat given to indolence, which is her greatest fault, but sober, observing, peculiarly clear and distinct in the faculty of memory, and disposed to exercise her own thoughts and follow her own judgment. Mary, my daughter, is the reverse of her in many particulars. She is singularly bold, somewhat imperious, and active of mind.[Pg 36] Her desire of knowledge is great, and her perseverance in everything she undertakes almost invincible. My own daughter is, I believe, very pretty. Fanny is by no means handsome, but, in general, prepossessing.

On the 3d of June Mary accompanied Christy back to Dundee, where she remained for the next ten months.

No account remains of her life there, but there can be doubt that her mental and intellectual powers matured rapidly, and that she learned, read, and thought far more than is common even with clever girls of her age. The girl who at seventeen is an intellectual companion for a Shelley cannot often have needed to be "excited to industry," unless indeed when she indulged in day-dreams, as, from her own account given in the preface to her novel of *Frankenstein*, we know she sometimes did. Proud of her parentage, idolising the memory of her mother, about whom she gathered and treasured every scrap of information she could obtain, and of whose history and writings she probably now learned more than she had done at home, accustomed from her childhood to the daily society of authors and literary men, the pen was her earliest toy, and now the attempt at original composition was her chosen occupation.

"As a child," she says, "I scribbled; and my favourite pastime, during the hours given me for recreation, was to 'write stories.' Still I had a dearer pleasure than this, which[Pg 37] was the formation of castles in the air,—the indulging in waking dreams,—the following up trains of thought which had for their subject the formation of a succession of imaginary incidents. My dreams were at once more fantastic and agreeable than my writings. In the latter I was a close imitator, rather doing as others had done than putting down the suggestions of my own mind. What I wrote was intended at least for one other eye—my childhood's companion and friend" (probably Isabel Baxter)—"but my dreams were all my own. I accounted for them to nobody; they were my refuge when annoyed, my dearest pleasure when free.

"I lived principally in the country as a girl, and passed a considerable time in Scotland. I made occasional visits to the more picturesque parts; but my habitual residence was on the blank and dreary northern shores of the Tay, near Dundee. Blank and dreary on retrospection I call them; they were not so to me then. They were the eyry of freedom, and the pleasant region where unheeded I could commune with the creatures of my fancy. I wrote then, but in a most commonplace style. It was beneath the trees of the grounds belonging to our house, or on the bleak sides of the woodless mountains near, that my true compositions, the airy flights of my imagination, were born and fostered. I did not make myself the heroine of my tales. Life appeared to me too commonplace an affair as regarded myself. I could not figure to myself that romantic woes or wonderful events would ever be my lot; but I was not confined to my own identity, and I could people the hours with creations far more interesting to me, at that age, than my own sensations."

From the entry in Godwin's diary, "M. W. G. at supper," for 30th March 1814, we learn that Mary returned to Skinner Street on that day. She now resumed her place in the home circle, a very different person from the little Mary who[Pg 38] went to Ramsgate in 1811. Although only sixteen and a half she was in the bloom of her girlhood, very pretty, very interesting in appearance, thoughtful and intelligent beyond her years. She did not settle down easily into her old place, and probably only realised gradually how much she had altered since she last lived at home. Perhaps, too, she saw that home in a new light. After the well-ordered, cheerful family life of the Baxters, the somewhat Bohemianism of Skinner Street may have seemed a little strange. A household with a philosopher for one of its heads, and a fussy, unscrupulous woman of business for the other, may have its amusing sides, and we have seen that it had; but it is not necessarily comfortable, still less sympathetic to a young and earnest nature, just awakening to a consciousness of the realities of life, at that transition stage when so much is chaotic and confusing to those who are beginning to think and to feel. One may well imagine that all was not smooth for poor Mary. Her stepmother's jarring temperament must have grated on her more keenly than ever after her long absence. Years and anxieties did not improve Mrs. Godwin's temper, nor bring refinement or a nice sense of honour to a nature singularly deficient in both. Mary must have had to take refuge from annoyance in day-dreams pretty frequently, and this was a sure and constant[Pg 39] source of irritation to her stepmother. Jane Clairmont, wilful, rebellious, witty, and probably a good deal spoilt, whose subsequent conduct shows that she was utterly unamenable to her mother's authority, was, at first, away at school. Fanny was the good angel of the house, but her persistent defence of every one attacked, and her determination to make the best of things and people as they were, seemed almost irritating to those who were smarting under daily and hourly little grievances. Compliance often looks like cowardice to the young and bold. Nor did Mary get any help from her father. A little affection and kindly sympathy from him would have gone a long way with her, for she loved him dearly. Long afterwards she alluded to his "calm, silent disapproval" when displeased, and to the bitter remorse and unhappiness it would cause her, although unspoken, and only instinctively felt by her. All her stepmother's scoldings would have failed to produce a like effect. But Godwin, though sincerely solicitous about the children's welfare, was self-concentrated, and had little real insight into character. Besides, he was, as usual, hampered about money matters; and when constant anxiety as to where to get his next loan was added to the preoccupation of authorship, and the unavoidable distraction of such details as reached him of the publishing business, he had little thought or attention to[Pg 40] bestow on the daughter who had arrived at so critical a time of her mental and moral history. He welcomed her home, but then took little more notice of her. If she and her stepmother disagreed, Godwin, when forced to take part in the matter, probably found it the best policy to side with his wife. Yet the situation would have been worth his attention. Here was this girl, Mary Wollstonecraft's daughter, who had left home a clever, unformed child, who had returned to it a maiden in her bloom, pretty and attractive, with ardour, ability, and ambition, with conscious powers that had not found their right use, with unsatisfied affections seeking an object. True, she might in time have found threads to gather up in her own home. But she was young, impatient, and unhappy. Mrs. Godwin was repellent, uncongenial, and very jealous of her. All that a daughter could do for Godwin seemed to be done by Fanny. When Jane came home it was on her that Mary was chiefly thrown for society. Her lively spirits and quick wit made her excellent company, and she was ready enough to make the most of grievances, and to head any revolt. Fanny, far more deserving of sisterly sympathy and far more in need of it, seemed to belong to the opposite camp.

Time, kindly judicious guidance, and sustained effort on her own part might have cleared Mary's[Pg 41] path and made things straight for her. Her heart was as sound and true as her intellect, but this critical time was rendered more dangerous, it may well be, by her knowledge of the existence of many theories on vexed subjects, making her feel keenly her own inexperience and want of a guide.

The guide she found was one who himself had wandered till now over many perplexing paths, led by the light of a restless, sleepless genius, and an inextinguishable yearning to find, to know, to do, to be the best.

Godwin's diary records on the 5th of May "Shelley calls." As far as can be known this was the first occasion since the dinner of the 11th of November 1812, when Mary Wollstonecraft Godwin saw Percy Bysshe Shelley.

[Pg 42]
CHAPTER IV
APRIL-JUNE 1814

Although she had seen Shelley only once, Mary had heard a good deal about him. More than two years before this time Godwin had received a letter from a stranger, a very young man, desirous of becoming acquainted with him. The writer had, it said, been under the impression that the great philosopher, the object of his reverential admiration, whom he now addressed, was one of the mighty dead. That such was not the case he had now learned for the first time, and the most ardent wish of his heart was to be admitted to the privilege of intercourse with one whom he regarded as "a luminary too bright for the darkness which surrounds him." "If," he concluded, "desire for universal happiness has any claim upon your preference, that desire I can exhibit."

Such neophytes never knelt to Godwin in vain. He did not, at first, feel specially interested in this one; still, the kindly tone of his reply led to further correspondence, in the course of which the [Pg 43] new disciple, Mr. Percy Bysshe Shelley, gave Godwin a sketch of the events of his past life. Godwin learned that his correspondent was the son of a country squire in Sussex, was heir to a baronetcy and a considerable fortune; that he had been expelled from Oxford for publishing, and refusing to deny the authorship of, a pamphlet called "The Necessity of Atheism"; that his father, having no sympathy either with his literary tastes or speculative views, and still less with his method of putting the latter in practice, had required from him certain concessions and promises which he had declined to make, and so had been cast off by his family, his father refusing to communicate with him, except through a solicitor, allowing him a sum barely enough for his own wants, and that professedly to "prevent his cheating strangers." That, undeterred by all this, he had, at nineteen, married a woman three years younger, whose "pursuits, hopes, fears, and sorrows" had been like his own; and that he hoped to devote his life and powers to the regeneration of mankind and society.

There was something remarkable about these letters, something that bespoke a mind, ill-balanced it might be, but yet of no common order. Whatever the worth of the writer's opinions, there could be no doubt that he had the gift of eloquence in their expression. Half interested [Pg 44] and half amused, with a vague perception of Shelley's genius, and a certain instinctive deference of which he could not divest himself towards the heir to £6000 a year, Godwin continued the correspondence with a frequency and an unreserve most flattering to the younger man.

Not long after this, the disciple announced that he had gone off, with his wife and her sister, to Ireland, for the avowed purpose of forwarding the Catholic Emancipation and the Repeal of the Union. His scheme was "the organisation of a society whose institution shall serve as a bond to its members for the purposes of virtue, happiness, liberty, and wisdom, by the means of intellectual opposition to grievances." He published and distributed an "Address to the Irish People," setting before them their grievances, their rights, and their duties.

This object Godwin regarded as an utter mistake, its practical furtherance as extremely perilous. Dreading the contagion of excitement, its tendency to prevent sober judgment and promote precipitate action, he condemned associations of men for any public purpose whatever. His calm temperament would fain have dissevered impulse and action altogether as cause and effect, and he had a shrinking, constitutional as well as philosophic, from any tendency to "strike while the iron is hot."

[Pg 45] "The thing most to be desired," he wrote, "is to keep up the intellectual, and in some sense the solitary fermentation, and to procrastinate the contact and consequent action." "Shelley! you are preparing a scene of blood," was his solemn warning.

Nothing could have been further from Shelley's thoughts than such a scene. Surprised and disappointed, he ingenuously confessed to Godwin that his association scheme had grown out of notions of political justice, first generated by Godwin's own book on that subject; and the mentor found himself in the position of an involuntary illustration of his own theory, expressed in the *Enquirer* (Essay XX), "It is by no means impossible that the books most pernicious in their effects that ever were produced, were written with intentions uncommonly elevated and pure."

Shelley, animated by an ardent enthusiasm of humanity, looked to association as likely to spread a contagion indeed, but a contagion of good. The revolution he preached was a Millennium.

If you are convinced of the truth of your cause, trust wholly to its truth; if you are not convinced, give it up. In no case employ violence; the way to liberty and happiness is never to transgress the rules of virtue and justice.

Before anything can be done with effect, habits of sobriety, regularity, and thought must be entered into and firmly resolved on.

I will repeat, that virtue and wisdom are necessary to true happiness and liberty.

[Pg 46]Before the restraints of government are lessened, it is fit that we should lessen the necessity for them. Before government is done away with, we must reform ourselves. It is this work which I would earnestly recommend to you. O Irishmen, reform yourselves.[1]

Whatever evil results Godwin may have apprehended from Shelley's proceedings, these sentiments taken in the abstract could not but enlist his sympathies to some extent on behalf of the deluded young optimist, nor did he keep the fact a secret. Shelley's letters, as well as the Irish pamphlet, were eagerly read and discussed by all the young philosophers of Skinner Street.

"You cannot imagine," Godwin wrote to him, "how much all the females of my family— Mrs. Godwin and three daughters—are interested in your letters and your history."

Publicly propounded, however, Shelley's sentiments proved insufficiently attractive to those to whom they were addressed. At a public meeting where he had ventured to enjoin on Catholics a tolerance so universal as to embrace not only Jews, Turks, and Infidels, but Protestants also, he narrowly escaped being mobbed. It was borne in upon him before long that the possibility, under existing conditions, of realising his scheme for associations of peace and virtue, was doubtful and distant. He abandoned his intention and left Ireland, professedly in submission to Godwin, but[Pg 47] in fact convinced by what he had seen. Godwin was delighted.

"Now I can call you a friend," he wrote, and the good understanding of the two was cemented.

After repeated but fruitless invitations from the Shelleys to the whole Godwin party to come and stay with them in Wales, Godwin, early in the autumn of this year (1812) actually made an expedition to Lynmouth, where his unknown friends were staying, in the hope of effecting a personal acquaintance, but his object was frustrated, the Shelleys having left the place just before he arrived.

They first met in London, in the month of October, and frequent, almost daily intercourse took place between the families. On the last day of their stay in town the Shelleys, with Eliza Westbrook, dined in Skinner Street. Mary Godwin, who had been for five months past in Scotland, had returned, as we know, with Christy Baxter the day before, and was, no doubt, very glad not to miss this opportunity of seeing the interesting young reformer of whom she had heard so much. His wife he had always spoken of as one who shared his tastes and opinions. No doubt they all thought her a fortunate woman, and Mary in after years would well recall her smiling face, and pink and white complexion, and her purple satin gown.

[Pg 48]During the year and a half that had elapsed since that time Mary had been chiefly away, and had heard little if anything of Shelley. In the spring of 1814, however, he came up to town to see her father on business,—business in which Godwin was deeply and solely concerned, about which he was desperately anxious, and in which Mary knew that Shelley was doing all in his power to help him. These matters had been going on for some time, when, on the 5th of May, he came to Skinner Street, and Mary and he renewed acquaintance. Both had altered since the last time they met. Mary, from a child had grown into a young, attractive, and interesting girl. Hers was not the sweet sensuous loveliness of her mother, but with her well-shaped head and intellectual brow, her fine fair hair and liquid hazel eyes, and a skin and complexion of singular whiteness and purity, she possessed beauty of a rare and refined type. She was somewhat below the medium height; very graceful, with drooping shoulders and swan-like throat. The serene eloquent eyes contrasted with a small mouth, indicative of a certain reserve of temperament, which, in fact, always distinguished her, and beneath which those who did not know her might not have suspected her vigour of intellect and fearlessness of thought.

Shelley, too, was changed; why, was in his[Pg 49] case not so evident. Mary would have heard how, just before her return home, he had been remarried to his wife; Godwin, the opponent of matrimony, having, mysteriously enough, been instrumental in procuring the licence for this superfluous ceremony; superfluous, as the parties had been quite legally married in Scotland three years before. His wife was not now with him in London. He was alone, and appeared saddened in aspect, ailing in health, unsettled and anxious in mind. It was impossible that Mary should not observe him with interest. She saw that, although so young a man, he not only could hold his own in discussion of literary, philosophical, or political questions with the wisest heads and deepest thinkers of his generation, but could throw new light on every subject he touched. His glowing imagination transfigured and idealised what it dwelt on, while his magical words seemed to recreate whatever he described. She learned that he was a poet. His conversation would call up her old day-dreams again, though, before it, they paled and faded like morning mists before the sun. She saw, too, that his disposition was most amiable, his manners gentle, his conversation absolutely free from suspicion of coarseness, and that he was a disinterested and devoted friend.

Before long she must have become conscious[Pg 50] that he took pleasure in talking with her. She could not but see that, while his melancholy and disquiet grew upon him every day, she possessed the power of banishing it for the time. Her presence illumined him; life and hopeful enthusiasm would flash anew from him if she was by. This intercourse stimulated all her intellectual powers, and its first effect was to increase her already keen desire of knowledge. To keep pace with the electric mind of this companion required some effort on her part, and she applied herself with renewed zeal to her studies. Nothing irritated her stepmother so much as to see her deep in a book, and in order to escape from Mrs. Godwin's petty persecution Mary used, whenever she could, to transport herself and her occupations to Old St. Pancras Churchyard, where she had been in the habit of coming to visit her mother's grave. There, under the shade of a willow tree, she would sit, book in hand, and sometimes read, but not always. The day-dreams of Dundee would now and again return upon her. How long she seemed to have lived since that time! Life no longer seemed "so commonplace an affair," nor yet her own part in it so infinitesimal if Shelley thought her conversation and companionship worth the having.

Before very long he had found out the secret of her retreat, and used to meet her there. He[Pg 51] revered the memory of Mary Wollstonecraft, and her grave was to him a consecrated shrine of which her daughter was the priestess.

By June they had become intimate friends, though Mary was still ignorant of the secret of his life.

On the 8th of June occurred the meeting described by Hogg in his *Life of Shelley*. The two friends were walking through Skinner Street when Shelley said to Hogg, "I must speak with Godwin; come in, I will not detain you long." Hogg continues—

I followed him through the shop, which was the only entrance, and upstairs we entered a room on the first floor; it was shaped like a quadrant. In the arc were windows; in one radius a fireplace, and in the other a door, and shelves with many old books. William Godwin was not at home. Bysshe strode about the room, causing the crazy floor of the ill-built, unowned dwelling-house to shake and tremble under his impatient footsteps. He appeared to be displeased at not finding the fountain of Political Justice.

"Where is Godwin?" he asked me several times, as if I knew. I did not know, and, to say the truth, I did not care. He continued his uneasy promenade; and I stood reading the names of old English authors on the backs of the venerable volumes, when the door was partially and softly opened. A thrilling voice called "Shelley!" A thrilling voice answered "Mary!" and he darted out of the room, like an arrow from the bow of the far-shooting king. A very young female, fair and fair-haired, pale indeed, and with a piercing look, wearing a frock of tartan, an unusual dress in London at that time, had called him out of the room. He was absent a very short time, a minute or two, and then returned.

[Pg 52]"Godwin is out, there is no use in waiting." So we continued our walk along Holborn.

"Who was that, pray?" I asked, "a daughter?"

"Yes."

"A daughter of William Godwin?"

"The daughter of Godwin and Mary."

Hogg asked no more questions, but something in this momentary interview and in the look of the fair-haired girl left an impression on his mind which he did not at once forget.

Godwin was all this time seeking and encouraging Shelley's visits. He was in feverish distress for money, bankruptcy was hanging over his head; and Shelley was exerting all his energies and influence to raise a large sum, it is said as much as £3000, for him. It is a melancholy fact that the philosopher had got to regard those who, in the thirsty search for truth and knowledge, had attached themselves to him, in the secondary light of possible sources of income, and, when in difficulties, he came upon them one after another for loans or advances of money, which, at first begged for as a kindness, came to be claimed by him almost as a right.

Shelley's own affairs were in a most unsatisfactory state. £200 a year from his father, and as much from his wife's father was all he had to depend upon, and his unsettled life and frequent journeys, generous disposition and careless ways, made fearful inroads on his narrow income, [Pg 53]notwithstanding the fact that he lived with Spartan frugality as far as his own habits were concerned. Little as he had, he never knew how little it was nor how far it would go, and, while he strained every nerve to save from ruin one whom he still considered his intellectual father, he was himself sorely hampered by want of money.

Visits to lawyers by Godwin, Shelley, or both, were of increasingly frequent occurrence during May; in June we learn of as many as two or three in a day. While this was going on, Shelley, the forlorn hope of Skinner Street, could not be lost sight of. If he seemed to find pleasure in Mary's society, this probably flattered Mary's father, who, though really knowing little of his child, was undoubtedly proud of her, her beauty, and her promise of remarkable talent. Like other fathers, he thought of her as a child, and, had there been any occasion for suspicion or remark, the fact of Shelley's being a married man with a lovely wife, would take away any excuse for dwelling on it. The Shelleys had not been favourites with Mrs. Godwin, who, the year before, had offended or chosen to quarrel with Harriet Shelley. The respective husbands had succeeded in smoothing over the difficulty, which was subsequently ignored. No love was lost, however, between the Shelleys and the head of the firm of M. J. Godwin & Co., who, however, was not now[Pg 54] likely to do or say anything calculated to drive from the house one who, for the present, was its sole chance of existence.

From the 20th of June until the end of the month Shelley was at Skinner Street every day, often to dinner.

By that time he and Mary had realised, only too well, the depth of their mutual feeling, and on some one day, what day we do not know, they owned it to each other. His history was poured out to her, not as it appears in the cold impartial light of after years perhaps, but as he felt it then, aching and smarting from life's fresh wounds and stings. She heard of his difficulties, his rebuffs, his mistakes in action, his disappointments in friendship, his fruitless sacrifices for what he held to be the truth; his hopes and his hopelessness, his isolation of soul and his craving for sympathy. She guessed, for he was still silent on this point, that he found it not in his home. She faced her feelings then; they were past mistake. But it never occurred to her mind that there was any possible future but a life's separation to souls so situated. She could be his friend, never anything more to him.

As a memento of that interview Shelley gave or sent her a copy of *Queen Mab*, his first published poem. This book (still in existence) has, written in pencil inside the cover, the name[Pg 55] "Mary Wollstonecraft Godwin," and, on the inner flyleaf, the words, "You see, Mary, I have not forgotten you." Under the printed dedication to his wife is the enigmatic but suggestive remark, carefully written in ink, "Count Slobendorf was about to marry a woman, who, attracted solely by his fortune, proved her selfishness by deserting him in prison."[2] On the flyleaves at the end Mary wrote in July 1814—

This book is sacred to me, and as no other creature shall ever look into it, I may write what I please. Yet what shall I write? That I love the author beyond all powers of expression, and that I am parted from him. Dearest and only love, by that love we have promised to each other, although I may not be yours, I can never be another's. But I am thine, exclusively thine.

By the kiss of love, the glance none saw beside,
The smile none else might understand,
The whispered thought of hearts allied,
The pressure of the thrilling hand.[3]

I have pledged myself to thee, and sacred is the gift. I remember your words. "You are now, Mary, going to mix with many, and for a moment I shall depart, but in the solitude of your chamber I shall be with you." Yes, you are ever with me, sacred vision.

But ah! I feel in this was given
A blessing never meant for me,
Thou art too like a dream from heaven
For earthly love to merit thee.[4]

[Pg 56]With this mutual consciousness, yet obliged inevitably to meet, thrown constantly in each other's way, Mary obliged too to look on Shelley as her father's benefactor and support, their situation was a miserable one. As for Shelley, when he had once broken silence he passed rapidly from tender affection to the most passionate love. His heart and brain were alike on fire, for at the root of his deep depression and unsettlement lay the fact, known as yet only to himself, of complete estrangement between himself and his wife.

[Pg 57]

CHAPTER V
June-August 1814

Perhaps of all the objects of Shelley's devotion up to this time, Harriet, his wife, was the only one with whom he had never, in the ideal sense, been in love. Possibly this was one reason that against her alone he never had the violent revulsion, almost amounting to loathing, which was the usual reaction after his other passionate illusions. He had eloped with her when they were but boy and girl because he found her ready to elope with him, and because he was persuaded that she was a victim of tyranny and oppression, which, to this modern knight-errant, was tantamount to an obligation laid on him to rescue her. Having eloped with her, he had married her, for her sake, and from a sense of chivalry, only with a quaint sort of apology to his friend Hogg for this early departure from his own principles and those of the philosophic writers who had helped to mould his views. His affection for his wife[Pg 58] had steadily increased after their marriage; she was fond of him and satisfied with her lot, and had made things very easy for him. She could not give him anything very deep in the way of love, but in return she was not very exacting; accommodating herself with good humour to all his vagaries, his changes of mood and plan, and his romantic friendships. Even the presence of her elder sister Eliza, who at an early period established herself as a member of their household, did not destroy although it did not add to their peace. It was during their stay in Scotland, in 1813, that the first shadow arose between them, and from this time Harriet seems to have changed. She became cold and indifferent. During the next winter, when they lived at Bracknell, she grew frivolous and extravagant, even yielding to habits of self-indulgence most repugnant to one so abstemious as Shelley. He, on his part, was more and more drawn away from the home which had become uncongenial by the fascinating society of his brilliant, speculative friend, Mrs. Boinville (the white-haired "Maimuna"), her daughter and sister. They were kind and encouraging to him, and their whole circle was cheerful, genial, and intellectual. This intimacy tended to widen the breach between husband and wife, while supplying none of the moral help which might have braced Shelley[Pg 59] to meet his difficulty. His letters and the stanza addressed to Mrs. Boinville[5] show the profound depression under which he laboured in April and May. His pathetic poem to Harriet, written in May, expresses only too plainly what he suffered from her alienation, and also his keen consciousness of the moral dangers that threatened him from the loosening of old ties, if left to himself unsupported by sympathy at home. But such feeling as Harriet had was at this time quite blunted. She had treated his unsettled depression and gloomy abstraction as coldness and sullen discontent, and met them with careless unconcern. Always a puppet in the hands of some one stronger than herself, she was encouraged by her elder sister, "the ever-present Eliza," the object of Shelley's abhorrence, to meet any want of attention on his part by this attitude of indifference; presumably on the assumption that men do not care for what they can have cheaply, and that the best way for a wife to keep a husband's affection is to show herself independent of it. Good-humoured and shallow, easy-going and fond of amusement, she probably[Pg 60] yielded to these counsels without difficulty. She was much admired by other men, and accepted their admiration willingly. From evidence which came to light not many years later, it appears Shelley thought he had reason to believe she had been misled by one of these admirers, and that he became aware of this in June 1814. No word of it was breathed by him at the time, and the painful story might never have been divulged but for subsequent events which dragged into publicity circumstances which he intended should be buried in oblivion. This is not a life of Shelley, and the evidence of all this matter,—such evidence, that is, as has escaped destruction,—must be looked for elsewhere. In the lawsuit which he undertook after Harriet's death to obtain possession of his children by her, he was content to state, "I was united to a woman of whom delicacy forbids me to say more than that we were disunited by incurable dissensions."

That time only confirmed his conviction of 1814 is clearly proved by his letter, written six years afterwards, to Southey, who had accused him of guilt towards both his first and second wives.

I take God to witness, if such a Being is now regarding both you and me, and I pledge myself if we meet, as perhaps you expect, before Him after death, to repeat the same in His presence, that you accuse me wrongfully. I am innocent of ill, either done or intended, the consequences you allude to[Pg 61] flowed in no respect from me. If you were my friend, I could tell you a history that would make you open your eyes, but I shall certainly never make the public my familiar confidant.

It is quite certain that in June 1814 Shelley, who had for months found his wife heartless, became convinced that she had also been faithless. A breach of the marriage vow was not, now or at any other time, regarded by him in the light of a heinous or unpardonable sin. Like his master Godwin, who held that right and wrong in these matters could only be decided by the circumstances of each individual case, he considered the vow itself to be the mistake, superfluous where it was based on mutual affection, tyrannic or false where it was not. Nor did he recognise two different laws, for men and for women, in these respects. His subsequent relations with Harriet show that, deeply as she had wounded him, he did not consider her criminally in fault. Could she indeed be blamed for applying in her own way the dangerous principles of which she had heard so much? But she had ceased to care for him, and the death of mutual love argued, to his mind, the loosening of the tie. He had been faithful to her; her faithlessness cut away the ground from under his feet and left him defenceless against a new affection.

No wonder that when his friend Peacock went, by his request, to call on him in London, he

[Pg 62]showed in his looks, in his gestures, in his speech, the state of a mind, "suffering like a little kingdom, the nature of an insurrection." His eyes were bloodshot, his hair and dress disordered. He caught up a bottle of laudanum and said, "I never part from this!" He added, "I am always repeating to myself your lines from Sophocles—

Man's happiest lot is not to be,
And when we tread life's thorny steep
Most blest are they, who, earliest free,
Descend to death's eternal sleep."

Harriet had been absent for some time at Bath, but now, growing anxious at the rarity of news from her husband, she wrote up to Hookham, his publisher, entreating to know what had become of him, and where he was.

Godwin, who called at Hookham's the next day, heard of this letter, and began at last to awaken to the consciousness that something he did not understand was going on between Shelley and his daughter. It is strange that Mrs. Godwin, a shrewd and suspicious woman, should not before now have called his attention to the fact. His diary for 8th July records a "Talk with Mary." What passed has not transpired. Probably Godwin "restricted himself to uttering his censures with seriousness and emphasis,"[6] probably Mary said little of any sort.

On the 14th of July Harriet Shelley came up to town, summoned thither by a letter from her husband. He informed her of his determination[Pg 63] to separate, and of his intention to take immediate measures securing her a sufficient income for her support. He fully expected that Harriet would willingly concur in this arrangement, but she did no such thing; perhaps she did not believe he would carry it out. She never at any time took life seriously; she looked on the rupture between herself and Shelley as trivial and temporary, and had no wish to make it otherwise. Godwin called on her two or three times; he was aware of the estrangement, and probably hoped by argument and discussion to restore matters to their old footing and bring peace and equanimity to his own household. But although Harriet was quite aware of Shelley's love for Godwin's daughter, and knew, too, that deeds were being prepared to assure her own separate maintenance, she said nothing to Godwin, nor did her family give him any hint. The impending elopement, with all its consequences to Godwin, were within her power to prevent, but she allowed matters to take their course. Godwin, evidently very uncomfortable, chronicles a "Talk with P. B. S.," and, on 22d July, a "Talk with Jane." But circumstances moved faster than he expected, and these many talks and discussions and complicated moves and counter-moves only made the position intolerable, and precipitated the final crisis. Towards the close of that month Shelley's confession was[Pg 64]wrung from him: he told Mary the whole truth, and how, though legally bound, he held himself morally free to offer himself to her if she would be his.

To her, passionately devoted to the one man who was and was ever to remain the sun and centre of her existence, the thought of a wife indifferent to him, hard to him, false to him, was sacrilege; it was torture. She had not been brought up to look on marriage as a divine institution; she had probably never even heard it discussed but on grounds of expediency. Harriet was his legal wife, so he could not marry Mary, but what of that, after all? if there was a sacrifice in her power to make for him, was not that the greatest joy, the greatest honour that life could have in store for her?

That her father would openly condemn her she knew, for she must have known that Godwin's practice did not move on the same lofty plane as his principles. Was he not at that moment making himself debtor to a man whose integrity he doubted? Had he not, in twice marrying, taken care to proclaim, both to his friends and the public, that he did so *in spite* of his opinions, which remained unchanged and unretracted, until some inconvenient application of them forced from him an expression of disapproval?

Her mother too, had she not held that ties[Pg 65] which were dead should be buried? and though not, like Godwin, condemning marriage as an institution, had she not been twice induced to form a connection which in one instance never was, in the other was not for some time consecrated by law? Who was Mary herself, that she should withstand one whom she felt to be the best as well as the cleverest man she had ever known? To talent she had been accustomed all her life, but here she saw something different, and what of all things calls forth most ardent response from a young and pure-minded girl, *a genius for goodness*; an aspiration and devotion such as she had dreamed of but never known, with powers which seemed to her absolutely inspired. She loved him, and she appreciated him,—as time abundantly showed,—rightly. She conceived that she wronged by her action no one but herself, and she did not hesitate. She pledged her heart and hand to Shelley for life, and she did not disappoint him, nor he her.

To the end of their lives, tried as they were to be by every kind of trouble, neither one nor the other ever repented the step they now took, nor modified their opinion of the grounds on which they took it. How Shelley regarded it in after years we have already seen. Mary, writing during her married life, when her judgment had been matured and her youthful buoyancy of spirit only too well sobered by stern and bitter experience, can find no[Pg 66] harder name for it than "an imprudence." Many years after, in 1825, alluding to Shelley's separation from Harriet, she remarks, "His justification is, to me, obvious." And at a later date still, when she had been seventeen years a widow, she wrote in the preface to her edition of Shelley's *Poems*—

I abstain from any remark on the occurrences of his private life, except inasmuch as the passions they engendered inspired his poetry. This is not the time to relate the truth, and I should reject any colouring of the truth. No account of these events has ever been given at all approaching reality in their details, either as regards himself or others; nor shall I further allude to them than to remark that the errors of action committed by a man as noble and generous as Shelley, may, as far as he only is concerned, be fearlessly avowed by those who loved him, in the firm conviction that, were they judged impartially, his character would stand in fairer and brighter light than that of any contemporary.

But they never "made the public their familiar confidant." They screened the erring as far as it was in their power to do so, although their reticence cost them dear, for it lent a colouring of probability to the slanders and misconstruction of all kinds which it was their constant fate to endure for others' sake, which pursued them to their lives' end, and beyond it.

Life, which is to no one what he expects, had many clouds for them. Mary's life reached its zenith too suddenly, and with happiness came care in undue proportion. The future of intellectual[Pg 67] expansion and creation which might have been hers was not to be fully realised, but perfections of character she might never have attained developed themselves as her nature was mellowed and moulded by time and by suffering.

Shelley's rupture with his first wife marks the end of his boyhood. Up to that time, thanks to his poetic temperament, his were the strong and simple, but passing impulses and feelings of a child. "A being of large discourse" he assuredly was, but not as yet "looking before and after." Now he was to acquire the doubtful blessing of that faculty. Like Undine when she became endued with a soul, he gained an immeasurable good, while he lost a something that never returned.

Early in the morning of 28th July 1814 Mary Godwin secretly left her father's house, accompanied by Jane Clairmont, and they started with Shelley in a post-chaise for Dover.

[Pg 68]
CHAPTER VI
AUGUST 1814-JANUARY 1816

From the day of their departure a joint journal was kept by Shelley and Mary, which tells their subsequent adventures and vicissitudes with the utmost candour and *naïveté*. A great deal of the earlier portion is written by Shelley, but after a time Mary becomes the principal diarist, and the latter part is almost entirely hers. Its account of their first wanderings in France and Switzerland was put into narrative form by her two or three years later, and published under the title *Journal of a Six Weeks' Tour*. But the transparent simplicity of the journal is invaluable, and carries with it an absolute conviction which no studied account can emulate or improve upon. Considerable portions are, therefore, given in their entirety.

That 28th of July was a hotter day than had been known in England for many years. Between the sultry heat and exhaustion from the excitement[Pg 69] and conflicting emotions of the last days, poor Mary was completely overcome.

"The heat made her faint," wrote Shelley, "it was necessary at every stage that she should repose. I was divided between anxiety for her health and terror lest our pursuers should arrive. I reproached myself with not allowing her sufficient time to rest, with conceiving any evil so great that the slightest portion of her comfort might be sacrificed to avoid it.

"At Dartford we took four horses, that we might outstrip pursuit. We arrived at Dover before four o'clock."

"On arriving at Dover," writes Mary,[7] "I was refreshed by a sea-bath. As we very much wished to cross the Channel with all possible speed, we would not wait for the packet of the following day (it being then about four in the afternoon), but hiring a small boat, resolved to make the passage the same evening, the seamen promising us a voyage of two hours.

"The evening was most beautiful; there was but little wind, and the sails flapped in the flagging breeze; the moon rose, and night came on, and with the night a slow, heavy swell and a fresh breeze, which soon produced a sea so violent as to toss the boat very much. I was dreadfully sea-sick, and, as is usually my custom when thus affected, I slept during the greater part of the night, awaking only from time to time to ask where we were, and to receive the dismal answer each time, 'Not quite halfway.'

"The wind was violent and contrary; if we could not reach Calais the sailors proposed making for Boulogne. They promised only two hours' sail from shore, yet hour after hour passed, and we were still far distant, when the moon sunk in the red and stormy horizon and the fast-flashing lightning became pale in the breaking day.

"We were proceeding slowly against the wind, when suddenly a thunder squall struck the sail, and the waves rushed [Pg 70]into the boat: even the sailors acknowledged that our situation was perilous; but they succeeded in reefing the sail; the wind was now changed, and we drove before the gale directly to Calais."

Journal (Shelley).—Mary did not know our danger; she was resting between my knees, that were unable to support her; she did not speak or look, but I felt that she was there. I had time in that moment to reflect, and even to reason upon death; it was rather a thing of discomfort and disappointment than horror to me. We should never be separated, but in death we might not know and feel our union as now. I hope, but my hopes are not unmixed with fear for what may befall this inestimable spirit when we appear to die.

The morning broke, the lightning died away, the violence of the wind abated. We arrived at Calais, whilst Mary still slept; we drove upon the sands. Suddenly the broad sun rose over France.

Godwin's diary for 28th July runs,

"*Five in the morning.* M. J. for Dover."

Mrs. Godwin, in fact, started in pursuit of the fugitives as soon as they were missed. Neither Shelley nor Mary were the objects of her anxiety, but her own daughter. Jane Clairmont, who cared no more for her mother than she did for any one else, had guessed Mary's secret or insinuated herself into her confidence some time before the final *dénouement* of the love-affair. Wild and wayward, ready for anything in the shape of a romantic adventure, and longing for freedom from the restraints of home, she had sympathised with, and perhaps helped Shelley and Mary. She was in no wise anxious to be left to mope alone, nor[Pg 71] to be exposed to cross-questioning she could ill have met. She claimed to escape with them as a return for her good offices, and whatever Mary may have thought or wished, Shelley was not one to leave her behind "in slavery." Mrs. Godwin arrived at Calais by the very packet the fugitives had refused to wait for.

Journal (Shelley).—In the evening Captain Davidson came and told us that a fat lady had arrived who said I had run away with her daughter; it was Mrs. Godwin. Jane spent the night with her mother.

July 30.—Jane informs us that she is unable to withstand the pathos of Mrs. Godwin's appeal. She appealed to the Municipality of Paris, to past slavery and to future freedom. I counselled her to take at least half an hour for consideration. She returned to Mrs. Godwin and informed her that she resolved to continue with us.

Mrs. Godwin departed without answering a word.

It is difficult to understand how this mother had so little authority over her own girl of sixteen. She might rule Godwin, but she evidently could not influence, far less rule her daughter. Shelley's influence, as far as it was exerted at all, was used in favour of Jane's remaining with them, and he paid dearly in after years for the heavy responsibility he now assumed.

The travellers proceeded to Paris, where they were obliged to remain longer than they intended, finding themselves so absolutely without money, nothing having been prearranged in their sudden flight, that Shelley had to sell his watch and chain[Pg 72] for eight napoleons. Funds were at last procured through Tavernier, a French man of business, and they were free to put into execution the plan they had resolved upon, namely, to *walk* through France, buying an ass to carry their portmanteau and one of them by turns.

Journal. August 8 (Mary).—Jane and Shelley go to the ass merchant; we buy an ass. The day spent in preparation for departure.

Their landlady tried to dissuade them from their design.

She represented to us that a large army had been recently disbanded, that the soldiers and officers wandered idle about the country, and that *les dames seroient certainement enlevées*. But we were proof against her arguments, and, packing up a few necessaries, leaving the rest to go by the diligence, we departed in a *fiacre* from the door of the hotel, our little ass following.[8]

Journal (Mary).—We set out to Charenton in the evening, carrying the ass, who was weak and unfit for labour, like the Miller and his Son.

We dismissed the coach at the barrier. It was dusk, and the ass seemed totally unable to bear one of us, appearing to sink under the portmanteau, though it was small and light. We were, however, merry enough, and thought the leagues short. We arrived at Charenton about ten. Charenton is prettily situated in a valley, through which the Seine flows, winding among banks variegated with trees. On looking at this scene C... (Jane) exclaimed, "Oh! this is beautiful enough; let us live here." This was her exclamation on every new scene, and as each surpassed the one before, she [Pg 73]cried, "I am glad we did not live at Charenton, but let us live here."[9]

August 9 (Shelley).—We sell our ass and purchase a mule, in which we much resemble him who never made a bargain but always lost half. The day is most beautiful.

(Mary).—About nine o'clock we departed; we were clad in black silk. I rode on the mule, which carried also our portmanteau. S. and C. (Jane) followed, bringing a small basket of provisions. At about one we arrived at Gros-Bois, where, under the shade of trees, we ate our bread and fruit, and drank our wine, thinking of Don Quixote and Sancho Panza.

Thursday, August 11 (Mary).—From Provins we came to Nogent. The town was entirely desolated by the Cossacks; the houses were reduced to heaps of white ruins, and the bridge was destroyed. Proceeding on our way we left the great road and arrived at St. Aubin, a beautiful little village situated among trees. This village was also completely destroyed. The inhabitants told us the Cossacks had not left one cow in the village. Notwithstanding the entreaties of the people, who eagerly desired us to stay all night, we continued our route to Trois Maisons, three long leagues farther, on an unfrequented road, and which in many places was hardly perceptible from the surrounding waste....

As night approached our fears increased that we should not be able to distinguish the road, and Mary expressed these fears in a very complaining tone. We arrived at Trois Maisons at nine o'clock. Jane went up to the first cottage to ask our way, but was only answered by unmeaning laughter. We, however, discovered a kind of an *auberge*, where, having in some degree satisfied our hunger by milk and sour bread, we retired to a wretched apartment to bed. But first let me observe that we discovered that the inhabitants were not in the habit of washing themselves, either when they rose or went to bed.

Friday, August 12.—We did not set out from here till eleven o'clock, and travelled a long league under the very eye of a[Pg 74] burning sun. Shelley, having sprained his leg, was obliged to ride all day.

Saturday, August 13 (Troyes).—We are disgusted with the excessive dirt of our habitation. Shelley goes to inquire about conveyances. He sells the mule for forty francs and the saddle for sixteen francs. In all our bargains for ass, saddle, and mule we lose more than fifteen napoleons. Money we can but little spare now. Jane and Shelley seek for a conveyance to Neufchâtel.

From Troyes Shelley wrote to Harriet, expressing his anxiety for her welfare, and urging her in her own interests to come out to Switzerland, where he, who would always remain her best and most disinterested friend, would procure for her some sweet retreat among the mountains. He tells her some details of their adventures in the simplest manner imaginable; never, apparently, doubting for a moment but that they would interest her as much as they did him. Harriet, it is needless to say, did not come. Had she done so, she would not have found Shelley, for, as the sequel shows, he was back in London almost as soon as she could have got to Switzerland.

Journal, August 14 (Mary).—At four in the morning we depart from Troyes, and proceed in the new vehicle to Vandeuvres. The village remains still ruined by the war. We rest at Vandeuvres two hours, but walk in a wood belonging to a neighbouring chateau, and sleep under its shade. The moss was so soft; the murmur of the wind in the leaves was sweeter than Æolian music; we forgot that we were in France or in the world for a time.

....

August 17.—The *voiturier* insists upon our passing the night[Pg 75] at the village of Mort. We go out on the rocks, and Shelley and I read part of *Mary*, a fiction. We return at dark, and, unable to enter the beds, we pass a few comfortless hours by the kitchen fireside.

Thursday, August 18.—We leave Mort at four. After some hours of tedious travelling, through a most beautiful country, we arrive at Noè. From the summit of one of the hills we see the whole expanse of the valley filled with a white, undulating mist, over which the piny hills pierced like islands. The sun had just risen, and a ray of the red light lay on the waves of this fluctuating vapour. To the west, opposite the sun, it seemed driven by the light against the rock in immense masses of foaming cloud until it becomes lost in the distance, mixing its tints with the fleecy sky. At Noè, whilst our postillion waited, we walked into the forest of pines; it was a scene of enchantment, where every sound and sight contributed to charm.

Our mossy seat in the deepest recesses of the wood was enclosed from the world by an impenetrable veil. On our return the postillion had departed without us; he left word that he expected to meet us on the road. We proceeded there upon foot to Maison Neuve, an *auberge* a league distant. At Maison Neuve he had left a message importing that he should proceed to Pontarlier, six leagues distant, and that unless he found us there he should return. We despatched a boy on horseback for him; he promised to wait for us at the next village; we walked two leagues in the expectation of finding him there. The evening was most beautiful; the horned moon hung in the light of sunset that threw a glow of unusual depth of redness above the piny mountains and the dark deep valleys which they included. At Savrine we found, according to our expectation, that M. le Voiturier had pursued his journey with the utmost speed. We engaged a *voiture* for Pontarlier. Jane very unable to walk. The moon becomes yellow and hangs close to the woody horizon. It is dark before we arrive at Pontarlier. The postillion tells many lies. We sleep, for the first time in France, in a clean bed.

[Pg 76]*Friday, August 19.*—We pursue our journey towards Neufchâtel. We pass delightful scenes of verdure surpassing imagination; here first we see clear mountain streams. We pass the barrier between France and Switzerland, and, after descending nearly a league, between lofty rocks covered with pines and interspersed with green glades, where the grass is short and soft and beautifully verdant, we arrive at St. Sulpice. The mule is very lame; we determined to engage another horse for the remainder of the way. Our *voiturier* had determined to leave us, and had taken measures to that effect. The mountains after St. Sulpice become loftier and more beautiful. Two leagues from Neufchâtel we see the Alps; hill after hill is seen extending its craggy outline before the other, and far behind all, towering above every feature of the scene, the snowy Alps; they are 100 miles distant; they look like those accumulated clouds of dazzling white that arrange themselves on the horizon in summer. This immensity staggers the imagination, and so far surpasses all conception that it requires an effort of the understanding to believe that they are indeed mountains. We arrive at Neufchâtel and sleep.

Saturday, August 20.—We consult on our situation. There are no letters at the *bureau de poste*; there cannot be for a week. Shelley goes to the banker's, who promises an answer in two hours; at the conclusion of the time he sends for Shelley, and, to our astonishment and consolation, Shelley returns staggering under the weight of a large canvas bag full of silver. Shelley alone looks grave on the occasion, for he alone clearly apprehends that francs and écus and louis d'or are like the white and flying cloud of noon, that is gone before one can say "Jack Robinson." Shelley goes to secure a place in the diligence; they are all taken. He meets there with a Swiss who speaks English; this man is imbued with the spirit of true politeness. He endeavours to perform real services, and seems to regard the mere ceremonies of the affair as things of very little value. He makes a bargain with a *voiturier* to take us to Lucerne for eighteen écus.

[Pg 77]We arrange to depart at four the next morning. Our Swiss friend appoints to meet us there.

Sunday, August 21.—Go from Neufchâtel at six; our Swiss accompanies us a little way out of town. There is a mist to-day, so we cannot see the Alps; the drive, however, is interesting, especially in the latter part of the day. Shelley and Jane talk concerning Jane's character. We arrive before seven at Soleure. Shelley and Mary go to the much-praised cathedral, and find it very modern and stupid.

Monday, August 22.—Leave Soleure at half-past five; very cold indeed, but we now again see the magnificent mountains of Le Valais. Mary is not well, and all are tired of wheeled machines. Shelley is in a jocosely horrible mood. We dine at Zoffingen, and sleep there two hours. In our drive after dinner we see the mountains of St. Gothard, etc. Change our plan of going over St. Gothard. Arrive tired to death; find at the room of the inn a horrible spinet and a case of stuffed birds. Sup at *table d'hôte*.

Tuesday, August 23.—We leave at four o'clock and arrive at Lucerne about ten. After breakfast we hire a boat to take us down the lake. Shelley and Mary go out to buy several needful things, and then we embark. It is a most divine day; the farther we advance the more magnificent are the shores of the lake—rock and pine forests covering the feet of the immense mountains. We read part of L'Abbé Barruel's *Histoire du Jacobinisme*. We land at Bessen, go to the wrong inn, where a most comical scene ensues. We sleep at Brunnen. Before we sleep, however, we look out of window.

Wednesday, August 24.—We consult on our situation. We cannot procure a house; we are in despair; the filth of the apartment is terrible to Mary; she cannot bear it all the winter. We propose to proceed to Fluelen, but the wind comes from Italy, and will not permit. At last we find a lodging in an ugly house they call the Château for one louis a month, which we take; it consists of two rooms. Mary and Shelley walk to the shore of the lake and read the description of the Siege of Jerusalem in Tacitus. We come home, look out of window and go to bed.

[Pg 78]*Thursday, August 25.*—We read Abbé Barruel. Shelley and Jane make purchases; we pack up our things and take possession of our house, which we have engaged for six months. Receive a visit from the *Médecin* and the old Abbé, whom, it must be owned, we do not treat with proper politeness. We arrange our apartment, and write part of Shelley's romance.

Friday, August 26.—Write the romance till three o'clock. Propose crossing Mount St. Gothard. Determine at last to return to England; only wait to set off till the washerwoman brings home our linen. The little Frenchman arrives with tubs and plums and scissors and salt. The linen is not dry; we are compelled to wait until to-morrow. We engage a boat to take us to Lucerne at six the following morning.

Saturday, August 27.—We depart at seven; it rains violently till just the end of our voyage. We conjecture the astonishment of the good people at Brunnen. We arrive at Lucerne, dine, then write a part of the romance, and read *Shakespeare*. Interrupted by Jane's horrors; pack up. We have engaged a boat for Basle.

Sunday, August 28.—Depart at six o'clock. The river is exceedingly beautiful; the waves break on the rocks, and the descents are steep and rapid. It rained the whole day. We stopped at Mettingen to dine, and there surveyed at our ease the horrid and slimy faces of our companions in voyage; our only wish was to absolutely annihilate such uncleanly animals, to which we might have addressed the boatman's speech to Pope: "'Twere easier for God to make entirely new men than attempt to purify such monsters as these." After a voyage in the rain, rendered disagreeable only by the presence of these loathsome "creepers," we arrive, Shelley much exhausted, at Dettingen, our resting-place for the night.

It never seems to have occurred to them before arriving in Switzerland that they had no money wherewith to carry out their further plans, that it was more difficult to obtain it abroad than at home,[Pg 79] and that the remainder of their little store would hardly suffice to take them back to England. No sooner thought, however, than done. They gave themselves no rest after their long and arduous journey, but started straight back viâ the Rhine, arriving in Rotterdam on 8th September with only twenty écus remaining, having been "horribly cheated." "Make arrangements, and talk of many things, past, present, and to come."

Journal. Friday, September 9.—We have arranged with a captain to take us to England—three guineas a-piece; at three o'clock we sail, and in the evening arrive at Marsluys, where a bad wind obliges us to stay.

Saturday, September 10.—We remain at Marsluys, Mary begins *Hate*, and gives Shelley the greater pleasure. Shelley writes part of his romance. Sleep at Marsluys. Wind contrary.

Sunday, September 11.—The wind becomes more favourable. We hear that we are to sail. Mary writes more of her *Hate*. We depart, cross the bar; the sea is horribly tempestuous, and Mary is nearly sick, nor is Shelley much better. There is an easterly gale in the night which almost kills us, whilst it carries us nearer our journey's end.

Monday, September 12.—It is calm; we remain on deck nearly the whole day. Mary recovers from her sickness. We dispute with one man upon the slave trade.

The wanderers arrived at last at Gravesend, not only penniless, but unable even to pay their passage money, or to discharge the hackney coach in which they drove about from place to place in search of assistance. At the time of Shelley's sudden flight, the deeds by which part of his income was transferred to Harriet were still in [Pg 80]preparation only, and he had, without thinking of the consequences of his act, written from Switzerland to his bankers, directing them to honour her calls for money, as far as his account allowed of it. She must have availed herself so well of this permission that now he found he could only obtain the sum he wanted by applying for it to her.

The relations between Shelley and Harriet, must, at first, have seemed to Mary as incomprehensible as they still do to readers of the *Journal*. Their interviews, necessarily very frequent in the next few months, were, on the whole, quite friendly. Shelley was kind and perfectly ingenuous and sincere; Harriet was sometimes "civil" and good tempered, sometimes cross and provoking. But on neither side was there any pretence of deep pain, of wounded pride or bitter constraint.

Journal. Tuesday, September 13.—We arrive at Gravesend, and with great difficulty prevail on the captain to trust us. We go by boat to London; take a coach; call on Hookham. T. H. not at home. C. treats us very ill. Call at Voisey's. Henry goes to Harriet. Shelley calls on her, whilst poor Mary and Jane are left in the coach for two whole hours. Our debt is discharged. Shelley gets clothes for himself. Go to Strafford Hotel, dine, and go to bed.

Wednesday, September 14.—Talk and read the newspaper. Shelley calls on Harriet, who is certainly a very odd creature; he writes several letters; calls on Hookham, and brings home Wordsworth's *Excursion*, of which we read a part, much [Pg 81]disappointed. He is a slave. Shelley engages lodgings, to which we remove in the evening.

Shelley now lost no time in putting himself in communication with Skinner Street, and on the first day after they settled in their new lodgings he addressed a letter to Godwin.

[Pg 82]

CHAPTER VII
SEPTEMBER 1814-MAY 1816

Whatever may have been Godwin's degree of responsibility for the opinions which had enabled Shelley to elope in all good faith with his daughter, and which saved her from serious scruple in eloping with Shelley, it would be impossible not to sympathise with the father's feelings after the event.

People do not resent those misfortunes least which they have helped to bring on themselves, and no one ever derived less consolation from his own theories than did Godwin from his, as soon as they were unpleasantly put into practice. He had done little to win his daughter's confidence, but he was keenly wounded by the proof she had given of its absence. His pride, as well as his affection, had suffered a serious blow through her departure and that of Jane. For a philosopher like him, accustomed to be looked up to and consulted on matters of education, such a failure in his own family was a public stigma. False[Pg 83] and malicious reports got about, which had an additional and peculiar sting from their originating partly in his well-known impecuniosity. It was currently rumoured that he had sold the two girls to Shelley for £800 and £700 respectively. No wonder that Godwin, accustomed to look down from a lofty altitude on such minor matters as money and indebtedness, felt now that he could not hold up his head. He shunned his old friends, and they, for the most part, felt this and avoided him. His home was embittered and spoilt. Mrs. Godwin, incensed at Jane's conduct, vented her wrath in abuse and invective on Shelley and Mary.

No one has thought it worth while to record how poor Fanny was affected by the first news of the family calamity. It must have reached her in Ireland, and her subsequent return home was dismal indeed. The loss of her only sister was a bitter grief to her; and, strong as was her disapproval of that sister's conduct, it must have given her a pang to feel that the culpable Jane had enjoyed Shelley's and Mary's confidence, while she who loved them with a really unselfish love, had been excluded from it. What could she now say or do to cheer Godwin? How parry Mrs. Godwin's inconsiderate and intemperate complaints and innuendos? No doubt Fanny had often stood up for Mary with her[Pg 84] stepmother, and now Mary herself had cut the ground from under her feet.

Charles Clairmont was at home again; ostensibly on the plea of helping in the publishing business, but as a fact idling about, on the lookout for some lucky opening. He cared no more than did Jane for the family (including his own mother) in Skinner Street: like every Clairmont, he was an adventurer, and promptly transferred his sympathies to any point which suited himself. To crown all, William, the youngest son, had become infected with the spirit of revolt, and had, as Godwin expresses it, "eloped for two nights," giving his family no little anxiety.

The first and immediate result of Shelley's letter to Godwin was *a visit to his windows* by Mrs. Godwin and Fanny, who tried in this way to get a surreptitious peep at the three truants. Shelley went out to them, but they would not speak to him. Late that evening, however, Charles Clairmont appeared. He was to be another thorn in the side of the interdicted yet indispensable Shelley. He did not mind having a foot in each camp, and had no scruples about coming as often and staying as long as he liked, or in retailing a large amount of gossip. They discussed William's escapade, and the various plans for the immuring of Jane, if she could be[Pg 85] caught. This did not predispose Jane to listen to the overtures subsequently made to her from time to time by her relatives.

Godwin replied to Shelley's letter, but declined all further communication with him except through a solicitor. Mrs. Godwin's spirit of rancour was such that, several weeks later, she, on one occasion, forbade Fanny to come down to dinner because she had received a lock of Mary's hair, probably conveyed to her by Charles Clairmont, who, in return, did not fail to inform Mary of the whole story. In spite, however, of this vehement show of animosity, Shelley was kept through one channel or another only too well informed of Godwin's affairs. Indeed, he was never suffered to forget them for long at a time. No sign of impatience or resentment ever appears in his journal or letters. Not only was Godwin the father of his beloved, but he was still, to Shelley, the fountain-head of wisdom, philosophy, and inspiration. Mary, too, was devoted to her father, and never wavered in her conviction that his inimical attitude proceeded from no impulse of his own mind, but that he was upheld in it by the influence and interference of Mrs. Godwin.

The journal of Shelley and Mary for the next few months is, in its extreme simplicity, a curious record of a most uncomfortable time; a medley of[Pg 86] lodgings, lawyers, money-lenders, bailiffs, wild schemes, and literary pursuits. Penniless themselves, they were yet responsible for hundreds and thousands of pounds of other people's debts; there was Harriet running up bills at shops and hotels and sending her creditors on to Shelley; Godwin perpetually threatened with bankruptcy, refusing to see the man who had robbed him of his daughter, yet with literally no other hope of support but his help; Jane Clairmont now, as for years to come, entirely dependent on them for everything; Shelley's friends quartering themselves on him all day and every day, often taking advantage of his love of society and intellectual friction, of Mary's youth and inexperience and compliant good-nature, to live at his expense, and, in one case at least, to obtain from him money which he really had not got, and could only borrow, at ruinous interest, on his expectations. He had frequently to be in hiding from bailiffs, change his lodgings, sleep at friends' houses or at different hotels, getting his letters when he could make a stealthy appointment to meet Mary, perhaps at St. Paul's, perhaps at some street corner or outside some coffee-house,—anywhere where he might escape observation. He was not always certain how far he could rely on those whom he had considered his friends, such as the brothers Hookham. Rightly or wrongly, he was led to imagine that[Pg 87] Harriet, from motives of revenge, was bent on ruining Godwin, and that for this purpose she would aid and abet in his own arrest, by persuading the Hookhams in such a case to refuse bail. The rumour of this conspiracy was conveyed to the Shelleys in a note from Fanny, who, for Godwin's sake and theirs, broke through the stern embargo laid on all communication.

Yet through all these troubles and bewilderments there went on a perpetual under-current of reading and study, thought and discussion. The actual existence was there, and all these external accidents of circumstance, the realities in ordinary lives, were, in these extraordinary lives, treated really as accidents, as passing hindrances to serious purpose, and no more.

Nothing but Mary's true love for Shelley and perfect happiness with him could have tided her over this time. Youth, however, was a wonderful helper, added to the unusual intellectual vigour and vivacity which made it possible for her, as it would be to few girls of seventeen, to forget the daily worries of life in reading and study. Perhaps at no time was the even balance of her nature more clearly manifested than now, when, after living through a romance that will last in story as long as the name of Shelley, her existence revolutionised, her sensibilities preternaturally stimulated, having taken, as it were, a life's experiences by[Pg 88] cumulation in a few months; weak and depressed in health, too, she still had sufficient energy and self-control to apply herself to a solid course of intellectual training.

Jane's presence added to their unsettlement, although at times it may have afforded them some amusement. Wilful, fanciful, with a sense of humour and many good impulses, but with that decided dash of charlatanism which characterised the Clairmonts, and little true sensibility, she was a willing disciple for any wild flights of fancy, and a keen participator in all impossible projects and harum-scarum makeshifts. Her presence stimulated and enlivened Shelley, her whims and fancies did not seriously affect, beyond amusing him, and she was an indefatigable companion for him in his walks and wanderings, now that Mary was becoming less and less able to go about. To Mary, however, she must often have been an incubus, a perpetual *third*, and one who, if sometimes useful, often gave a great deal of trouble too. She did not bring to Mary, as she did to Shelley, the charm of novelty; nor does the unfolding of one girl's character present to another girl whose character is also in process of development such attractive problems as it does to a young and speculative man. Mary was too noble by nature and too perfectly in accord with Shelley to indulge in actual jealousy of Jane's companionship with[Pg 89]him; still, she must often have had a weary time when those two were scouring the town on their multifarious errands; misunderstandings, also, would occur, only to be removed by long and patient explanation. Jane (or "Clara," as about this time she elected to call herself, in preference to her own less romantic name) was hardly more than a child, and in some respects a very childish child. Excitable and nervous, she had no idea of putting constraint upon herself for others' sake, and gave her neighbours very little rest, as she preferred any amount of scenes to humdrum quiet. She and Shelley would sit up half the night, amusing themselves with wild speculations, natural and supernatural, till she would go off into hysterics or trances, or, when she had at last gone to bed, would walk in her sleep, see phantoms, and frighten them all with her terrors. In the end she was invariably brought to poor Mary, who, delicate in health, had gone early to rest, but had to bestir herself to bring Jane to reason, and to "console her with her all-powerful benevolence," as Shelley describes it.

Every page of the journal testifies to the extreme youth of the writers; likely and unlikely events are chronicled with equal simplicity. Where all is new, one thing is not more startling than another; and the commonplaces of everyday life may afford more occasion for [Pg 90]surprise than the strangest anomalies. Specimens only of the diary can be given here, and they are best given without comment.

Sunday, September 18.—Mary receives her first lesson in Greek. She reads the *Curse of Kehama*, while Shelley walks out with Peacock, who dines. Shelley walks part of the way home with him. Curious account of Harriet. We talk, study a little Greek, and go to bed.

Tuesday, September 20.—Shelley writes to Hookham and Tavernier; goes with Hookham to Ballachy's. Mary reads *Political Justice* all the morning. Study Greek. In the evening Shelley reads *Thalaba* aloud.

Monday, September 26.—Shelley goes with Peacock to Ballachy's, and engages lodgings at Pancras. Visit from Mrs. Pringer. Read *Political Justice* and the *Empire of the Nairs*.

Tuesday, September 27.—Read *Political Justice*; finish the *Nairs*; pack up and go to our lodgings in Somers Town.

Friday, September 30.—After breakfast walk to Hampstead Heath. Discuss the possibility of converting and liberating two heiresses; arrange a plan on the subject.... Peacock calls; talk with him concerning the heiresses and Marian, arrange his marriage.

Sunday, October 2.—Peacock comes after breakfast; walk over Primrose Hill; sail little boats; return a little before four; talk. Read *Political Justice* in the evening; talk.

Monday, October 3.—Read *Political Justice*. Hookham calls. Walk with Peacock to the Lake of Nangis and set off little fire-boats. After dinner talk and let off fireworks. Talk of the west of Ireland plan.

Wednesday, October 5.—Peacock at breakfast. Walk to the Lake of Nangis and sail fire-boats. Read *Political Justice*. Shelley reads the *Ancient Mariner* aloud. Letter from Harriet, very civil. £400 for £2400.

Friday, October 7 (Shelley).—Read *Political Justice*. Peacock calls. Jane, for some reason, refuses to walk. We[Pg 91] traverse the fields towards Hampstead. Under an expansive oak lies a dead calf; the cow, lean from grief, is watching it. (Contemplate subject for poem.) The sunset is beautiful. Return at 9. Peacock departs. Mary goes to bed at half-past 8; Shelley sits up with Jane. Talk of oppression and reform, of cutting squares of skin from the soldiers' backs. Jane states her conception of the subterranean community of women. Talk of Hogg, Harriet, Miss Hitchener, etc. At 1 o'clock Shelley observes that it is the witching time of night; he inquires soon after if it is not horrible to feel the silence of night tingling in our ears; in half an hour the question is repeated in a different form; at 2 they retire awestruck and hardly daring to breathe. Shelley says to Jane, "Good-night;" his hand is leaning on the table; he is conscious of an expression in his countenance which he cannot repress. Jane hesitates. "Good-night" again. She still hesitates.

"Did you ever read the tragedy of *Orra*?" said Shelley.

"Yes. How horribly you look!—take your eyes off."

"Good-night" again, and Jane runs to her room. Shelley, unable to sleep, kissed Mary, and prepared to sit beside her and read till morning, when rapid footsteps descended the stairs. Jane was there; her countenance was distorted most unnaturally by horrible dismay—it beamed with a whiteness that seemed almost like light; her lips and cheeks were of one deadly hue; the skin of her face and forehead was drawn into innumerable wrinkles; the lineaments of terror that could not be contained; her hair came prominent and erect; her eyes were wide and staring, drawn almost from the sockets by the convulsion of the muscles; the eyelids were forced in, and the eyeballs, without any relief, seemed as if they had been newly inserted, in ghastly sport, in the sockets of a lifeless head. This frightful spectacle endured but for a few moments—it was displaced by terror and confusion, violent indeed, and full of dismay, but human. She asked me if I had touched her pillow (her tone was that of dreadful alarm). I said, "No, no! if you will come into the room I will tell you."[Pg 92] I informed her of Mary's pregnancy; this seemed to check her violence. She told me that a pillow placed upon her bed had been removed, in the moment that she turned her eyes away to a chair at some distance, and evidently by no human power. She was positive as to the facts of her self-possession and calmness. Her manner convinced me that she was not deceived. We continued to sit by the fire, at intervals engaging in awful conversation relative to the nature of these mysteries. I read part of *Alexy*; I repeated one of my own poems. Our conversation, though intentionally directed to other topics, irresistibly recurred to these. Our candles burned low; we feared they would not last until daylight. Just as the dawn was struggling with moonlight, Jane remarked in me that unutterable expression which had affected her with so much horror before; she described it as expressing a mixture of deep sadness and conscious power over her. I covered my face with my hands, and spoke to her in the most studied gentleness. It was ineffectual; her horror and agony increased even to the most dreadful convulsions. She shrieked and writhed on the floor. I ran to Mary; I communicated in few words the state of Jane. I brought her to Mary. The convulsions gradually ceased, and she slept. At daybreak we examined her apartment and found her pillow on the chair.

Saturday, October 8 (Mary).—Read *Political Justice*. We walked out; when we return Shelley talks with Jane, and I read *Wrongs of Women*. In the evening we talk and read.

Tuesday, October 11.—Read *Political Justice*. Shelley goes to the Westminster Insurance Office. Study Greek. Peacock dines. Receive a refusal about the money....

Have a good-humoured letter from Harriet, and a cold and even sarcastic one from Mrs. Boinville. Shelley reads the *History of the Illuminati*, out of Barruel, to us.

Wednesday, October 12.—Read *Political Justice*. A letter from Marshall; Jane goes there. When she comes home we go to Cheapside; returning, an occurrence. Deliberation until 7; burn the letter; sleep early.

[Pg 93]*Thursday, October 13.*—Communicate the burning of the letter. Much dispute and discussion concerning its probable contents. Alarm. Determine to quit London; send for £5 from Hookham. Change our resolution. Go to the play. The extreme depravity and disgusting nature of the scene; the inefficacy of acting to encourage or maintain the delusion. The loathsome sight of men personating characters which do not and cannot belong to them. Shelley displeased with what he saw of Kean. Return. Alarm. We sleep at the Stratford Hotel.

Friday, October 14 (Shelley).—Jane's insensibility and incapacity for the slightest degree of friendship. The feelings occasioned by this discovery prevent me from maintaining any measure in security. This highly incorrect; subversion of the first principles of true philosophy; characters, particularly those which are unformed, may change. Beware of weakly giving way to trivial sympathies. Content yourself with one great affection—with a single mighty hope; let the rest of mankind be the subjects of your benevolence, your justice, and, as human beings, of your sensibility; but, as you value many hours of peace, never suffer more than one even to approach the hallowed circle. Nothing should shake the truly great spirit which is not sufficiently mighty to destroy it.

Peacock calls. I take some interest in this man, but no possible conduct of his would disturb my tranquillity.... Converse with Jane; her mind unsettled; her character unformed; occasion of hope from some instances of softness and feeling; she is not entirely insensible to concessions, new proofs that the most exalted philosophy, the truest virtue, consists in an habitual contempt of self; a subduing of all angry feelings; a sacrifice of pride and selfishness. When you attempt benefit to either an individual or a community, abstain from imputing it as an error that they despise or overlook your virtue. These are incidental reflections which arise only indirectly from the circumstances recorded.

Walk with Peacock to the pond; talk of Marian and Greek metre. Peacock dines. In the evening read Cicero and the[Pg 94] *Paradoxa*. Night comes; Jane walks in her sleep, and groans horribly; listen for two hours; at length bring her to Mary. Begin *Julius*, and finish the little volume of Cicero.

The next morning the chimney board in Jane's room is found to have walked leisurely into the middle of the room, accompanied by the pillow, who, being very sleepy, tried to get into bed again, but sat down on his back.

Saturday, October 15 (Mary).—After breakfast read *Political Justice*. Shelley goes with Peacock to Ballachy's. A disappointment; it is put off till Monday. They then go to Homerton. Finish *St. Leon*. Jane writes to Marshall. A letter from my Father. Talking; Jane and I walk out. Shelley and Peacock return at 6. Shelley advises Jane not to go. Jane's letter to my Father. A refusal. Talk about going away, and, as usual, settle nothing.

Wednesday, October 19.—Finish *Political Justice*, read *Caleb Williams*. Shelley goes to the city, and meets with a total failure. Send to Hookham. Shelley reads a part of *Comus* aloud.

Thursday, October 20.—Shelley goes to the city. Finish *Caleb Williams*; read to Jane. Peacock calls; he has called on my father, who will not speak about Shelley to any one but an attorney. Oh! philosophy!...

Saturday, October 22.—Finish the *Life of Alfieri*. Go to the tomb (Mary Wollstonecraft's), and read the *Essay on Sepulchres* there. Shelley is out all the morning at the lawyer's, but nothing is done....

In the evening a letter from Fanny, warning us of the Hookhams. Jane and Shelley go after her; they find her, but Fanny runs away.

Monday, October 24.—Read aloud to Jane. At 11 go out to meet Shelley. Walk up and down Fleet Street; call at Peacock's; return to Fleet Street; call again at Peacock's; return to Pancras; remain an hour or two. People call; I suppose bailiffs. Return to Peacock's. Call at the coffee-house; see Shelley; he has been to Ballachy's. Good hopes; to be decided Thursday morning. Return to Peacock's; dine[Pg 95] there; get money. Return home in a coach; go to bed soon, tired to death.

Thursday, October 25.—Write to Shelley. Jane goes to Fanny.... Call at Peacock's; go to the hotel; Shelley not there. Go back to Peacock's. Peacock goes to Shelley. Meet Shelley in Holborn. Walk up and down Bartlett's Buildings.... Come with him to Peacock's; talk with him till 10; return to Pancras without him. Jane in the dumps all evening about going away.

Wednesday, October 26.—A visit from Shelley's old friends;[10] they go away much disappointed and very angry. He has written to T. Hookham to ask him to be bail. Return to Pancras about 4. Read all the evening.

Thursday, October 27.—Write to Fanny all morning. We had received letters from Skinner Street in the morning. Fanny is very doleful, and C. C. contradicts in one line what he had said in the line before. After two go to St. Paul's; meet Shelley; go with him in a coach to Hookham's; H. is out; return; leave him and proceed to Pancras. He has not received a definitive answer from Ballachy; meet a money-lender, of whom I have some hopes. Read aloud to Jane in the evening. Jane goes to sleep. Write to Shelley. A letter comes enclosing a letter from Hookham consenting to justify bail. Harriet has been to work there against my Father.

Tuesday, November 1.—Learn Greek all morning. Shelley goes to the 'Change. Jane calls.[11] People want their money; won't send up dinner, and we are all very hungry. Jane goes to Hookham. Shelley and I talk about her character. Jane returns without money. Writes to Fanny about coming to see her; she can't come. Writes to Charles. Goes to Peacock to send him to us with some eatables; he is out. Charles promises to see her. She returns to Pancras; he goes there, and tells the dismal state of the Skinner Street affairs. Shelley[Pg 96] goes to Peacock's; comes home with cakes. Wait till T. Hookham sends money to pay the bill. Shelley returns to Pancras. Have tea, and go to bed. Shelley goes to Peacock's to sleep.

These are two specimens of the notes constantly passing between them.

MARY TO SHELLEY.

25th October.

For what a minute did I see you yesterday. Is this the way, my beloved, we are to live till the 6th? In the morning when I wake I turn to look on you. Dearest Shelley, you are solitary and uncomfortable. Why cannot I be with you, to cheer you and press you to my heart? Ah! my love, you have no friends; why, then, should you be torn from the only one who has affection for you? But I shall see you to-night, and this is the hope I shall live on through the day. Be happy, dear Shelley, and think of me! I know how tenderly you love me, and how you repine at your absence from me. When shall we be free of treachery? I send you the letter I told you of from Harriet, and a letter we received yesterday from Fanny; the history of this interview I will tell you when I come. I was so dreadfully tired yesterday that I was obliged to take a coach home. Forgive this extravagance, but I am so very weak at present, and I had been so agitated through the day, that I was not able to stand; a morning's rest, however, will set me quite right again; I shall be well when I meet you this evening. Will you be at the door of the coffee-house at 5 o'clock, as it is disagreeable to go into those places. I shall be there exactly at that time, and we can go into St. Paul's, where we can sit down.

I send you *Diogenes*, as you have no books. Hookham was so ill-tempered as not to send the book I asked for. So this is the end of my letter, dearest love.

What do they mean?[12] I detest Mrs. Godwin; she plagues[Pg 97] my father out of his life; and these——Well, no matter. Why will Godwin not follow the obvious bent of his affections, and be reconciled to us? No; his prejudices, the world, and *she*—all these forbid it. What am I to do? trust to time, of course, for what else can I do. Good-night, my love; to-morrow I will seal this blessing on your lips. Press me, your own Mary, to your heart. Perhaps she will one day have a father; till then be everything to me, love; and, indeed, I will be a good girl, and never vex you. I will learn Greek and——but when shall we meet when I may tell you all this, and you will so sweetly reward me? But good-night; I am wofully tired, and so sleepy. One kiss—well, that is enough—to-morrow!

SHELLEY TO MARY.

28th October.

MY BELOVED MARY—I know not whether these transient meetings produce not as much pain as pleasure. What have I said? I do not mean it. I will not forget the sweet moments when I saw your eyes—the divine rapture of the few and fleeting kisses. Yet, indeed, this must cease; indeed, we must not part thus wretchedly to meet amid the comfortless tumult of business; to part I know not how.

Well, dearest love, to-morrow—to-morrow night. That eternal clock! Oh! that I could "fright the steeds of lazy-paced Time." I do not think that I am less impatient now than formerly to repossess—to entirely engross—my own treasured love. It seems so unworthy a cause for the slightest separation. I could reconcile it to my own feelings to go to prison if they would cease to persecute us with interruptions. Would it not be better, my heavenly love, to creep into the loathliest cave so that we might be together.

Mary, love, we must be united; I will not part from you again after Saturday night. We must devise some scheme. I must return. Your thoughts alone can waken mine to energy; my mind without yours is dead and cold as the dark midnight river when the moon is down. It seems as if you[Pg 98] alone could shield me from impurity and vice. If I were absent from you long, I should shudder with horror at myself; my understanding becomes undisciplined without you. I believe I must become in Mary's hands what Harriet was in mine. Yet how differently disposed—how devoted and affectionate—how, beyond measure, reverencing and adoring—the intelligence that governs me! I repent me of this simile; it is unjust; it is false. Nor do I mean that I consider you much my superior, evidently as you surpass me in originality and simplicity of mind. How divinely sweet a task it is to imitate each other's excellences, and each moment to become wiser in this surpassing love, so that, constituting but one being, all real knowledge may be comprised in the maxim γνωθι σεαυτον—(know thyself)—with infinitely more justice than in its narrow and common application. I enclose you Hookham's note; what do you think of it? My head aches; I am not well; I am tired with this comfortless estrangement from all that is dear to me. My own dearest love, good-night. I meet you in Staples Inn at twelve to-morrow—half an hour before twelve. I have written to Hooper and Sir J. Shelley.

Journal. Thursday. November 3 (Mary).—Work; write to Shelley; read Greek grammar. Receive a letter from Mr. Booth; so all my hopes are over there. Ah! Isabel; I did not think you would act thus. Read and work in the evening. Receive a letter from Shelley. Write to him.

[Letter not transcribed here.]

Sunday, November 6.—Talk to Shelley. He writes a great heap of letters. Read part of *St. Leon*. Talk with him all evening; this is a day devoted to Love in idleness. Go to sleep early in the evening. Shelley goes away a little before 10.

Wednesday, November 9.—Pack up all morning; leave Pancras about 3; call at Peacock's for Shelley; Charles Clairmont has been for £8. Go to Nelson Square. Jane gloomy; she is very sullen with Shelley. Well, never mind, my love—we are happy.

Thursday, November 10.—Jane is not well, and does not[Pg 99] speak the whole day. We send to Peacock's, but no good news arrives. Lambert has called there, and says he will write. Read a little of *Petronius*, a most detestable book. Shelley is out all the morning. In the evening read Louvet's *Memoirs*—go to bed early. Shelley and Jane sit up till 12, talking; Shelley talks her into a good humour.

Sunday, November 13.—Write in the morning; very unwell all day. Fanny sends a letter to Jane to come to Blackfriars Road; Jane cannot go. Fanny comes here; she will not see me; hear everything she says, however. They think my letter cold and *indelicate*! God bless them. Papa tells Fanny if she sees me he will never speak to her again; a blessed degree of liberty this! He has had a very impertinent letter from Christy Baxter. The reason she comes is to ask Jane to Skinner Street to see Mrs. Godwin, who they say is dying. Jane has no clothes. Fanny goes back to Skinner Street to get some. She returns. Jane goes with her. Shelley returns (he had been to Hookham's); he disapproves. Write and read. In the evening talk with my love about a great many things. We receive a letter from Jane saying she is very happy, and she does not know when she will return. Turner has called at Skinner Street; he says it is too far to Nelson Square. I am unwell in the evening.

Journal. November 14 (Shelley).—Mary is unwell. Receive a note from Hogg; cloth from Clara. I wish this girl had a resolute mind. Without firmness understanding is impotent, and the truest principles unintelligible. Charles calls to confer concerning Lambert; walk with him. Go to 'Change, to Peacock's, to Lambert's; receive £30. In the evening Hogg calls; perhaps he still may be my friend, in spite of the radical differences of sympathy between us; he was pleased with Mary; this was the test by which I had previously determined to judge his character. We converse on many interesting subjects, and Mary's illness disappears for a time.

Thursday, November 15 (Shelley).—Disgusting dreams have occupied the night.

(Mary).—Very unwell. Jane calls; converse with her.[Pg 100] She goes to Skinner Street; tells Papa that she will not return; comes back to Nelson Square with Shelley; calls at Peacock's. Shelley read aloud to us in the evening out of Adolphus's *Lives*.

Wednesday, November 16.—Very ill all day. Shelley and Jane out all day shopping about the town. Shelley reads *Edgar Huntley* to us. Shelley and Jane go to Hookham's. Hogg comes in the meantime; he stops all the evening. Shelley writes his critique till half-past 3.

Saturday, November 19.—Very ill. Shelley and Jane go out to call at Mrs. Knapp's; she receives Jane kindly; promises to come and see me. I go to bed early. Charles Clairmont calls in the evening, but I do not see him.

Sunday, November 20.—Still very ill; get up very late. In the evening Shelley reads aloud out of the *Female Revolutionary Plutarch*. Hogg comes in the evening.... Get into an argument about virtue, in which Hogg makes a sad bungle; quite muddled on the point, I perceive.

Tuesday, November 29.—Work all day. Heigh ho! Clara and Shelley go before breakfast to Parker's. After breakfast, Shelley is as badly off as I am with my work, for he is out all day with those lawyers. In the evening Shelley and Jane go in search of Charles Clairmont; they cannot find him. Read *Philip Stanley*—very stupid.

Tuesday, December 6.—Very unwell. Shelley and Clara walk out, as usual, to heaps of places. Read *Agathon*, which I do not like so well as *Peregrine*.... A letter from Hookham, to say that Harriet has been brought to bed of a son and heir. Shelley writes a number of circular letters of this event, which ought to be ushered in with ringing of bells, etc., for it is the son *of his wife*. Hogg comes in the evening; I like him better, though he vexed me by his attachment to sporting. A letter from Harriet confirming the news, in a letter from a *deserted wife*!! and telling us he has been born a week.

Wednesday, December 7.—Clara and Shelley go out together; Shelley calls on the lawyers and on Harriet, who treats him with insulting selfishness; they return home wet and very tired. Read *Agathon*. I like it less to-day; he discovers[Pg 101] many opinions which I think detestable. Work. In the evening Charles Clairmont comes. Hear that Place is trying to raise £1200 to pay Hume on Shelley's *post obit*; affairs very bad in Skinner Street; afraid of a call for the rent; all very bad. Shelley walks home with Charles Clairmont; goes to Hookham's about the £100 to lend my Father. Hookham out. He returns; very tired. Work in the evening.

Thursday, December 8.—Shelley and Clara go to Hookham's; get the £90 for my father; they are out, as usual, all morning. Finish *Agathon*. I do not like it; Wieland displays some most detestable opinions; he is one of those men who alter all their opinions when they are about forty, and then think it will be the same with every one, and that they are themselves the only proper monitors of youth. Work. When Shelley and Clara return, Shelley goes to Lambert's; out. Work. In the evening Hogg comes; talk about a great number of things; he is more sincere this evening than I have seen him before. Odd dreams.

Friday, December 16.—Still ill; heigh ho! Finish *Jane Talbot*. Hume calls at half-past 12; he tells of the great distress in Skinner Street; I do not see him. Hookham calls; hasty little man; he does not stay long. In the evening Hogg comes. Shelley and Clara are at first out; they have been to look for Charles Clairmont; they find him, and walk with him some time up and down Ely Place. Shelley goes to sleep early; very tired. We talk about flowers and trees in the evening; a country conversation.

Saturday, December 17.—Very ill. Shelley and Clara go to Pike's; when they return, Shelley goes to walk round the Square. Talk with Shelley in the evening; he sleeps, and I lie down on the bed. Jane goes to Pike's at 9. Charles Clairmont comes, and talks about several things. Mrs. Godwin did not allow Fanny to come down to dinner on her receiving a lock of my hair. Fanny of course behaves slavishly on the occasion. He goes at half-past 11.

Sunday, December 18.—Better, but far from well. Pass a very happy morning with Shelley. Charles Clairmont comes at[Pg 102] dinner-time, the Skinner Street folk having gone to dine at the Kennie's. Jane and he take a long walk together. Shelley and I are left alone. Hogg comes after Clara and her brother return. C. C. flies from the field on his approach. Conversation as usual. Get worse towards night.

Monday, December 19 (Shelley).—Mary rather better this morning. Jane goes to Hume's about Godwin's bills; learn that Lambert is inclined, but hesitates. Hear of a woman—supposed to be the daughter of the Duke of Montrose—who has the head of a hog. *Suetonius* is finished, and Shelley begins the *Historia Augustana*. Charles Clairmont comes in the evening; a discussion concerning female character. Clara imagines that I treat her unkindly; Mary consoles her with her all-powerful benevolence. I rise (having already gone to bed) and speak with Clara; she was very unhappy; I leave her tranquil.

Tuesday, December 20 (Mary).—Shelley goes to Pike's; take a short walk with him first. Unwell. A letter from Harriet, who threatens Shelley with her lawyer. In the evening read *Emilia Galotti*. Hogg comes. Converse of various things. He goes at twelve.

Wednesday, December 21 (Shelley).—Mary is better. Shelley goes to Pike's, to the Insurance Offices, and the lawyer's; an agreement entered into for £3000 for £1000. A letter from Wales, offering *post obit*. Shelley goes to Hume's; Mary reads Miss Baillie's plays in the evening. Shelley goes to bed at 8; Mary at 11.

Saturday, December 24 (Mary).—Read *View of French Revolution*. Walk out with Shelley, and spend a dreary morning waiting for him at Mr. Peacock's. In the evening Hogg comes. I like him better each time; it is a pity that he is a lawyer; he wasted so much time on that trash that might be spent on better things.

Sunday, December 25.—Christmas Day. Have a very bad side-ache in the morning, so I rise late. Charles Clairmont comes and dines with us. In the afternoon read Miss Baillie's plays. Hogg spends the evening with us; conversation, as usual.

[Pg 103]*Monday, December 26* (Shelley).—The sweet Maie asleep; leave a note with her. Walk with Clara to Pike's, etc. Go to Hampstead and look for a house; we return in a return-chaise; find that Laurence has arrived, and consult for Mary; she has read Miss Baillie's plays all day. Mary better this evening. Shelley very much fatigued; sleeps all the evening. Read *Candide*.

Tuesday, December 27 (Mary).—Not very well; Shelley very unwell. Read *De Montfort*, and talk with Shelley in the evening. Read *View of the French Revolution*. Hogg comes in the evening; talk of heaps of things. Shelley's odd dream.

Wednesday, December 28.—Shelley and Clara out all the morning. Read *French Revolution* in the evening. Shelley and I go to Gray's Inn to get Hogg; he is not there; go to Arundel Street; can't find him. Go to Garnerin's. Lecture on electricity; the gases, and the phantasmagoria; return at half-past 9. Shelley goes to sleep. Read *View of French Revolution* till 12; go to bed.

Friday, December 30.—Shelley and Jane go out as usual. Read Bryan Edwards's *Account of West Indies*. They do not return till past seven, having been locked into Kensington Gardens; both very tired. Hogg spends the evening with us.

Saturday, December 31 (Shelley).—The poor Maie was very weak and tired all day. Shelley goes to Pike's and Humes' and Mrs. Peacock's;[13] return very tired, and sleeps all the evening. The Maie goes to sleep early. New Year's Eve.

In January 1815 Shelley's grandfather, Sir Bysshe, died, and his father, Mr. Timothy Shelley, succeeded to the baronetcy and estate. By an arrangement with his father, according to which he relinquished all claim on a certain portion of his patrimony, Shelley now became possessed of £1000 a year (£200 a year of which he at once set[Pg 104] apart for Harriet), as well as a considerable sum of ready money for the relief of his present necessities. £200 of this he also sent to Harriet to pay her debts. The next few entries in the journal were, however, written before this event.

Thursday, January 5 (Mary).—Go to breakfast at Hogg's; Shelley leaves us there and goes to Hume's. When he returns we go to Newman Street; see the statue of Theoclea; it is a divinity that raises your mind to all virtue and excellence; I never beheld anything half so wonderfully beautiful. Return home very ill. Expect Hogg in the evening, but he does not come. Too ill to read.

Friday, January 6.—Walk to Mrs. Peacock's with Clara. Walk with Hogg to Theoclea; she is ten thousand times more beautiful to-day than ever; tear ourselves away. Return to Nelson Square; no one at home. Hogg stays a short time with me. Shelley had stayed at home till 2 to see Ryan;[14] he does not come. Goes out about business. In the evening Shelley and Clara go to Garnerin's.... Very unwell. Hogg comes. Shelley and Clara return at ten. Conversation as usual. Shelley reads "Ode to France" aloud, and repeats the poem to "Tranquillity." Talk with Shelley afterwards for some time; at length go to sleep. Shelley goes out and sits in the other room till 5; I then call him. Talk. Shelley goes to sleep; at 8 Shelley rises and goes out.

The next entry is made during Shelley's short absence in Sussex, after his grandfather's death. Clara had accompanied him on his journey.

(*Date between January 7 and January 13*).—Letter from Peacock to say that he is in prison.... His debt is £40....[Pg 105] Write to Peacock and send him £2. Hogg dines with me and spends the evening; letter from Hookham.

Friday, January 13.—A letter from Clara. While I am at breakfast Shelley and Clara arrive. The will has been opened, and Shelley is referred to Whitton. His father would not allow him to enter Field Place; he sits before the door and reads *Comus*. Dr. Blocksome comes out; tells him that his father is very angry with him. Sees my name in Milton.... Hogg dines, and spends the evening with us.

Sunday, January 24.—In the evening Shelley, Clara, and Hogg sleep. Read Gibbon.... Hogg goes at half-past 11. Shelley and Clara explain as usual.

Monday, January 30.—Work all day. Shelley reads Livy. In the evening Shelley reads *Paradise Regained* aloud, and then goes to sleep. Hogg comes at 9. Talk and work. Hogg sleeps here.

Wednesday, February 1.—Read Gibbon (end of vol. i.) Shelley reads Livy in the evening. Work. Shelley and Clara sleep. Hogg comes and sleeps here. Mrs. Hill calls.

Sunday, February 5.—Read Gibbon. Take a long walk in Kensington Gardens and the Park; meet Clairmont as we return, and hear that my father wishes to see a copy of the codicil, because he thinks Shelley is acting rashly. All this is very odd and inconsistent, but I never quarrel with inconsistency; folks must change their minds. After dinner talk. Shelley finishes Gibbon's *Memoirs* aloud. Clara, Shelley, and Hogg sleep. Read Gibbon. Shelley writes to Longdill and Clairmont. Hogg ill, but we cannot persuade him to stay; he goes at half-past 11.

Wednesday, February 8.—Ash Wednesday. So Hogg stays all day. We are to move to-day, so Shelley and Clara go out to look for lodgings. Hogg and I pack, and then talk. Shelley and Clara do not return till 3; they have not succeeded; go out again; they get apartments at Hans Place; move. In the evening talk and read Gibbon. Letters. Pike calls; insolent plague. Hogg goes at half-past 11.

Tuesday, February 14 (Shelley).—Shelley goes to Longdill's[Pg 106] and Hayward's, and returns feverish and fatigued. Maie finishes the third volume of Gibbon. All unwell in the evening. Hogg comes and puts us to bed. Hogg goes at half-past 11.

In this month, probably on the 22d (but that page of the diary is torn), when they had been hardly more than a week in their last new lodgings, a little girl was born. Although her confinement was premature, Mary had a favourable time; the infant, a scarcely seven months' child, was not expected to live; it survived, however, for some days. It might possibly have been saved, had it had an ordinary chance of life given it, but, on the ninth day of its existence, the whole family moved yet again to new lodgings. How the young mother ever recovered from the fatigues, risks, and worries she had to go through at this critical time may well be wondered. It is more than probable that the unreasonable demands made on her strength and courage during this month and those which preceded it laid the foundation of much weak health later on. The child was sacrificed. Four days after the move it was found in the morning dead by its mother's side. The poor little thing was a mere passing episode in Shelley's troubled, hurried existence. Only to Mary were its birth and death a deep and permanent experience. Apart from her love for Shelley, her affections had been chiefly of the intellectual kind, and even in her relation with him mental affinity had[Pg 107] played a great part. A new chord in her temperament was set vibrating by the advent of this baby, the maternal one, quite absent from her disposition before, and which was to assert itself at last as the keynote of her nature.

Hogg, who was almost constantly with them at this time, seems to have been kind, helpful, and sympathetic.

The baby's birth was too much for Fanny Godwin's endurance and fortitude. Up to this time she had, in accordance with what she conceived to be her duty, held aloof from the Shelleys, but, the barrier once broken down, she came repeatedly to see them. Mrs. Godwin showed that she had a soft spot in her heart by sending Mary, through Fanny, a present of linen, no doubt most welcome at this unprepared-for crisis. Beyond this she was unrelenting. Her pride, however, was not so strong as her feminine curiosity, which she indulged still by parading before the windows and trying to get peeps at the people behind them. She was annoyed with Fanny, who now, however, held her own course, feeling that her duty could not be all on one side while her family consented to be dependent, and that every moment of her father's peace and safety were due entirely to this Shelley whom he would not see.

Journal, February 22 (Shelley) (after the baby's birth).—Maie perfectly well and at ease. The child is not quite seven[Pg 108] months; the child not expected to live. Shelley sits up with Maie, much exhausted and agitated. Hogg sleeps here.

Thursday, February 23.—Mary quite well; the child unexpectedly alive, but still not expected to live. Hogg returns in the evening at half-past 7. Shelley writes to Fanny requesting her to come and see Maie. Fanny comes and remains the whole night, the Godwins being absent from home. Charles comes at 11 with linen from Mrs. Godwin. Hogg departs at 11. £30 from Longdill.

Friday, February 24.—Maie still well; favourable symptoms in the child; we may indulge some hopes. Hogg calls at 2. Fanny departs. Dr. Clarke calls; confirms our hopes of the child. Shelley finishes second volume of Livy, p. 657. Hogg comes in the evening. Shelley very unwell and exhausted.

Saturday, February 25.—The child very well; Maie very well also; drawing milk all day. Shelley is very unwell.

Sunday, February 26 (Mary).—Maie rises to-day. Hogg comes; talk; she goes to bed at 6. Hogg calls at the lodgings we have taken. Read *Corinne*. Shelley and Clara go to sleep. Hogg returns; talk with him till past 11. He goes. Shelley and Clara go down to tea. Just settling to sleep when a knock comes to the door; it is Fanny; she came to see how we were; she stays talking till half-past 3, and then leaves the room that Shelley and Mary may sleep. Shelley has a spasm.

Monday, February 27.—Rise; talk and read *Corinne*. Hogg comes in the evening. Shelley and Clara go out about a cradle....

Tuesday, February 28.—I come downstairs; talk, nurse the baby, read *Corinne*, and work. Shelley goes to Pemberton about his health.

Wednesday, March 1.—Nurse the baby, read *Corinne*, and work. Shelley and Clara out all morning. In the evening Peacock comes. Talk about types, editions, and Greek letters all the evening. Hogg comes. They go away at half-past 11. Bonaparte invades France.

[Pg 109]*Thursday, March 2.*—A bustle of moving. Read *Corinne*. I and my baby go about 3. Shelley and Clara do not come till 6. Hogg comes in the evening.

Friday, March 3.—Nurse my baby; talk, and read *Corinne*. Hogg comes in the evening.

Saturday, March 4.—Read, talk, and nurse. Shelley reads the *Life of Chaucer*. Hogg comes in the evening and sleeps.

Sunday, March 5.—Shelley and Clara go to town. Hogg here all day. Read *Corinne* and nurse my baby. In the evening talk. Shelley finishes the *Life of Chaucer*. Hogg goes at 11.

Monday, March 6.—Find my baby dead. Send for Hogg. Talk. A miserable day. In the evening read *Fall of the Jesuits*. Hogg sleeps here.

Tuesday, March 7.—Shelley and Clara go after breakfast to town. Write to Fanny. Hogg stays all day with us; talk with him, and read the *Fall of the Jesuits* and *Rinaldo Rinaldini*. Not in good spirits. Hogg goes at 11. A fuss. To bed at 3.

Wednesday, March 8.—Finish *Rinaldini*. Talk with Shelley. In very bad spirits, but get better; sleep a little in the day. In the evening net. Hogg comes; he goes at half-past 11. Clara has written for Fanny, but she does not come.

Thursday, March 9.—Read and talk. Still think about my little baby. 'Tis hard, indeed, for a mother to lose a child. Hogg and Charles Clairmont come in the evening. C. C. goes at 11. Hogg stays all night. Read Fontenelle, *Plurality of Worlds*.

Friday, March 10.—Hogg's holidays begin. Shelley, Hogg, and Clara go to town. Hogg comes back soon. Talk and net. Hogg now remains with us. Put the room to rights.

Saturday, March 11.—Very unwell. Hogg goes to town. Talk about Clara's going away; nothing settled; I fear it is hopeless. She will not go to Skinner Street; then our house[Pg 110] is the only remaining place, I see plainly. What is to be done? Hogg returns. Talk, and Hogg reads the *Life of Goldoni* aloud.

Sunday, March 4.—Talk a great deal. Not well, but better. Very quiet all the morning, and happy, for Clara does not get up till 4. In the evening read Gibbon, fourth volume; go to bed at 12.

Monday, March 13.—Shelley and Clara go to town. Stay at home; net, and think of my little dead baby. This is foolish, I suppose; yet, whenever I am left alone to my own thoughts, and do not read to divert them, they always come back to the same point—that I was a mother, and am so no longer. Fanny comes, wet through; she dines, and stays the evening; talk about many things; she goes at half-past 9. Cut out my new gown.

Tuesday, March 14.—Shelley calls on Dr. Pemberton. Net till breakfast. Shelley reads *Religio Medici* aloud, after Hogg has gone to town. Work; finish Hogg's purse. Shelley and I go upstairs and talk of Clara's going; the prospect appears to me more dismal than ever; not the least hope. This is, indeed, hard to bear. In the evening Hogg reads Gibbon to me. Charles Clairmont comes in the evening.

Sunday, March 19.—Dream that my little baby came to life again; that it had only been cold, and that we rubbed it before the fire, and it lived. Awake and find no baby. I think about the little thing all day. Not in good spirits. Shelley is very unwell. Read Gibbon. Charles Clairmont comes. Hogg goes to town till dinner-time. Talk with Charles Clairmont about Skinner Street. They are very badly off there. I am afraid nothing can be done to save them. C. C. says that he shall go to America; this I think a rather wild project in the Clairmont style. Play a game of chess with Clara. In the evening Shelley and Hogg play at chess. Shelley and Clara walk part of the way with Charles Clairmont. Play chess with Hogg, and then read Gibbon.

Monday, March 20.—Dream again about my baby. Work[Pg 111] after breakfast, and then go with Shelley, Hogg, and Clara to Bullock's Museum; spend the morning there. Return and find more letters for A. Z.—one from a "Disconsolate Widow."[15]

Wednesday, March 22.—Talk, and read the papers. Read Gibbon all day. Charles Clairmont calls about Shelley lending £100. We do not return a decisive answer.

....

Thursday, March 23.—Read Gibbon. Shelley reads Livy. Walk with Shelley and Hogg to Arundel Street. Read *Le Diable Boiteux*. Hear that Bonaparte has entered Paris. As we come home, meet my father and Charles Clairmont.... C. C. calls; he tells us that Papa saw us, and that he remarked that Shelley was so beautiful, it was a pity he was so wicked.

....

Tuesday, March 28.—Work in the morning and then walk out to look at house.

Saturday, April 8.—Peacock comes at breakfast-time; Hogg and he go to town. Read *L'Esprit des Nations*. Settle to go to Virginia Water.

....

Sunday, April 9.—Rise at 8. Charles Clairmont comes to breakfast at 10. Read some lines of Ovid before breakfast; after, walk with Shelley, Hogg, Clara, and C. C. to pond in Kensington Gardens; return about 2. C. C. goes to Skinner Street. Read Ovid with Hogg (finish second fable). Shelley reads Gibbon and *Pastor Fido* with Clara. In the evening read *L'Esprit des Nations*. Shelley reads Gibbon, *Pastor Fido*, and the story of Myrrha in Ovid.

Monday, April 10.—Read Voltaire before breakfast. After breakfast work. Shelley passes the morning with Harriet, who is in a surprisingly good humour. Mary reads third fable of Ovid: Shelley and Clara read *Pastor Fido*. Shelley reads Gibbon. Mrs. Godwin after dinner parades before the[Pg 112] windows. Talk in the evening with Hogg about mountains and lakes and London.

Tuesday, April 11.—Work in the morning. Receive letters from Skinner Street to say that Mamma had gone away in the pet, and had stayed out all night. Read fourth and fifth fables of Ovid.... After tea, work. Charles Clairmont comes.

Saturday, April 15.—Read Ovid till 3. Shelley and Clara finish *Pastor Fido*, and then go out about Clara's lottery ticket; draws. Clara's ticket comes up a prize. She buys two desks after dinner. Read Ovid (ninety-five lines). Shelley and Clara begin *Orlando Furioso*. A very grim dream.

Friday, April 21.—After breakfast go with Shelley to Peacock's. Shelley goes to Longdill's. Read third canto of the *Lord of the Isles*. Return about 2. Shelley goes to Harriet to procure his son, who is to appear in one of the courts. After dinner look over W. W.'s poems. After tea read forty lines of Ovid. Fanny comes and gives us an account of Hogan's threatened arrest of my Father. Shelley walks home part of the way with her. Very sleepy. Shelley reads one canto of Ariosto.

Saturday, April 22.—Read a little of Ovid. Shelley goes to Harriet's about his son. Work. Fanny comes. Shelley returns at 4; he has been much teased with Harriet. He has been to Longdill's, Whitton's, etc., and at length has got a promise that he shall appear Monday. After dinner Fanny goes. Read sixty lines of Ovid. Shelley and Clara read to the middle of the fourteenth canto of Ariosto.

Shortly after this several leaves of the journal are lost.

Friday, May 5.—After breakfast to Marshall's,[16] but do not see him. Go to the Tomb. Shelley goes to Longdill's. Return soon. Read Spenser; construe Ovid.... After dinner talk with Shelley; then Shelley and Clara go out.... Fanny[Pg 113] comes; she tells us of Marshall's servant's death. Papa is to see Mrs. Knapp to-morrow. Read Spenser. Walk home with Fanny and with Shelley.... Shelley reads Seneca.

Monday, May 8.—Go out with Shelley to Mrs. Knapp; not at home. Buy Shelley a pencil-case. Return at 1. Read Spenser. Go again with Shelley to Mrs. Knapp; she cannot take Clara. Read Spenser after dinner. Clara goes out with Shelley. Talk with Jefferson (Hogg); write to Marshall. Read Spenser. They return at 8. Very tired; go to bed early. Jefferson scolds.

Wednesday, May 10.—Not very well; rise late. Walk to Marshall's, and talk with him for an hour. Go with Jefferson and Shelley to British Museum—attend most to the statues; return at 2. Construe Ovid. After dinner construe Ovid (100 lines); finish second book of Spenser, and read two cantos of the third. Shelley reads Seneca every day and all day.

Friday, May 12.—Not very well. After breakfast read Spenser. Shelley goes out with his friend; he returns first. Construe Ovid (90 lines); read Spenser. Jefferson returns at half-past 4, and tells us that poor Sawyer is to be hung. These blessed laws! After dinner read Spenser. Read over the Ovid to Jefferson, and construe about ten lines more. Read Spenser. Shelley and the lady walk out. After tea, talk; write Greek characters. Shelley and his friend have a last conversation.

Saturday, May 13.—Clara goes; Shelley walks with her. C. C. comes to breakfast; talk. Shelley goes out with him. Read Spenser all day (finish Canto 8, Book V.) Jefferson does not come till 5. Get very anxious about Shelley; go out to meet him; return; it rains. Shelley returns at half-past 6; the business is finished. After dinner Shelley is very tired, and goes to sleep. Read Ovid (60 lines). C. C. comes to tea. Talk of pictures.

(Mary).—A tablespoonful of the spirit of aniseed, with a small quantity of spermaceti.

[Pg 114](Shelley)—9 drops of human blood, 7 grains of gunpowder, ½ oz. of putrified brain, 13 mashed grave worms—the Pecksie's doom salve.

The Maie and her Elfin Knight.

I begin a new journal with our regeneration.

[Pg 115]

CHAPTER VIII
MAY 1815-SEPTEMBER 1816

"Our regeneration" meant, in other words, the departure of Jane or "Clara" Clairmont who, on the plea of needing change of air, went off by herself into cottage lodgings at Lynmouth, in North Devon. She had never shown any very great desire to go back to her family in Skinner Street, but even had it been otherwise, objections had now been raised to her presence there which made her return difficult if not impossible. Fanny Godwin's aunts, Everina Wollstonecraft and Mrs. Bishop, were Principals of a select Ladies' School in Dublin, and intended that, on their own retirement, their niece should succeed them in its management. They strongly objected now to her associating with Miss Clairmont, pointing out that, even if her morals were not injured, her professional prospects must be marred by the fact being generally known of her connection and companionship with a girl who undoubtedly had run away from home, and who was, untruly[Pg 116] but not groundlessly, reported to be concerned in a notorious scandal.

Her continued presence in the Shelley household, a thing probably never contemplated at the time of their hurried flight, was manifestly undesirable, on many grounds. To Mary it was a perpetual trial, and must, in the end, have tended towards disagreement between her and Shelley, while it put Clara herself at great and unjust social disadvantage. Not that she heeded that, or regretted the barrier that divided her from Skinner Street, where poverty and anxiety and gloom reigned paramount, and where she would have been watched with ceaseless and unconcealed suspicion. She had heard that her relations had even discussed the advisability of immuring her in a convent if she could be caught,—but she did not mean to be caught. She advertised for a situation as companion; nothing, however, came of this. An idea of sending her to board in the family of a Mrs. Knapp seems to have been entertained for some months both by Godwins and Shelleys, Charles Clairmont probably acting as a medium between the two households. But, after appearing well disposed at first, Mrs. Knapp thought better of the plan. She did not want, and would not have Clara. The final project, that of the Lynmouth lodgings, was a sudden idea, suddenly carried[Pg 117] out, and devised with the Shelleys independently of the Godwins, who were not consulted, nor even informed, until it had been put into execution. So much is to be gathered from the letter which Clara wrote to Fanny a fortnight after her arrival.

CLARA TO FANNY.

Sunday, 28th May 1815.

MY DEAR FANNY—Mary writes me that you thought me unkind in not letting you know before my departure; indeed, I meant no unkindness, but I was afraid if I told you that it might prevent my putting a plan into execution which I preferred before all the Mrs. Knapps in the world. Here I am at liberty; there I should have been under a perpetual restraint. Mrs. Knapp is a forward, impertinent, superficial woman. Here there are none such; a few cottages, with little, rosy-faced children, scolding wives, and drunken husbands. I wish I had a more amiable and romantic picture to present to you, such as shepherds and shepherdesses, flocks and madrigals; but this is the truth, and the truth is best at all times. I live in a little cottage, with jasmine and honeysuckle twining over the window; a little downhill garden full of roses, with a sweet arbour. There are only two gentlemen's seats here, and they are both absent. The walks and shrubberies are quite open, and are very delightful. Mr. Foote's stands at top of the hill, and commands distant views of the whole country. A green tottering bridge, flung from rock to rock, joins his garden to his house, and his side of the bridge is a waterfall. One tumbles directly down, and then flows gently onward, while the other falls successively down five rocks, and seems like water running down stone steps. I will tell you, so far, that it is a valley I live in, and perhaps one you may have seen. Two ridges of mountains enclose the village, which is situated at the west end. A river, which you may step over, runs at the foot of the mountains, and[Pg 118] trees hang so closely over, that when on a high eminence you sometimes lose sight of it for a quarter of a mile. One ridge of hills is entirely covered with luxuriant trees, the opposite line is entirely bare, with long pathways of slate and gray rocks, so that you might almost fancy they had once been volcanic. Well, enough of the valleys and the mountains.

You told me you did not think I should ever be able to live alone. If you knew my constant tranquillity, how cheerful and gay I am, perhaps you would alter your opinion. I am perfectly happy. After so much discontent, such violent scenes, such a turmoil of passion and hatred, you will hardly believe how enraptured I am with this dear little quiet spot. I am as happy when I go to bed as when I rise. I am never disappointed, for I know the extent of my pleasures; and let it rain or let it be fair weather, it does not disturb my serene mood. This is happiness; this is that serene and uninterrupted rest I have long wished for. It is in solitude that the powers concentre round the soul, and teach it the calm, determined path of virtue and wisdom. Did you not find this—did you not find that the majestic and tranquil mountains impressed deep and tranquil thoughts, and that everything conspired to give a sober temperature of mind, more truly delightful and satisfying than the gayest ebullitions of mirth?

> The foaming cataract and tall rock
> Haunt me like a passion.

Now for a little chatting. I was quite delighted to hear that Papa had at last got £1000. Riches seem to fly from genius. I suppose, for a month or two, you will be easy—pray be cheerful. I begin to think there is no situation without its advantages. You may learn wisdom and fortitude in adversity, and in prosperity you may relieve and soothe. I feel anxious to be wise; to be capable of knowing the best; of following resolutely, however painful, what mature and serious thought may prescribe; and of acquiring a prompt and vigorous judgment, and powers capable of execution. What are you reading? Tell Charles, with my best love, that I will[Pg 119] never forgive him for having disappointed me of Wordsworth, which I miss very much. Ask him, likewise, to lend me his Coleridge's poems, which I will take great care of. How is dear Willy? How is every one? If circumstances get easy, don't you think Papa and Mamma will go down to the seaside to get up their health a little? Write me a very long letter, and tell me everything. How is your health? Now do not be melancholy; for heaven's sake be cheerful; so young in life, and so melancholy! The moon shines in at my window, there is a roar of waters, and the owls are hooting. How often do I not wish for a curfew!—"swinging slow with sullen roar!" Pray write to me. Do, there's a good Fanny.—Affectionately yours,

M. J. CLAIRMONT.

Miss Fanny Godwin,
41 Skinner Street, Snow Hill, London.

How long this delightful life of solitude lasted is not exactly known. For a year after this time both Clara's journal and that of Shelley and Mary are lost, and the next thing we hear of Clara is her being in town in the spring of 1816, when she first made Lord Byron's acquaintance.

Mary, at any rate, enjoyed nearly a year of comparative peace and *tête-à-tête* with Shelley, which, after all she had gone through, must have been happiness indeed. Had she known that it was the only year she would ever pass with him without the presence of a third person, it may be that—although her loyalty to Shelley stood every test—her heart might have sunk within her. But, happily for her, she could not foresee this. Her letter from Clifton shows that Clara's shadow haunted[Pg 120] her at times. Still she was happy, and at peace. Her health, too, was better; and, though always weighed down by Godwin's anxieties, she and Shelley were, themselves, free for once from the pinch of actual penury and the perpetual fear of arrest.

In June they made a tour in South Devon, and very probably paid Clara a visit in her rural retirement; after which Mary stayed for some time at Clifton, while Shelley travelled about looking for a country house to suit them. It was during one of his absences that Mary wrote to him the letter referred to above.

MARY TO SHELLEY.

CLIFTON, *27th July 1815.*

MY BELOVED SHELLEY—What I am now going to say is not a freak from a fit of low spirits, but it is what I earnestly entreat you to attend to and comply with.

We ought not to be absent any longer; indeed we ought not. I am not happy at it. When I retire to my room, no sweet love; after dinner, no Shelley; though I have heaps of things *very particular* to say; in fine, either you must come back, or I must come to you directly. You will say, shall we neglect taking a house—a dear home? No, my love, I would not for worlds give up that; but I know what seeking for a house is, and, trust me, it is a very, *very* long job, too long for one love to undertake in the absence of the other. Dearest, I know how it will be; we shall both of us be put off, day after day, with the hopes of the success of the next day's search, for I am frightened to think how long. Do you not see it in this light, my own love? We have been now a long time separated, and a house is not yet in sight; and even if you should fix on one, which I do not hope for in less than a[Pg 121] week, then the settling, etc. Indeed, my love, I cannot bear to remain so long without you; so, if you will not give me leave, expect me without it some day; and, indeed, it is very likely that you may, for I am quite sick of passing day after day in this hopeless way.

Pray, is Clara with you? for I have inquired several times and no letters; but, seriously, it would not in the least surprise me, if you have written to her from London, and let her know that you are without me, that she should have taken some such freak.

The Dormouse has hid the brooch; and, pray, why am I for ever and ever to be denied the sight of my case? Have you got it in your own possession? or where is it? It would give me very great pleasure if you would send it me. I hope you have not already appropriated it, for if you have I shall think it un-Pecksie of you, as Maie was to give it you with her own hands on your birthday; but it is of little consequence, for I have no hope of seeing you on that day; but I am mistaken, for I have hope and certainty, for if you are not here on or before the 3d of August, I set off on the 4th, in early coach, so as to be with you in the evening of that dear day at least.

To-morrow is the 28th of July. Dearest, ought we not to have been together on that day? Indeed we ought, my love, as I shall shed some tears to think we are not. Do not be angry, dear love; your Pecksie is a good girl, and is quite well now again, except a headache, when she waits so anxiously for her love's letters.

Dearest, best Shelley, pray come to me; pray, pray do not stay away from me! This is delightful weather, and you better, we might have a delightful excursion to Tintern Abbey. My dear, dear love, I most earnestly, and with tearful eyes, beg that I may come to you if you do not like to leave the searches after a house.

It is a long time to wait, even for an answer. To-morrow may bring you news, but I have no hope, for you only set off to look after one in the afternoon, and what can be done at that hour of the day? You cannot.

[Pg 122]They finally settled on a house at Bishopsgate just outside Windsor Park, where they passed several months of tranquillity and comparative health; perhaps the most peacefully happy time that Shelley had ever known or was ever to know. Shadows he, too, had to haunt him, but he was young, and the reaction from the long-continued strain of anxiety, fear, discomfort, and ill-health was so strong that it is no wonder if he yielded himself up to its influence. The summer was warm and dry, and most of the time was passed out of doors. They visited the source of the Thames, making the voyage in a wherry from Windsor to Cricklade. Charles Clairmont was of the party, and Peacock also, who gives a humorous account of the expedition, and of the cure he effected of Shelley's ailments by his prescription of "three mutton chops, well peppered." Shelley was at this time a strict vegetarian. Mary, Peacock says, kept a diary of the excursion, which, however, has been lost. Shelley's "Stanzas in the churchyard of Lechlade" were an enduring memento of the occasion. At Bishopsgate, under the oak shades of Windsor Great Park, he composed *Alastor*, the first mature production of his genius, and at Bishopsgate Mary's son William was born, on 24th January 1816.

The list of books read during 1815 by Shelley[Pg 123] and Mary is worth appending, as giving some idea of their wonderful mental activity and insatiable thirst for knowledge, and the singular sympathy which existed between them in these intellectual pursuits.

LIST OF BOOKS READ IN 1815.
MARY.
*Those marked * Shelley read also.*
Posthumous Works. 3 vols.
Sorrows of Werter.
Don Roderick. By Southey.
*Gibbon's Decline and Fall 12 vols.
*Gibbon's Life and Letters. 1st Edition. 2 vols.
*Lara.
New Arabian Knights. 3 vols.
Corinna.
Fall of the Jesuits.
Rinaldo Rinaldini.
Fontenelle's Plurality of Worlds.
Hermsprong.
Le Diable Boiteux.
Man as he is.
Rokeby.
Ovid's Metamorphoses in Latin.
*Wordsworth's Poems.
*Spenser's Fairy Queen.
*Life of the Phillips.
*Fox's History of James II.
The Reflector.
Fleetwood.
Wieland.
Don Carlos.
*Peter Wilkins.
Rousseau's Confessions.

Leonora: a Poem.
Emile.
*Milton's Paradise Lost.
*Life of Lady Hamilton.
De l'Allemagne. By Madame de Staël.
Three vols, of Barruet.
*Caliph Vathek.
Nouvelle Heloise.
*Kotzebue's Account of his Banishment to Siberia.
Waverley.
Clarissa Harlowe.
Robertson's History of America.
*Virgil.
*Tale of a Tub.
*Milton's Speech on Unlicensed Printing.
*Curse of Kehama.
*Madoc.
La Bible Expliquée.
Lives of Abelard and Heloise.
*The New Testament.
*Coleridge's Poems.
[Pg 124]First vol. of Système de la Nature.
Castle of Indolence.
Chatterton's Poems.
*Paradise Regained.
Don Carlos.
*Lycidas.
*St. Leon.
Shakespeare's Plays (part of which Shelley read aloud).
*Burke's Account of Civil Society.
*Excursion.
Pope's Homer's Illiad.
*Sallust.
Micromejas.
*Life of Chaucer.
Canterbury Tales.
Peruvian Letters.
Voyages round the World.
Plutarch's Lives.
*Two vols, of Gibbon.
Ormond.
Hugh Trevor.
*Labaume's History of the Russian War.
Lewis's Tales.
Castle of Udolpho.
Guy Mannering.
*Charles XII by Voltaire.
Tales of the East.

SHELLEY.

Pastor Fido.
Orlando Furioso.
Livy's History.
Seneca's Works.
Tasso's Gerusalemme Liberata.
Tasso's Aminta.
Two vols. of Plutarch in Italian.
Some of the Plays of Euripides.
Seneca's Tragedies.
Reveries of Rousseau.
Hesoid.
Novum Organum.

Alfieri's Tragedies.
Theocritus.
Ossian.
Herodotus.
Thucydides.
Homer.
Locke on the Human Understanding.
Conspiration de Rienzi.
History of Arianism.
Ockley's History of the Saracens.
Madame de Staël sur la Literature.

These months of rest were needed to fit them for the year of shocks, of blows, of conflicting emotions which was to follow. As usual, the first disturbing cause was Clara Clairmont. Early in 1816 she was in town, possibly with her brother Charles, with whom she kept up[Pg 125] correspondence, and with whom (thanks to funds provided by Shelley) she had in the autumn been travelling, or paying visits. She now started one of her "wild projects in the Clairmont style," which brought as its consequence the overshadowing of her whole life. She thought she would like to go on the stage, and she applied to Lord Byron, then connected with the management of Drury Lane Theatre, for some theatrical employment. The fascination of Byron's poetry, joined to his very shady social reputation, surrounded him with a kind of romantic mystery highly interesting to a wayward, audacious young spirit, attracted by anything that excited its curiosity. Clara never went on the stage. But she became Byron's mistress. Their connection lasted but a short time. Byron quickly tired of her, and when importuned with her or her affairs, soon came to look on her with positive antipathy. Nothing in Clara's letters to him[17]goes to prove that she was very deeply in love with him. The episode was an excitement and an adventure: one, to him, of the most trivial nature, but fraught with tragic indirect results to her, and, through her, to the Shelleys. They, although they knew of her acquaintance with Byron, were in complete and unsuspecting ignorance of its intimate nature. It might have been imagined[Pg 126] that Clara would confide in them, and would even rejoice in doing so. But she had, on the contrary, a positive horror and dread of their finding out anything about her secret. She told Byron who Mary was, one evening when she knew they were to meet, but implored him beforehand to talk only on general subjects, and, if possible, not even to mention her name.

This introduction probably took place in March, when Shelley and Mary were, for a short time, staying up in town. Shelley was occupied in transacting business, which had reference, as usual, to Godwin's affairs. A suit in Chancery was proceeding, to enable him to sell, to his father, the reversion of a portion of his estates. Short of obtaining this permission, he could not assist Godwin to the full extent demanded and expected by this latter, who chose to say, and was encouraged by his man of business to think that, if Shelley did not get the money, it was owing to slackness of effort or inclination on his part. The suit was, however, finally decided against Shelley. The correspondence between him and Godwin was painful in the highest degree, and must have embittered Mary's existence.

Godwin, while leaving no stone unturned to get as much of Shelley's money as possible, and while exerting himself with feverish activity to control and direct to his own advantage the legal[Pg 127] negotiations for disposal of part of the Shelley estates, yet declined personal communication with Shelley, and wrote to him in insulting terms, carrying sophistry so far as to assert that his dignity (save the mark!) would be compromised, not by taking Shelley's money, but by taking it in the form of a cheque made out in his, Godwin's, own name. Small wonder if Shelley was wounded and indignant. More than any one else, Godwin had taught and encouraged him to despise what he would have called prejudice.

"In my judgment," wrote Shelley, "neither I, nor your daughter, nor her offspring, ought to receive the treatment which we encounter on every side. It has perpetually appeared to me to have been your especial duty to see that, so far as mankind value your good opinion, we were dealt justly by, and that a young family, innocent, and benevolent, and united should not be confounded with prostitutes and seducers. My astonishment—and I will confess, when I have been treated with most harshness and cruelty by you, my indignation—has been extreme, that, knowing as you do my nature, any consideration should have prevailed on you to be thus harsh and cruel. I lamented also over my ruined hopes, of all that your genius once taught me to expect from your virtue, when I found that for yourself, your family, and your creditors, you would submit to that communication with me which you once rejected and abhorred, and which no pity for my poverty or sufferings, assumed willingly for you, could avail to extort. Do not talk of *forgiveness* again to me, for my blood boils in my veins, and my gall rises against all that bears the human form, when I think of what I, their benefactor and ardent lover, have endured of enmity and contempt from you and from all mankind."

[Pg 128]That other, ordinary, people should resent his avowed opposition to conventional morality was, even to Shelley, less of an enigma than that Godwin, from whom he expected support, should turn against him. Yet he never could clearly realise the aspect which his relations with Mary bore to the world, who merely saw in him a married man who had deserted his wife and eloped with a girl of sixteen. He thought people should understand all he knew, and credit him with all he did not tell them; that they should sympathise and fraternise with him, and honour Mary the more, not the less, for what she had done and dared. Instead of this, the world accepted his family's estimate of its unfortunate eldest son, and cut him. It is no wonder that, as Peacock puts it, "the spirit of restlessness came over him again," and drove him abroad once more. His first intention was to settle with Mary and their infant child in some remote region of Scotland or Northern England. But he was at all times delicate, and he longed for balmy air and sunny skies. To these motives were added Clara's wishes, and, as she herself states, her pressing solicitations. Byron, she knew, was going to Geneva, and she persuaded the Shelleys to go there also, in the hope and intention of meeting him. Shelley had read and admired several of Byron's poems, and the prospect of possible companionship with a[Pg 129] kindred mind was now and at all times supremely attractive to him. He had made repeated, but fruitless efforts to get a personal interview with Godwin, in the hope, probably, of coming to some definite understanding as to his hopelessly involved and intricate affairs. Godwin went off to Scotland on literary business and was absent all April. Before he returned Shelley, Mary, and Clara had started for Switzerland. The Shelleys were still ignorant and unsuspecting of the intrigue between Byron and Clara. Byron, knowing of Clara's wish to follow him to Geneva, enjoined her on no account to come alone or without protection, as he knew she was capable of doing; hence her determinate wish that the Shelleys should come. She wrote to Byron from Paris to tell him that she was so far on her way, accompanied by "the whole tribe of Otaheite philosophers," as she styles her friends and escort. Just before sailing from Dover Shelley wrote to Godwin, who was still in Scotland, telling him finally of the unsuccessful issue to his Chancery suit, of his doubtful and limited prospects of income or of ability to pay more than £300 for Godwin, and that only some months hence. He referred again to his painful position in England, and his present determination to remain abroad,—perhaps for ever,—with the exception of a possible, solitary, visit to London, should business make this inevitable.[Pg 130] He touched on his old obligations to Godwin, assuring him of his continued respect and admiration in spite of the painful past, and of his regret for any too vehement words he might have used.

It is unfortunate for me that the part of your character which is least excellent should have been met by my convictions of what was right to do. But I have been too indignant, I have been unjust to you—forgive me—burn those letters which contain the records of my violence, and believe that however what you erroneously call fame and honour separate us, I shall always feel towards you as the most affectionate of friends.

The travellers reached Geneva by the middle of May; their arrival preceding that of Byron by several days. A letter written by Mary Shelley from their first resting-place, the Hôtel de Sécheron, the descriptive portions of which were afterwards published by her, with the *Journal of a Six Weeks' Tour*, gives a graphic account of their journey and their first impressions of Geneva.

HÔTEL DE SÉCHERON, GENEVA,
17th May 1816.

We arrived at Paris on the 8th of this month, and were detained two days for the purpose of obtaining the various signatures necessary to our passports, the French Government having become much more circumspect since the escape of Lavalette. We had no letters of introduction, or any friend in that city, and were therefore confined to our hotel, where we were obliged to hire apartments for the week, although, when we first arrived, we expected to be detained one night only; for in Paris there are no houses where you can be accommodated with apartments by the day.

The manners of the French are interesting, although less[Pg 131] attractive, at least to Englishmen, than before the last invasion of the Allies; the discontent and sullenness of their minds perpetually betrays itself. Nor is it wonderful that they should regard the subjects of a Government which fills their country with hostile garrisons, and sustains a detested dynasty on the throne, with an acrimony and indignation of which that Government alone is the proper object. This feeling is honourable to the French, and encouraging to all those of every nation in Europe who have a fellow-feeling with the oppressed, and who cherish an unconquerable hope that the cause of liberty must at length prevail.

Our route after Paris as far as Troyes lay through the same uninteresting tract of country which we had traversed on foot nearly two years before, but on quitting Troyes we left the road leading to Neufchâtel, to follow that which was to conduct us to Geneva. We entered Dijon on the third evening after our departure from Paris, and passing through Dôle, arrived at Poligny. This town is built at the foot of Jura, which rises abruptly from a plain of vast extent. The rocks of the mountain overhang the houses. Some difficulty in procuring horses detained us here until the evening closed in, when we proceeded by the light of a stormy moon to Champagnolles, a little village situated in the depth of the mountains. The road was serpentine and exceedingly steep, and was overhung on one side by half-distinguished precipices, whilst the other was a gulf, filled by the darkness of the driving clouds. The dashing of the invisible streams announced to us that we had quitted the plains of France, as we slowly ascended amidst a violent storm of wind and rain, to Champagnolles, where we arrived at twelve o'clock the fourth night after our departure from Paris. The next morning we proceeded, still ascending among the ravines and valleys of the mountain. The scenery perpetually grows more wonderful and sublime; pine forests of impenetrable thickness and untrodden, nay, inaccessible expanse spread on every side. Sometimes the dark woods descending follow the route into the valleys, the distorted trees struggling with knotted roots[Pg 132] between the most barren clefts; sometimes the road winds high into the regions of frost, and then the forests become scattered, and the branches of the trees are loaded with snow, and half of the enormous pines themselves buried in the wavy drifts. The spring, as the inhabitants informed us, was unusually late, and indeed the cold was excessive; as we ascended the mountains the same clouds which rained on us in the valleys poured forth large flakes of snow thick and fast. The sun occasionally shone through these showers, and illuminated the magnificent ravines of the mountains, whose gigantic pines were, some laden with snow, some wreathed round by the lines of scattered and lingering vapour; others darting their spires into the sunny sky, brilliantly clear and azure.

As the evening advanced, and we ascended higher, the snow, which we had beheld whitening the overhanging rocks, now encroached upon our road, and it snowed fast as we entered the village of Les Rousses, where we were threatened by the apparent necessity of passing the night in a bad inn and dirty beds. For, from that place there are two roads to Geneva; one by Nion, in the Swiss territory, where the mountain route is shorter and comparatively easy at that time of the year, when the road is for several leagues covered with snow of an enormous depth; the other road lay through Gex, and was too circuitous and dangerous to be attempted at so late an hour in the day. Our passport, however, was for Gex, and we were told that we could not change its destination; but all these police laws, so severe in themselves, are to be softened by bribery, and this difficulty was at length overcome. We hired four horses, and ten men to support the carriage, and departed from Les Rousses at six in the evening, when the sun had already far descended, and the snow pelting against the windows of our carriage assisted the coming darkness to deprive us of the view of the lake of Geneva and the far-distant Alps.

The prospect around, however, was sufficiently sublime to command our attention—never was scene more awfully desolate. The trees in these regions are incredibly large, and stand in[Pg 133] scattered clumps over the white wilderness; the vast expanse of snow was chequered only by these gigantic pines, and the poles that marked our road; no river nor rock-encircled lawn relieved the eye, by adding the picturesque to the sublime. The natural silence of that uninhabited desert contrasted strangely with the voices of the men who conducted us, who, with animated tones and gestures, called to one another in a *patois* composed of French and Italian, creating disturbance where, but for them, there was none. To what a different scene are we now arrived! To the warm sunshine, and to the humming of sun-loving insects. From the windows of our hotel we see the lovely lake, blue as the heavens which it reflects, and sparkling with golden beams. The opposite shore is sloping and covered with vines, which, however, do not so early in the season add to the beauty of the prospect. Gentlemen's seats are scattered over these banks, behind which rise the various ridges of black mountains, and towering far above, in the midst of its snowy Alps, the majestic Mont Blanc, highest and queen of all. Such is the view reflected by the lake; it is a bright summer scene without any of that sacred solitude and deep seclusion that delighted us at Lucerne. We have not yet found out any very agreeable walks, but you know our attachment to water excursions. We have hired a boat, and every evening, at about six o'clock, we sail on the lake, which is delightful, whether we glide over a glassy surface or are speeded along by a strong wind. The waves of this lake never afflict me with that sickness that deprives me of all enjoyment in a sea-voyage; on the contrary, the tossing of our boat raises my spirits and inspires me with unusual hilarity. Twilight here is of short duration, but we at present enjoy the benefit of an increasing moon, and seldom return until ten o'clock, when, as we approach the shore, we are saluted by the delightful scent of flowers and new-mown grass, and the chirp of the grasshoppers, and the song of the evening birds.

We do not enter into society here, yet our time passes swiftly and delightfully.

We read Latin and Italian during the heats of noon, and[Pg 134] when the sun declines we walk in the garden of the hotel, looking at the rabbits, relieving fallen cockchafers, and watching the motions of a myriad of lizards, who inhabit a southern wall of the garden. You know that we have just escaped from the gloom of winter and of London; and coming to this delightful spot during this divine weather, I feel as happy as a new-fledged bird, and hardly care what twig I fly to, so that I may try my new-found wings. A more experienced bird may be more difficult in its choice of a bower; but, in my present temper of mind, the budding flowers, the fresh grass of spring, and the happy creatures about me that live and enjoy these pleasures, are quite enough to afford me exquisite delight, even though clouds should shut out Mont Blanc from my sight. Adieu!

M. S.

On the 25th of May Byron, accompanied by his young Italian physician, Polidori, and attended by three men-servants, arrived at the Hôtel de Sécheron. It was now that he and Shelley became for the first time personally acquainted; an acquaintance which, though it never did and never could ripen quite into friendship, developed with time and circumstances into an association more or less familiar which lasted all Shelley's life. After the arrival of the English Milord and his retinue, the hotel quarters probably became less quiet and comfortable, and before June the Shelleys, with Clare[18] (who, while her secret remained a secret, must have found it inexpedient to live under the same roof with Byron) moved to a cottage on the other side of the lake, near Coligny; known as[Pg 135] Maison Chapuis, but sometimes called Campagne Mont Alègre.

CAMPAGNE CHAPUIS, NEAR COLIGNY,
1st June.

You will perceive from my date that we have changed our residence since my last letter. We now inhabit a little cottage on the opposite shore of the lake, and have exchanged the view of Mont Blanc and her snowy *aiguilles* for the dark frowning Jura, behind whose range we every evening see the sun sink, and darkness approaches our valley from behind the Alps, which are then tinged by that glowing rose-like hue which is observed in England to attend on the clouds of an autumnal sky when daylight is almost gone. The lake is at our feet, and a little harbour contains our boat, in which we still enjoy our evening excursions on the water. Unfortunately we do not now enjoy those brilliant skies that hailed us on our first arrival to this country. An almost perpetual rain confines us principally to the house; but when the sun bursts forth it is with a splendour and heat unknown in England. The thunderstorms that visit us are grander and more terrific than I have ever seen before. We watch them as they approach from the opposite side of the lake, observing the lightning play among the clouds in various parts of the heavens, and dart in jagged figures upon the piny heights of Jura, dark with the shadow of the overhanging clouds, while perhaps the sun is shining cheerily upon us. One night we *enjoyed* a finer storm than I had ever before beheld. The lake was lit up, the pines on Jura made visible, and all the scene illuminated for an instant, when a pitchy blackness succeeded, and the thunder came in frightful bursts over our heads amid the darkness.

But while I still dwell on the country around Geneva, you will expect me to say something of the town itself; there is nothing, however, in it that can repay you for the trouble of walking over its rough stones. The houses are high, the streets narrow, many of them on the ascent, and no public building of any beauty to attract your eye, or any architecture[Pg 136] to gratify your taste. The town is surrounded by a wall, the three gates of which are shut exactly at ten o'clock, when no bribery (as in France) can open them. To the south of the town is the promenade of the Genevese, a grassy plain planted with a few trees, and called Plainpalais. Here a small obelisk is erected to the glory of Rousseau, and here (such is the mutability of human life) the magistrates, the successors of those who exiled him from his native country, were shot by the populace during that revolution which his writings mainly contributed to mature, and which, notwithstanding the temporary bloodshed and injustice with which it was polluted, has produced enduring benefits to mankind, which not all the chicanery of statesmen, nor even the great conspiracy of kings, can entirely render vain. From respect to the memory of their predecessors, none of the present magistrates ever walk in Plainpalais. Another Sunday recreation for the citizens is an excursion to the top of Mont Salère. This hill is within a league of the town, and rises perpendicularly from the cultivated plain. It is ascended on the other side, and I should judge from its situation that your toil is rewarded by a delightful view of the course of the Rhone and Arne, and of the shores of the lake. We have not yet visited it. There is more equality of classes here than in England. This occasions a greater freedom and refinement of manners among the lower orders than we meet with in our own country. I fancy the haughty English ladies are greatly disgusted with this consequence of republican institutions, for the Genevese servants complain very much of their *scolding*, an exercise of the tongue, I believe, perfectly unknown here. The peasants of Switzerland may not however emulate the vivacity and grace of the French. They are more cleanly, but they are slow and inapt. I know a girl of twenty who, although she had lived all her life among vineyards, could not inform me during what month the vintage took place, and I discovered she was utterly ignorant of the order in which the months succeed one another. She would not have been surprised if I had talked of the burning sun and delicious fruits of December, or of[Pg 137] the frosts of July. Yet she is by no means deficient in understanding.

The Genevese are also much inclined to puritanism. It is true that from habit they dance on a Sunday, but as soon as the French Government was abolished in the town, the magistrates ordered the theatre to be closed, and measures were taken to pull down the building.

We have latterly enjoyed fine weather, and nothing is more pleasant than to listen to the evening song of the wine-dressers. They are all women, and most of them have harmonious although masculine voices. The theme of their ballads consists of shepherds, love, flocks, and the sons of kings who fall in love with beautiful shepherdesses. Their tunes are monotonous, but it is sweet to hear them in the stillness of evening, while we are enjoying the sight of the setting sun, either from the hill behind our house or from the lake.

Such are our pleasures here, which would be greatly increased if the season had been more favourable, for they chiefly consist in such enjoyments as sunshine and gentle breezes bestow. We have not yet made any excursion in the environs of the town, but we have planned several, when you shall again hear of us; and we will endeavour, by the magic of words, to transport the ethereal part of you to the neighbourhood of the Alps, and mountain streams, and forests, which, while they clothe the former, darken the latter with their vast shadows.—Adieu! M.

Less than a fortnight after this Byron also left the hotel, annoyed beyond endurance by the unbounded curiosity of which he was the object. He established himself at the Villa Diodati, on the hill above the Shelleys' cottage, from which it was separated by a vineyard. Both he and Shelley were devoted to boating, and passed much time on the water, on one occasion narrowly escaping being drowned. Visits from one house[Pg 138] to the other were of daily occurrence. The evenings were generally spent at Diodati, when the whole party would sit up into the small hours of the morning, discussing all possible and impossible things in earth and heaven. In temperament Shelley and Byron were indeed radically opposed to each other, but the intellectual intercourse of two men, alike condemned to much isolation from their kind by their gifts, their dispositions, and their misfortunes, could not but be a source of enjoyment to each. Despite his deep grain of sarcastic egotism, Byron did justice to Shelley's sincerity, simplicity, and purity of nature, and appreciated at their just value his mental powers and literary accomplishments. On the other hand, Shelley's admiration of Byron's genius was simply unbounded, while he apprehended the mixture of gold and clay in Byron's disposition with singular acuteness. His was the "pure mind that penetrateth heaven and hell." But at Geneva the two men were only finding each other out, and, to Shelley at least, any pain arising from difference of feeling or opinion was outweighed by the intense pleasure and refreshment of intellectual comradeship.

Naturally fond of society, and indeed requiring its stimulus to elicit her best powers, Mary yet took a passive rather than an active share in these *symposia*. Looking back on them many years[Pg 139] afterwards she wrote: "Since incapacity and timidity always prevented my mingling in the nightly conversations of Diodati, they were, as it were, entirely *tête-à-tête* between my Shelley and Albè."[19] But she was a keen, eager listener. Nothing escaped her observation, and none of this time was ever obliterated from her memory.

To the intellectual ferment, so to speak, of the Diodati evenings, working with the new experiences and thoughts of the past two years, is due the conception of the story by which, as a writer, she is best remembered, the ghastly but powerful allegorical romance of *Frankenstein*. In her introduction to a late edition of this work (part of which has already been quoted here) Mary Shelley has herself told the history of its origin.

In the summer of 1816 we visited Switzerland, and became the neighbours of Lord Byron. At first we spent our pleasant hours on the lake, or wandering on its shores, and Lord Byron, who was writing the third canto of *Childe Harold*, was the only one among us who put his thoughts upon paper. These, as he brought them successively to us, clothed in all the light and harmony of poetry, seemed to stamp as divine the glories of heaven and earth, whose influences we partook with him.

But it proved a wet, ungenial summer, and incessant rain often confined us for days to the house. Some volumes of ghost stories, translated from the German into French, fell into our hands. There was the history of the Inconstant Lover, who, when he thought to clasp the bride to whom he had pledged his vows, found himself in the arms of the pale ghost[Pg 140] of her whom he had deserted. There was the tale of the sinful founder of his race, whose miserable doom it was to bestow the kiss of death on all the younger sons of his fated house, just when they reached the age of promise. His gigantic shadowy form, clothed, like the ghost in Hamlet, in complete armour, but with the beaver up, was seen at midnight, by the moon's fitful beams, to advance slowly along the gloomy avenue. The shape was lost beneath the shadow of the castle walls; but soon a gate swung back, a step was heard, the door of the chamber opened, and he advanced to the couch of the blooming youths, cradled in healthy sleep. Eternal sorrow sat upon his face as he bent down and kissed the forehead of the boys, who from that hour withered like flowers snapt upon the stalk. I have not seen these stories since then, but their incidents are as fresh in my mind as if I had read them yesterday. "We will each write a ghost story," said Byron; and his proposition was acceded to. There were four of us. The noble author began a tale, a fragment of which he printed at the end of his poem of Mazeppa. Shelley, more apt to embody ideas and sentiments in the radiance of brilliant imagery, and in the music of the most melodious verse that adorns our language, than to invent the machinery of a story, commenced one founded on the experiences of his early life. Poor Polidori had some terrible idea about a skull-headed lady, who was so punished for peeping through a keyhole—what to see I forget—something very shocking and wrong of course; but when she was reduced to a worse condition than the renowned Tom of Coventry he did not know what to do with her, and he was obliged to despatch her to the tomb of the Capulets, the only place for which she was fitted. The illustrious poets also, annoyed by the platitude of prose, speedily relinquished their ungrateful task. I busied myself to *think of a story*,—a story to rival those which had excited us to this task. One that would speak to the mysterious fears of our nature, and awaken thrilling horror—one to make the reader dread to look round, to curdle the blood and quicken the beatings of the heart. If I did not accomplish these things my ghost story would be[Pg 141] unworthy of its name. I thought and wondered—vainly. I felt that blank incapability of invention which is the greatest misery of authorship, when dull Nothing replies to our anxious invocations. "*Have you thought of a story?*" I was asked each morning, and each morning I was forced to reply with a mortifying negative.

Everything must have a beginning, to speak in Sanchean phrase: and that beginning must be linked to something that went before. The Hindoos give the world an elephant to support it, but they make the elephant stand upon a tortoise. Invention, it must be humbly admitted, does not consist in creating out of void, but out of chaos; the materials must, in the first place, be afforded: it can give form to dark shapeless substances, but cannot bring into being the substance itself. In all matters of discovery and invention, even of those that appertain to the imagination, we are continually reminded of the story of Columbus and his egg. Invention consists in the capacity of seizing on the capabilities of a subject, and in the power of moulding and fashioning ideas suggested to it.

Many and long were the conversations between Lord Byron and Shelley, to which I was a devout but nearly silent listener. During one of these various philosophical doctrines were discussed, and, among others, the nature of the principle of life, and whether there was any probability of its ever being discovered and communicated. They talked of the experiments of Dr. Darwin (I speak not of what the doctor really did, or said that he did, but, as more to my purpose, of what was then spoken of as having been done by him), who preserved a piece of vermicelli in a glass case till by some extraordinary means it began to move with voluntary motion. Not thus, after all, would life be given. Perhaps a corpse would be reanimated; galvanism had given token of such things; perhaps the component parts of a creature might be manufactured, brought together, and endued with vital warmth.

Night waned upon this talk, and even the witching hour had gone by, before we retired to rest. When I placed my head upon my pillow I did not sleep, nor could I be said to[Pg 142] think. My imagination, unbidden, possessed and guided me, gifting the successive images that arose in my mind with a vividness far beyond the usual bounds of reverie. I saw—with shut eyes, but acute mental vision,—I saw the pale student of unhallowed arts kneeling beside the thing he had put together—I saw the hideous phantasm of a man stretched out, and then, on the working of some powerful engine, show signs of life, and stir with an uneasy, half vital motion. Frightful must it be; for supremely frightful would be the effect of any human endeavour to mock the stupendous mechanism of the Creator of the world. His success would terrify the artist; he would rush away from his odious handiwork, horrorstricken. He would hope that, left to itself, the slight spark which he had communicated would fade; that this thing, which had received such imperfect animation, would subside into dead matter; and he might sleep in the belief that the silence of the grave would quench for ever the transient existence of the hideous corpse which he had looked upon as the cradle of life. He sleeps; but he is awakened; he opens his eyes; behold the horrid thing stands at his bedside, opening his curtains, and looking on him with yellow, watery, but speculative eyes.

I opened mine in terror. The idea so possessed my mind that a thrill of fear ran through me, and I wished to exchange the ghastly image of my fancy for the realities around. I see them still; the very room, the dark *parquet*, the closed shutters, with the moonlight struggling through, and the sense I had that the glassy lake and white high Alps were beyond. I could not so easily get rid of my hideous phantom; still it haunted me. I must try to think of something else. I recurred to my ghost story—my tiresome unlucky ghost story. O! if I could only contrive one which would frighten my reader as I myself had been frightened that night!

Swift as light and as cheering was the idea that broke in upon me. "I have found it! What terrified me will terrify others; and I need only describe the spectre which had haunted my midnight pillow." On the morrow I announced that I had *thought of a story*. I began that day with the[Pg 143] words, *It was on a dreary night of November*, making only a transcript of the grim terrors of my waking dream.

At first I thought of but a few pages—of a short tale; but Shelley urged me to develop the idea at greater length. I certainly did not owe the suggestion of one incident, nor scarcely of one train of feeling, to my husband, and yet, but for his incitement, it would never have taken the form in which it was presented to the world. From this declaration I must except the preface. As far as I can recollect, it was entirely written by him.

Every one now knows the story of the "Modern Prometheus,"—the student who, having devoted himself to the search for the principle of life, discovers it, manufactures an imitation of a human being, endows it with vitality, and having thus encroached on divine prerogative, finds himself the slave of his own creature, for he has set in motion a force beyond his power to control or annihilate. Aghast at the actual and possible consequences of his own achievement, he recoils from carrying it out to its ultimate end, and stops short of doing what is necessary to render this force independent. The being has, indeed, the perception and desire of goodness; but is, by the circumstances of its abnormal existence, delivered over to evil, and Frankenstein, and all whom he loves, fall victims to its vindictive malice. Surely no girl, before or since, has imagined, and carried out to its pitiless conclusion so grim an idea.

Mary began her rough sketch of this story[Pg 144] during the absence of Shelley and Byron on a voyage round the lake of Geneva; the memorable excursion during which Byron wrote the *Prisoner of Chillon* and great part of the third canto of *Childe Harold*, and Shelley conceived the idea of that "Hymn to Intellectual Beauty," which may be called his confession of faith. When they returned they found Mary hard at work on the fantastic speculation which possessed her mind and exerted over it a fascination and a power of excitement beyond that of the sublime external nature which inspired the two poets.

When, in July, she set off with Shelley and Clare on a short tour to the Valley of Chamounix, she took her MS. with her. They visited the Mer de Glace, and the source of the Arveiron. The magnificent scenery which inspired Shelley with his poem on "Mont Blanc," and is described by Mary in the extracts from her journal which follow, served her as a fitting background for the most preternatural portions of her romance.

Tuesday, July 23 (Chamounix).—In the morning, after breakfast, we mount our mules to see the source of the Arveiron. When we had gone about three parts of the way, we descended and continued our route on foot, over loose stones, many of which were an enormous size. We came to the source, which lies (like a stage) surrounded on the three sides by mountains and glaciers. We sat on a rock, which formed the fourth, gazing on the scene before us. An immense glacier was on our left, which continually rolled stones to its[Pg 145] foot. It is very dangerous to be directly under this. Our guide told us a story of two Hollanders who went, without any guide, into a cavern of the glacier, and fired a pistol there, which drew down a large piece on them. We see several avalanches, some very small, others of great magnitude, which roared and smoked, overwhelming everything as it passed along, and precipitating great pieces of ice into the valley below. This glacier is increasing every day a foot, closing up the valley. We drink some water of the Arveiron and return. After dinner think it will rain, and Shelley goes alone to the glacier of Boison. I stay at home. Read several tales of Voltaire. In the evening I copy Shelley's letter to Peacock.

Wednesday, July 24.—To-day is rainy; therefore we cannot go to Col de Balme. About 10 the weather appears clearing up. Shelley and I begin our journey to Montanvert. Nothing can be more desolate than the ascent of this mountain; the trees in many places having been torn away by avalanches, and some half leaning over others, intermingled with stones, present the appearance of vast and dreadful desolation. It began to rain almost as soon as we left our inn. When we had mounted considerably we turned to look on the scene. A dense white mist covered the vale, and tops of scattered pines peeping above were the only objects that presented themselves. The rain continued in torrents. We were wetted to the skin; so that, when we had ascended halfway, we resolved to turn back. As we descended, Shelley went before, and, tripping up, fell upon his knee. This added to the weakness occasioned by a blow on his ascent; he fainted, and was for some minutes incapacitated from continuing his route.

We arrived wet to the skin. I read *Nouvelles Nouvelles*, and write my story. Shelley writes part of letter.

....

Saturday, July 27.—It is a most beautiful day, without a cloud. We set off at 12. The day is hot, yet there is a fine breeze. We pass by the Great Waterfall, which presents an aspect of singular beauty. The wind carries it away from the[Pg 146] rock, and on towards the north, and the fine spray into which it is entirely dissolved passes before the mountain like a mist.

The other cascade has very little water, and is consequently not so beautiful as before. The evening of the day is calm and beautiful. Evening is the only time I enjoy travelling. The horses went fast, and the plain opened before us. We saw Jura and the Lake like old friends. I longed to see my pretty babe. At 9, after much inquiring and stupidity, we find the road, and alight at Diodati. We converse with Lord Byron till 12, and then go down to Chapuis, kiss our babe, and go to bed.

Circumstances had modified Shelley's previous intention of remaining permanently abroad, and the end of August found him moving homeward.

The following extracts from Mary's diary give a sketch of their life during the few weeks preceding their return to England.

Sunday, July 28 (Montalègre).—I read Voltaire's *Romans*. Shelley reads Lucretius, and talks with Clare. After dinner he goes out in the boat with Lord Byron, and we all go up to Diodati in the evening. This is the second anniversary since Shelley's and my union.

Monday, July 29.—Write; read Voltaire and Quintus Curtius. A rainy day, with thunder and lightning. Shelley finishes Lucretius, and reads Pliny's *Letters*.

Tuesday, July 30.—Read Quintus Curtius. Shelley read Pliny's *Letters*. After dinner we go up to Diodati, and stay the evening.

Thursday, August 1.—Make a balloon for Shelley, after which he goes up to Diodati, to dine and spend the evening. Read twelve pages of Curtius. Write, and read the *Rêveries of Rousseau*. Shelley reads Pliny's *Letters*.

Friday, August 2.—I go to the town with Shelley, to buy a telescope for his birthday present. In the evening Lord Byron and he go out in the boat, and, after their return,[Pg 147] Shelley and Clare go up to Diodati; I do not, for Lord Byron did not seem to wish it. Shelley returns with a letter from Longdill, which requires his return to England. This puts us in bad spirits. I read *Rêveries* and *Adèle et Théodore de Madame de Genlis*, and Shelley reads Pliny's *Letters*.

Saturday, August 3.—Finish the first volume of *Adèle*, and write. After dinner write to Fanny, and go up to Diodati, where I read the *Life of Madame du Deffand*. We come down early and talk of our plans. Shelley reads Pliny's *Letters*, and writes letters.

Sunday, August 4.—Shelley's birthday. Write; read *Tableau de famille*. Go out with Shelley in the boat, and read to him the fourth book of Virgil. After dinner we go up to Diodati, but return soon. I read Curtius with Shelley, and finish the first volume, after which we go out in the boat to set up the balloon, but there is too much wind; we set it up from the land, but it takes fire as soon as it is up. I finish the *Rêveries of Rousseau*. Shelley reads and finishes Pliny's *Letters*, and begins the *Panegyric of Trajan*.

Wednesday, August 7.—Write, and read ten pages of Curtius. Lord Byron and Shelley go out in the boat. I translate in the evening, and afterwards go up to Diodati. Shelley reads Tacitus.

Friday, August 9.—Write and translate; finish *Adèle*, and read a little Curtius. Shelley goes out in the boat with Lord Byron in the morning and in the evening, and reads Tacitus. About 3 o'clock we go up to Diodati. We receive a long letter from Fanny.

FANNY TO MARY.

LONDON, *29th July 1816.*

MY DEAR MARY—I have just received yours, which gave me great pleasure, though not quite so satisfactory a one as I could have wished. I plead guilty to the charge of having written in some degree in an ill humour; but if you knew how I am harassed by a variety of trying circumstances, I am sure you would feel for me. Besides other plagues, I was oppressed[Pg 148] with the most violent cold in my head when I last wrote you that I ever had in my life. I will now, however, endeavour to give as much information from England as I am capable of giving, mixed up with as little spleen as possible. I have received Jane's letter, which was a very dear and a very sweet one, and I should have answered it but for the dreadful state of mind I generally labour under, and which I in vain endeavour to get rid of. From your and Jane's description of the weather in Switzerland, it has produced more mischief abroad than here. Our rain has been as constant as yours, for it rains every day, but it has not been accompanied by violent storms. All accounts from the country say that the corn has not yet suffered, but that it is yet perfectly green; but I fear that the sun will not come this year to ripen it. As yet we have had fires almost constantly, and have just got a few strawberries. You ask for particulars of the state of England. I do not understand the causes for the distress which I see, and hear dreadful accounts of, every day; but I know that they really exist. Papa, I believe, does not think much, or does not inquire, on these subjects, for I never can get him to give me any information. From Mr. Booth I got the clearest account, which has been confirmed by others since. He says that it is the "Peace" that has brought all this calamity upon us; that during the war the whole Continent were employed in fighting and defending their country from the incursions of foreign armies; that England alone was free to manufacture in peace; that our manufactories, in consequence, employed several millions, and at higher wages, than were wanted for our own consumption. Now peace is come, foreign ports are shut, and millions of our fellow-creatures left to starve. He also says that we have no need to manufacture for ourselves—that we have enough of the various articles of our manufacture to last for seven years—and that the going on is only increasing the evil. They say that in the counties of Staffordshire and Shropshire there are 26,000 men out of employment, and without the means of getting any. A few weeks since there were several parties of colliers, who came as far as St. Albans[Pg 149] and Oxford, dragging coals in immense waggons, without horses, to the Prince Regent at Carlton House; one of these waggons was said to be conducted by a hundred colliers. The Ministers, however, thought proper, when these men had got to the distance from London of St. Albans, to send Magistrates to them, who paid them handsomely for their coals, and gave them money besides, telling them that coming to London would only create disturbance and riot, without relieving their misery; they therefore turned back, and the coals were given away to the poor people of the neighbourhood where they were met. This may give you some idea of the misery suffered. At Glasgow, the state of wretchedness is worse than anywhere else. Houses that formerly employed two or three hundred men now only employ three or four individuals. There have been riots of a very serious nature in the inland counties, arising from the same causes. This, joined to this melancholy season, has given us all very serious alarm, and helped to make me write so dismally. They talk of a change of Ministers; but this can effect no good; it is a change of the whole system of things that is wanted. Mr. Owen, however, tells us to cheer up, for that in two years we shall feel the good effect of his plans; he is quite certain that they will succeed. I have no doubt that he will do a great deal of good; but how he can expect to make the rich give up their possessions, and live in a state of equality, is too romantic to be believed. I wish I could send you his Address to the People of New Lanark, on the 1st of January 1816, on the opening of the Institution for the Formation of Character. He dedicates it "To those who have no private ends to accomplish, who are honestly in search of truth for the purpose of ameliorating the condition of society, and who have the firmness to follow the truth, wherever it may lead, without being turned aside from the pursuit by the *prepossessions or prejudices of any part of mankind.*"

This dedication will give you some idea of what sort of an Address it is. This Address was delivered on a Sunday evening, in a place set apart for the purposes of religion, and brought hundreds of persons from the regular clergymen to[Pg 150] hear his profane Address,—against all religions, governments, and all sorts of aristocracy,—which, he says, was received with the greatest attention and highly approved. The outline of his plan is this: "That no human being shall work more than two or three hours every day; that they shall be all equal; that no one shall dress but after the plainest and simplest manner; that they be allowed to follow any religion, as they please; and that their [studies] shall be Mechanics and Chemistry." I hate and am sick at heart at the misery I see my fellow-beings suffering, but I own I should not like to live to see the extinction of all genius, talent, and elevated generous feeling in Great Britain, which I conceive to be the natural consequence of Mr. Owen's plan. I am not either wise enough, philosophical enough, nor historian enough, to say what will make man plain and simple in manners and mode of life, and at the same time a poet, a painter, and a philosopher; but this I know, that I had rather live with the Genevese, as you and Jane describe, than live in London, with the most brilliant beings that exist, in its present state of vice and misery. So much for Mr. Owen, who is, indeed, a very great and good man. He told me the other day that he wished our Mother were living, as he had never before met with a person who thought so exactly as he did, or who would have so warmly and zealously entered into his plans. Indeed, there is nothing very promising in a return to England at least for some time to come, for it is better to witness misery in a foreign country than one's own, unless you have the means of relieving it. I wish I could send you the books you ask for. I should have sent them, if Longdill had not said he was not sending—that he expected Shelley in England. I shall send again immediately, and will then send you *Christabel* and the "Poet's" *Poems.* Were I not a dependent being in every sense of the word, but most particularly in money, I would send you other things, which perhaps you would be glad of. I am much more interested in Lord Byron since I have read all his poems. When you left England I had only read *Childe Harold* and his smaller poems. The pleasure he has[Pg 151] excited in me, and gratitude I owe him for having cheered several gloomy hours, makes me wish for a more finished portrait, both of his *mind* and *countenance*. From *Childe Harold* I gained a very ill impression of him, because I conceived it was *himself*,—notwithstanding the pains he took to tell us it was an imaginary being. The *Giaour*, *Lara*, and the *Corsair* make me justly style him a poet. Do in your next oblige me by telling me the minutest particulars of him, for it is from the *small things* that you learn most of character. Is his face as fine as in your portrait of him, or is it more like the other portrait of him? Tell me also if he has a pleasing voice, for that has a great charm with me. Does he come into your house in a careless, friendly, dropping-in manner? I wish to know, though not from idle curiosity, whether he was capable of acting in the manner that the London scandal-mongers say he did? You must by this time know if he is a profligate in principle—a man who, like Curran, gives himself unbounded liberty in all sorts of profligacy. I cannot think, from his writings, that he can be such a *detestable being*. Do answer me these questions, for where I love the poet I should like to respect the man. Shelley's boat excursion with him must have been very delightful. I think Lord Byron never writes so well as when he writes descriptions of water scenes; for instance, the beginning of the *Giaour*. There is a fine expressive line in *Childe Harold*: "Blow, swiftly blow, thou keen compelling gale," etc. There could have been no difference of sentiment in this divine excursion; they were both poets, equally alive to the charms of nature and the eloquent writing of Rousseau. I long very much to read the poem the "Poet" has written on the spot where Julie was drowned. When will they come to England? Say that you have a friend who has few pleasures, and is very impatient to read the poems written at Geneva. If they are not to be published, may I see them in manuscript? I am angry with Shelley for not writing himself. It is impossible to tell the good that POETS do their fellow-creatures, at least those that can feel. Whilst I read I am a poet. I am inspired[Pg 152] with good feelings—feelings that create perhaps a more permanent good in me than all the everyday preachments in the world; it counteracts the dross which one gives on the everyday concerns of life, and tells us there is something yet in the world to aspire to—something by which succeeding ages may be made happy and perhaps better. If Shelley cannot accomplish any other good, he can this divine one. Laugh at me, but do not be angry with me, for taking up your time with my nonsense. I have sent again to Longdill, and he has returned the same answer as before. I can [not], therefore, send you *Christabel*. Lamb says it ought never to have been published; that no one understands it; and *Kubla Khan* (which is the poem he made in his sleep) is nonsense. Coleridge is living at Highgate; he is living with an apothecary, to whom he pays £5 a week for board, lodging, and medical advice. The apothecary is to take care that he does not take either opium or spirituous liquors. Coleridge, however, was tempted, and wrote to a chemist he knew in London to send a bottle of laudanum to Mr. Murray's in Albemarle Street, to be enclosed in a parcel of books to him; his landlord, however, felt the parcel outside, and discovered the fatal bottle. Mr. Morgan told me the other day that Coleridge improved in health under the care of the apothecary, and was writing fast a continuation of *Christabel*.

You ask me if Mr. Booth mentioned Isabel's having received a letter from you. He never mentioned your name to me, nor I to him; but he told Mamma that you had written a letter to her from Calais. He is gone back, and promises to bring Isabel next year. He has given us a volume of his *poetry*—*true, genuine poetry*—not such as Coleridge's or Wordsworth's, but Miss Seward's and Dr. Darwin's—

Dying swains to sighing Delias.

You ask about old friends; we have none, and see none. Poor Marshal is in a bad way; we see very little of him. Mrs. Kenny is going immediately to live near Orleans, which is better for her than living in London, afraid of her creditors.[Pg 153] The Lambs have been spending a month in the neighbourhood of Clifton and Bristol; they were highly delighted with Clifton. Sheridan is dead. Papa was very much grieved at his death. William and he went to his funeral. He was buried in the Poets' Corner of Westminster Abbey, attended by all the high people. Papa has visited his grave many times since. I am too young to remember his speeches in Parliament. I never admired his style of play-writing. I cannot, therefore, sympathise in the elegant tributes to his memory which have been paid by all parties. Those things which I have heard from all parties of his drunkenness I cannot admire. We have had one great pleasure since your departure, in viewing a fine collection of the Italian masters at the British Institution. Two of the Cartoons are there. Paul preaching at Athens is the finest picture I ever beheld.... I am going again to see this Exhibition next week, before it closes, when I shall be better able to tell you which I most admire of Raphael, Titian, Leonardo da Vinci, Domenichino, Claude, S. Rosa, Poussin, Murillo, etc., and all of which cannot be too much examined. I only wish I could have gone many times. Charles's letter has not yet arrived. Do give me every account of him when you next hear from him. I think it is of great consequence the mode of life he now pursues, as it will most likely decide his future good or ill doing. You ask what I mean by "plans with Mr. Blood?" I meant a residence in Ireland. However, I will not plague you with them till I understand them myself. My Aunt Everina will be in London next week, when my future fate will be decided. I shall then give you a full and clear account of what my unhappy life is to be spent in, etc. I left it to the end of my letter to call your attention most seriously to what I said in my last letter respecting Papa's affairs. They have now a much more serious and threatening aspect than when I last wrote to you. You perhaps think that Papa has gained a large sum by his novel engagement, which is not the case. He could make no other engagement with Constable than that they should share the profits equally between them, which, if the novel is successful, is an[Pg 154]advantageous bargain. Papa, however, prevailed upon him to advance £200, to be deducted hereafter out of the part he is to receive; and if two volumes of the novel are not forthcoming on the 1st of January 1817, Constable has a promissory note to come upon papa for the £200. This £200 I told you was appropriated to Davidson and Hamilton, who had lent him £200 on his *Caleb Williams* last year; so that you perceive he has as yet gained nothing on his novel, and all depends upon his future exertions. He has been very unwell and very uneasy in his mind for the last week, unable to write; and it was not till this day I discovered the cause, which has given me great uneasiness. You seem to have forgotten Kingdon's £300 to be paid at the end of June. He has had a great deal of plague and uneasiness about it, and has at last been obliged to give Kingdon his promissory note for £300, payable on demand, so that every hour is not safe. Kingdon is no friend, and the money Government money, and it cannot be expected he will show Papa any mercy. I dread the effect on his health. He cannot sleep at night, and is indeed very unwell. This he concealed from Mamma and myself until this day. Taylor of Norwich has also come upon him again; he says, owing to the distress of the country, he must have the money for his children; but I do not fear him like Kingdon. Shelley said in his letter, some weeks ago, that the £300 should come the end of June. Papa, therefore, acted upon that promise. From your last letter I perceive you think I colour my statements. I assure you I am most anxious, when I mention these unfortunate affairs, to speak the truth, and nothing but the truth, as it is. I think it my duty to tell you the real state of the case, for I know you deceive yourself about things. If Papa could go on with his novel in good spirits, I think it would perhaps be his very best. He said the other day that he was writing upon a subject no one had ever written upon before, and that it would require great exertion to make it what he wished. Give my love to Jane; thank her for her letter. I will write to her next week, though I consider this long tiresome one as[Pg 155] addressed to you all. Give my love also to Shelley; tell him, if he goes any more excursions, nothing will give me more pleasure than a description of them. Tell him I like your [ ][20] tour best, though I should like to visit *Venice* and *Naples*. Kiss dear William for me; I sometimes consider him as my child, and look forward to the time of my old age and his manhood. Do you dip him in the lake? I am much afraid you will find this letter much too long; if it affords you any pleasure, oblige me by a long one in return, but write small, for Mamma complains of the postage of a double letter. I pay the full postage of all the letters I send, and you know I have not a *sous* of my own. Mamma is much better, though not without rheumatism. William is better than he ever was in his life. I am not well; my mind always keeps my body in a fever; but never mind me. Do entreat J. to attend to her eyes. Adieu, my dear Sister. Let me entreat you to consider seriously all that I have said concerning your Father.—Yours, very affectionately,

FANNY.

Journal, Saturday, August 10.—Write to Fanny. Shelley writes to Charles. We then go to town to buy books and a watch for Fanny. Read Curtius after my return; translate. In the evening Shelley and Lord Byron go out in the boat. Translate, and when they return go up to Diodati. Shelley reads Tacitus. A writ of arrest comes from Polidori, for having "cassé ses lunettes et fait tomber son chapeau" of the apothecary who sells bad magnesia.

....

Monday, August 12.—Write my story and translate. Shelley goes to the town, and afterwards goes out in the boat with Lord Byron. After dinner I go out a little in the boat, and then Shelley goes up to Diodati. I translate in the evening, and read *Le Vieux de la Montagne*, and write. Shelley, in coming down, is attacked by a dog, which delays him; we send up for him, and Lord Byron comes down; in the meantime Shelley returns.

[Pg 156]*Wednesday, August 14.*—Read *Le Vieux de la Montagne*; translate. Shelley reads Tacitus, and goes out with Lord Byron before and after dinner. Lewis[21] comes to Diodati. Shelley goes up there, and Clare goes up to copy. Remain at home, and read *Le Vieux de la Montagne*.

....

Friday, August 16.—Write, and read a little of Curtius; translate; read *Walther* and some of *Rienzi*. Lord Byron goes with Lewis to Ferney. Shelley writes, and reads Tacitus.

Saturday, August 17.—Write, and finish *Walther*. In the evening I go out in the boat with Shelley, and he afterwards goes up to Diodati. Began one of Madame de Genlis's novels. Shelley finishes Tacitus. Polidori comes down. Little babe is not well.

Sunday, August 18.—Talk with Shelley, and write; read Curtius. Shelley reads Plutarch in Greek. Lord Byron comes down, and stays here an hour. I read a novel in the evening. Shelley goes up to Diodati, and Monk Lewis.

....

Tuesday, August 20.—Read Curtius; write; read *Herman d'Unna*. Lord Byron comes down after dinner, and remains with us until dark. Shelley spends the rest of the evening at Diodati. He reads Plutarch.

Wednesday, August 21.—Shelley and I talk about my story. Finish *Herman d'Unna* and write. Shelley reads Milton. After dinner Lord Byron comes down, and Clare and Shelley go up to Diodati. Read *Rienzi*.

Friday, August 23.—Shelley goes up to Diodati, and then in the boat with Lord Byron, who has heard bad news of Lady Byron, and is in bad spirits concerning it.... Letters arrive from Peacock and Charles. Shelley reads Milton.

Saturday, August 24.—Write. Shelley goes to Geneva. Read. Lord Byron and Shelley sit on the wall before dinner. After I talk with Shelley, and then Lord Byron comes down and spends an hour here. Shelley and he go up together.

....

[Pg 157]*Monday, August 26.*—Hobhouse and Scroop Davis come to Diodati. Shelley spends the evening there, and reads *Germania*. Several books arrive, among others Coleridge's *Christabel*, which Shelley reads aloud to me before going to bed.

....

Wednesday, August 28.—Packing. Shelley goes to town. Work. Polidori comes down, and afterwards Lord Byron. After dinner we go upon the water; pack; and Shelley goes up to Diodati. Shelley reads *Histoire de la Révolution par Rabault*.

Thursday, August 29.—We depart from Geneva at 9 in the morning.

They travelled to Havre *via* Dijon, Auxerre, and Villeneuve; allowing only a few hours for visiting the palaces of Fontainebleau and Versailles, and the Cathedral of Rouen. From Havre they sailed to Portsmouth, where, for a short time, they separated. Shelley went to stay with Peacock, who was living at Great Marlow, and had been looking about there for a house to suit his friends. Mary and Clare proceeded to Bath, where they were to spend the next few months.

Journal, Tuesday, September 10.—Arrive at Bath about 2. Dine, and spend the evening in looking for lodgings. Read Mrs. Robinson's *Valcenga*.

Wednesday, September 11.—Look for lodgings; take some, and settle ourselves. Read the first volume of *The Antiquary*, and work.

[Pg 158]

CHAPTER IX
SEPTEMBER 1816-FEBRUARY 1817

Trouble had, for some time past, been gathering in heavy clouds. Godwin's affairs were in worse plight than ever, and the Shelleys, go where they might, were never suffered to forget them. Fanny constituted herself his special pleader, and made it evident that she found it hard to believe Shelley could not, if he chose, get more money than he did for Mary's father. Her long letters, bearing witness in every line to her great natural intelligence and sensibility, excite the deepest pity for her, and not a little, it must be added, for those to whom they were addressed. The poor girl's life was, indeed, a hard one, and of all her trials perhaps the most insurmountable was that inherited melancholy of the Wollstonecraft temperament which permitted her no illusions, no moments, even, of respite from care in unreasoning gaiety such as are incidental to most young and healthy natures. Nor, although she won every one's respect and most people's liking, had she the inborn gift of inspiring devotion or arousing enthusiasm. She[Pg 159] was one of those who give all and take nothing. The people she loved all cared for others more than they did for her, or cared only for themselves. Full of warmth and affection and ideal aspirations; sympathetically responsive to every poem, every work of art appealing to imagination, she was condemned by her temperament and the surroundings of her life to idealise nothing, and to look at all objects as they presented themselves to her, in the light of the very commonest day.

Less pressing than Godwin, but still another disturbing cause, was Charles Clairmont, who was travelling abroad in search, partly of health, partly of occupation; had found the former, but not the latter, and, of course, looked to Shelley as the magician who was to realise all his plans for him. Of his discursive letters, which are immensely long, in a style of florid eloquence, only a few specimen extracts can find room here. One, received by Shelley and Mary at Geneva, openly confesses that, though it was a year since he had left England, he had abstained, as yet, from writing to Skinner Street, being as unsettled as ever, and having had nothing to speak of but his pleasures;—having in short been going on "just like a butterfly,—though still as a butterfly of the best intentions." He proceeds to describe the country, his manner of living there, his health,—he details his symptoms, and sets forth at length the[Pg 160]various projects he might entertain, and the marvellous cheapness of one and all of them, if only he could afford to have any projects at all. He enumerates items of expenditure connected with one of his schemes, and concludes thus—

I lay this proposal before you, without knowing anything of your finances, which, I fear, cannot be in too flourishing a situation. You will, I trust, consider of the thing, and treat it as frankly as it has been offered. I know you too well not to know you would do for me all in your power. Have the goodness to write to me as instantly as possible.

And Shelley did write,—so says the journal.

Last not least, there was Clare. At what point of all this time did her secret become known to Shelley and Mary? No document as yet has seen the light which informs us of this. Perhaps some day it may. Unfortunately for biographers and for readers of biography, Mary's journal is almost devoid of personal gossip, or indeed of personalities of any kind. Her diary is a record of outward facts, and, occasionally, of intellectual impressions; no intimate history and no one else's affairs are confided to it. No change of tone is perceptible anywhere. All that can be asserted is that they knew nothing of it when they went to Geneva. In the absence of absolute proof to the contrary it is impossible to believe that they were not aware of it when they came back. Clare was an expecting mother. For four months they had all been in daily intercourse with Byron, who[Pg 161] never was or could be reticent, and who was not restrained either by delicacy or consideration for others from saying what he chose. But when and how the whole affair was divulged and what its effect was on Shelley and Mary remains a mystery. From this time, however, Clare resumed her place as a member of their household. It cannot have been a matter of satisfaction to Mary: domestic life was more congenial without Clare's presence than with it, but now that there was a true reason for her taking shelter with them, Mary's native nobility of heart was equal to the occasion, and she gave help, support, and confidence, ungrudgingly and without stint. Never in her journal, and only once in her letters does any expression of discontent appear. They settled down together in their lodgings at Bath, but on the 19th of September Mary set out to join Shelley at Marlow for a few days, leaving Clara in charge of little Willy and the Swiss nurse Elise. On the 25th both were back at Bath, where they resumed their quiet, regular way of life, resting and reading. But this apparent peace was not to be long unbroken. Letters from Fanny followed each other in quick succession, breathing nothing but painful, perpetual anxiety.

FANNY TO MARY.

26th September 1816.

MY DEAR MARY—I received your letter last Saturday, which rejoiced my heart. I cannot help envying your calm, [Pg 162]contented disposition, and the calm philosophical habits of life which pursue you, or rather which pursue you everywhere. I allude to your description of the manner in which you pass your days at Bath, when most women would hardly have recovered from the fatigues of such a journey as you had been taking. I am delighted to hear such pleasing accounts of your William; I should like to see him, dear fellow; the change of air does him infinite good, no doubt. I am very glad you have got Jane a pianoforte; if anything can do her good and restore her to industry, it is music. I think I gave her all the music here; however, I will look again for what I can find. I am angry with Shelley for not giving me an account of his health. All that I saw of him gave me great uneasiness about him, and as I see him but seldom, I am much more alarmed perhaps than you, who are constantly with him. I hope that it is only the London air which does not agree with him, and that he is now much better; however, it would have been kind to have said so.

Aunt Everina and Mrs. Bishop left London two days ago. It pained me very much to find that they have entirely lost their little income from Primrose Street, which is very hard upon them at their age. Did Shelley tell you a singular story about Mrs. B. having received an annuity which will make up in part for her loss?

Poor Papa is going on with his novel, though I am sure it is very fatiguing to him, though he will not allow it; he is not able to study as much as formerly without injuring himself; this, joined to the plagues of his affairs, which he fears will never be closed, make me very anxious for him. The name of his novel is *Manderville, or a Tale of the Seventeenth Century*. I think, however, you had better not mention the name to any one, as he wishes it not to be announced at present. Tell Shelley, as soon as he knows certainly about Longdill, to write, that he may be eased on that score, for it is a great weight on his spirits at present. Mr. Owen is come to town to prepare for the meeting of Parliament. There never was so devoted a being as he is; and it certainly must end in his doing a great deal of good, though not the good he talks of.

[Pg 163]Have you heard from Charles? He has never given us a single line. I am afraid he is doing very ill, and has the conscience not to write a parcel of lies. Beg the favour of Shelley, to copy for me his poem on the scenes at the foot of Mont Blanc, and tell him or remind him of a letter which you said he had written on these scenes; you cannot think what a treasure they would be to me; remember you promised them to me when you returned to England. Have you heard from Lord Byron since he visited those sublime scenes? I have had great pleasure since I saw Shelley in going over a fine gallery of pictures of the Old Masters at Dulwich. There was a St. Sebastian by Guido, the finest picture I ever saw; there were also the finest specimens of Murillo, the great Spanish painter, to be found in England, and two very fine Titians. But the works of art are not to be compared to the works of nature, and I am never satisfied. It is only poets that are eternal benefactors of their fellow-creatures, and the real ones never fail of giving us the highest degree of pleasure we are capable of; they are, in my opinion, nature and art united, and as such never fading.

Do write to me immediately, and tell me you have got a house, and answer those questions I asked you at the beginning of this letter.

Give my love to Shelley, and kiss William for me. Your affectionate Sister,

FANNY.

When Shelley sold to his father the reversion of a part of his inheritance, he had promised to Godwin a sum of £300, which he had hoped to save from the money thus obtained. Owing to certain conditions attached to the transaction by Sir Timothy Shelley, this proved to be impossible. The utmost Shelley could do, and that only by leaving himself almost without resources, was to send something over £200; a bitter disappointment[Pg 164] to Godwin, who had given a bill for the full amount. Shelley had perhaps been led by his hopes, and his desire to serve Godwin, to speak in too sanguine a tone as to his prospect of obtaining the money, and the letter announcing his failure came, Fanny wrote, "like a thunderclap." In her disappointment she taxed Shelley with want of frankness, and Shelley and Mary both with an apparent wish to avoid the subject of Godwin's affairs.

"You know," she writes, "the peculiar temperature of Papa's mind (if I may so express myself); you know he cannot write when pecuniary circumstances overwhelm him; you know that it is of the utmost consequence, for *his own* and the *world's sake* that he should finish his novel; and is it not your and Shelley's duty to consider these things, and to endeavour to prevent, as far as lies in your power, giving him unnecessary pain and anxiety?"

To the Shelleys, who had strained every nerve to obtain this money, unmindful of the insulting manner in which such assistance was demanded and received by Godwin, these appeals to their sense of duty must have been exasperating. Nor were matters mended by hearing of sundry scandalous reports abroad concerning themselves—reports sedulously gathered by Mrs. Godwin, and of which Fanny thought it her duty to inform them, so as to put them on their guard. They, on their part, were indignant, especially with Mrs. Godwin, who had evidently, they surmised, gone[Pg 165] out of her way to collect this false information, and had helped rather than hindered its circulation; and they expressed themselves to this effect. Fanny stoutly defended her stepmother against these attacks.

Mamma and I are not great friends, but, always alive to her virtues, I am anxious to defend her from a charge so foreign to her character.... I told Shelley these (scandalous reports), and I still think they originated with your servants and Harriet, whom I know has been very industrious in spreading false reports about you. I at the same time advised Shelley always to keep French servants, and he then seemed to think it a good plan. You are very careless, and are for ever leaving your letters about. English servants like nothing so much as scandal and gossip; but this you know as well as I, and this is the origin of the stories that are told. And this you choose to father on Mamma, who (whatever she chooses to say in a passion to me alone) is the woman the most incapable of such low conduct. I do not say that her inferences are always the most just or the most amiable, but they are always confined to myself and Papa. Depend upon it you are perfectly safe as long as you keep your French servant with you.... I have now to entreat you, Shelley, to tell Papa exactly what you can and what you cannot do, for he does not seem to know what you mean in your letter. I know that you are most anxious to do everything in your power to complete your engagement to him, and to do anything that will not ruin yourself to save him;

but he is not convinced of this, and I think it essential to his peace that he should be convinced of this. I do not on any account wish you to give him false hopes. Forgive me if I have expressed myself unkindly. My heart is warm in your cause, and I am *anxious, most anxious*, that Papa should feel for you as I do, both for your own and his sake.... All that I have said about Mamma proceeds from the hatred I have of talking and petty scandal, which, though[Pg 166] trifling in itself, often does superior persons much injury, though it cannot proceed from any but vulgar souls in the first instance.

This letter was crossed by Shelley's, enclosing more than £200—insufficient, however, to meet the situation or to raise the heavy veil of gloom which had settled on Skinner Street. Fanny could bear it no longer. Despairing gloom from Godwin, whom she loved, and who in his gloom was no philosopher; sordid, nagging, angry gloom from "Mamma," who, clearly enough, did not scruple to remind the poor girl that she had been a charge and a burden to the household (this may have been one of the things she only "chose to say in a passion, to Fanny alone"); her sisters gone, and neither of them in complete sympathy with her; no friends to cheer or divert her thoughts! A plan had been under consideration for her residing with her relatives in Ireland, and the last drop of bitterness was the refusal of her aunt, Everina Wollstonecraft, to have her. What was left for her? Much, if she could have believed it, and have nerved herself to patience. But she was broken down and blinded by the strain of over endurance. On the 9th of October she disappeared from home. Shelley and Mary in Bath suspected nothing of the impending crisis. The journal for that week is as follows—

Saturday, October 5 (Mary).—Read Clarendon and Curtius; walk with Shelley. Shelley reads Tasso.

[Pg 167]*Sunday, October 6* (Shelley).—On this day Mary put her head through the door and said, "Come and look; here's a cat eating roses; she'll turn into a woman; when beasts eat these roses they turn into men and women."

(Mary).—Read Clarendon all day; finish the eleventh book. Shelley reads Tasso.

Monday, October 7.—Read Curtius and Clarendon; write. Shelley reads *Don Quixote* aloud in the evening.

Tuesday, October 8.—Letter from Fanny (this letter has not been preserved). Drawing lesson. Walk out with Shelley to the South Parade; read Clarendon, and draw. In the evening work, and Shelley reads *Don Quixote*; afterwards read *Memoirs of the Princess of Bareith* aloud.

Wednesday, October 9.—Read Curtius; finish the *Memoirs*; draw. In the evening a very alarming letter comes from Fanny. Shelley goes immediately to Bristol; we sit up for him till 2 in the morning, when he returns, but brings no particular news.

Thursday, October 10.—Shelley goes again to Bristol, and obtains more certain trace. Work and read. He returns at 11 o'clock.

Friday, October 11.—He sets off to Swansea. Work and read.

Saturday, October 12.—He returns with the worst account. A miserable day. Two letters from Papa. Buy mourning, and work in the evening.

From Bristol Fanny had written not only to the Shelleys, but to the Godwins, accounting for her disappearance, and adding, "I depart immediately to the spot from which I hope never to remove."

During the ensuing night, at the Mackworth Arms Inn, Swansea, she traced the following words—

[Pg 168]I have long determined that the best thing I could do was to put an end to the existence of a being whose birth was unfortunate, and whose life has only been a series of pain to those persons who have hurt their health in endeavouring to promote her welfare. Perhaps to hear of my death may give you pain, but you will soon have the blessing of forgetting that such a creature ever existed as....

This note and a laudanum bottle were beside her when, next morning, she was found lying dead.

The persons for whose sake it was—so she had persuaded herself—that she committed this act were reduced to a wretched condition by the blow. Shelley's health was shattered; Mary profoundly miserable; Clare, although by her own avowal feeling less affection for Fanny than might have been expected, was shocked by the dreadful manner of her death, and infected by the contagion of the general gloom. She was not far from her confinement, and had reasons enough of her own for any amount of depression.

Godwin was deeply afflicted; to him Fanny was a great and material loss, and the last remaining link with a happy past. As usual, public comment was the thing of all others from which he shrank most, and in the midst of his first sorrow his chief anxiety was to hide or disguise the painful story from the world. In writing (for the first time) to Mary he says—

Do not expose us to those idle questions which, to a mind in anguish, is one of the severest of all trials. We are at this moment in doubt whether, during the first shock, we shall not[Pg 169] say that she is gone to Ireland to her aunt, a thing that had been in contemplation. Do not take from us the power to exercise our own discretion. You shall hear again to-morrow.

What I have most of all in horror is the public papers, and I thank you for your caution, as it may act on this.

We have so conducted ourselves that not one person in our home has the smallest apprehension of the truth. Our feelings are less tumultuous than deep. God only knows what they may become.

Charles Clairmont was not informed at all of Fanny's death; a letter from him a year later contains a message to her. Mrs. Godwin busied herself with putting the blame on Shelley. Four years later she informed Mrs. Gisborne that the three girls had been simultaneously in love with Shelley, and that Fanny's death was due to jealousy of Mary! This shows that the Shelleys' instinct did not much mislead them when they held Mary's stepmother responsible for the authorship and diffusion of many of those slanders which for years were to affect their happiness and peace. Any reader of Fanny's letters can judge how far Mrs. Godwin's allegation is borne out by actual facts; and to any one knowing aught of women and women's lives these letters afford clue enough to the situation and the story, and further explanation is superfluous. Fanny was fond of Shelley, fond enough even to forgive him for the trouble he had brought on their home, but her part was throughout that of a long-suffering sister, one, too, to whose lot it always fell to say all the[Pg 170]disagreeable things that had to be said—a truly ungrateful task. Her loyalty to the Godwins, though it could not entirely divide her from the Shelleys, could and did prevent any intimacy of friendship with them. Her enlightened, liberal mind, and her generous, loving heart had won Shelley's recognition and his affection, and in a moment a veil was torn from his eyes, revealing to him unsuspected depths of suffering, sacrifice, and heroism—now it was too late. How much more they might have done for Fanny had they understood what she endured! There was he, Shelley, offering sympathy and help to the oppressed and the miserable all the world over, and here,—here under his very eyes, this tragic romance was acted out to the death.

Her voice did quiver as we parted,
Yet knew I not that heart was broken
From which it came,—and I departed,
Heeding not the words then spoken—
Misery, ah! misery!
This world is all too wide for thee.

If the echo of those lines reached Fanny in the world of shadows, it may have calmed the restless spirit with the knowledge that she had not lived for nothing after all.

During the next two months another tragedy was silently advancing towards its final catastrophe. Shelley was anxious for intelligence of Harriet and her children; she had, however, [Pg 171]disappeared, and he could discover no clue to her whereabouts. Mr. Peacock, who, during June, had been in communication with her on money matters, had now, apparently, lost sight of her. The worry of Godwin's money-matters and the fearful shock of Fanny's self-sought death, followed as it was by collapse of his own health and nerves, probably withdrew Shelley's thoughts from the subject for a time. In November, however, he wrote to Hookham, thinking that he, to whom Harriet had once written to discover Shelley's whereabouts, might now know or have the means of finding out where she was living. No answer came, however, to these inquiries for some weeks, during which Shelley, Mary, and Clare lived in their seclusion, reading Lucian and Horace, Shakespeare, Gibbon, and Locke; in occasional correspondence with Skinner Street, through Mrs. Godwin, who was now trying what she could do to obtain money loans (probably raised on Shelley's prospects), requisite, not only to save Godwin from bankruptcy, but to repay Shelley a small fraction of what he had given and lent, and without which he was unable to pay his own way.

The plan for settling at Marlow was still pending, and on the 5th of December Shelley went there again to stay with Mr. Peacock and his mother, and to look about for a residence to suit him. Mary during his absence was somewhat[Pg 172] tormented by anxiety for his fragile health; fearful, too, lest in his impulsive way he should fall in love with the first pretty place he saw, and burden himself with some unsuitable house, in the idea of settling there "for ever," Clare and all. To that last plan she probably foresaw the objections more clearly than Shelley did. But her cheery letters are girlish and playful.

5th December 1816.

SWEET ELF—I got up very late this morning, so that I could not attend Mr. West. I don't know any more. Good-night.

NEW BOND STREET, BATH,
6th December 1816.

SWEET ELF—I was awakened this morning by my pretty babe, and was dressed time enough to take my lesson from Mr. West, and (thank God) finished that tedious ugly picture I have been so long about. I have also finished the fourth chapter of *Frankenstein*, which is a very long one, and I think you would like it. And where are you? and what are you doing? my blessed love. I hope and trust that, for my sake, you did not go outside this wretched day, while the wind howls and the clouds seem to threaten rain. And what did my love think of as he rode along—did he think about our home, our babe, and his poor Pecksie? But I am sure you did, and thought of them all with joy and hope. But in the choice of a residence, dear Shelley, pray be not too quick or attach yourself too much to one spot. Ah! were you indeed a winged Elf, and could soar over mountains and seas, and could pounce on the little spot. A house with a lawn, a river or lake, noble trees, and divine mountains, that should be our little mouse-hole to retire to. But never mind this; give me a garden, and *absentia* Claire, and I will thank my love for many favours. If you, my love, go to London, you will perhaps try to procure a good Livy, for I wish very much to read it. I must[Pg 173] be more industrious, especially in learning Latin, which I neglected shamefully last summer at intervals, and those periods of not reading at all put me back very far.

The *Morning Chronicle*, as you will see, does not make much of the riots, which they say are entirely quelled, and you would be almost inclined to say, "Out of the mountain comes forth a mouse," although, I daresay, poor Mrs. Platt does not think so.

The blue eyes of your sweet Boy are staring at me while I write this; he is a dear child, and you love him tenderly, although I fancy that your affection will increase when he has a nursery to himself, and only comes to you just dressed and in good humour; besides when that comes to pass he will be a wise little man, for he improves in mind rapidly. Tell me, shall you be happy to have another little squaller? You will look grave on this, but I do not mean anything.

Leigh Hunt has not written. I would advise a letter addressed to him at the *Examiner* Office, if there is no answer to-morrow. He may not be at the Vale of Health, for it is odd that he does not acknowledge the receipt of so large a sum. There have been no letters of any kind to-day.

Now, my dear, when shall I see you? Do not be very long away; take care of yourself and take a house. I have a great fear that bad weather will set in. My airy Elf, how unlucky you are! I shall write to Mrs. Godwin to-morrow; but let me know what you hear from Hayward and papa, as I am greatly interested in those affairs. Adieu, sweetest; love me tenderly, and think of me with affection when anything pleases you greatly.—Your affectionate girl

MARY.

I have not asked Clare, but I dare say she would send her love, although I dare say she would scold you well if you were here. Compliments and remembrances to Dame Peacock and Son, but do not let them see this.

Sweet, adieu!

Percy　　　　　　　　　　B.　　　　　　　　　　Shelley,　　　　　　　　　　Esq., Great Marlow, Bucks.

[Pg 174]On 6th December the journal records—

Letter from Shelley; he has gone to visit Leigh Hunt.

This was the beginning of a lifelong intimacy.

On the 14th Shelley returned to Bath, and on the very next day a letter from Hookham informed him that on the 9th Harriet's body had been taken out of the Serpentine. She had disappeared three weeks before that time from the house where she was living. An inquest had been held at which her name was given as Harriet Smith; little or no information about her was given to the jury, who returned a verdict of "Found drowned."

Life and its complications had proved too much for the poor silly woman, and she took the only means of escape she saw open to her. Her piteous story was sufficiently told by the fact that when she drowned herself she was not far from her confinement. But it would seem from subsequent evidence that harsh treatment on the part of her relatives was what finally drove her to despair. She had lived a fast life, but had been, nominally at any rate, under her father's protection until a comparatively short time before her disappearance, when some act or occurrence caused her to be driven from his house. From that moment she sank lower and lower, until at last, deserted by one—said to be a groom—to whom she had looked for protection, she killed herself.

[Pg 175]It is asserted that she had had, all her life, an avowed proclivity to suicide. She had been fond, in young and happy days, of talking jocosely about it, as silly girls often do; discoursing of "some scheme of self-destruction as coolly as another lady would arrange a visit to an exhibition or a theatre."[22] But it is a wide dreary waste that lies between such an idea and the grim reality,—and poor Harriet had traversed it.

Shelley's first thought on receiving the fatal news was of his children. His sensations were those of horror, not of remorse. He never spoke or thought of Harriet with harshness, rather with infinite pity, but he never regarded her save in the light of one who had wronged him and failed him,—whom he had left, indeed, but had forgiven, and had tried to save from the worst consequences of her own acts. Her dreadful death was a shock to him of which he said (to Byron) that he knew not how he had survived it; and he regarded her father and sister as guilty of her blood. But Fanny's death caused him acuter anguish than Harriet's did.

As for Mary, she regarded the whole Westbrook family as the source of grief and shame to Shelley. Harriet she only knew for a frivolous, heartless, faithless girl, whom she had never had the faintest cause to respect, hardly even to pity.[Pg 176] Poor Harriet was indeed deserving of profound commiseration, and no one could have known and felt this more than Mary would have done, in later years. But she heard one side of the case only, and that one the side on which her own strongest feelings were engaged. She was only nineteen, with an exalted ideal of womanly devotion; and at nineteen we may sternly judge what later on we may condemn indeed, but with a depth of pity quite beyond the power of its object to fathom or comprehend.

No comment whatever on the occurrence appears in her journal. She threw herself ardently into Shelley's eagerness to get possession of his elder children; ready, for his sake, to love them as her own.

It could not but occur to her that her own position was altered by this event, and that nothing now stood between her and her legal marriage to Shelley and acknowledgment as his wife. So completely, however, did they regard themselves as united for all time by indissoluble ties that she thought of the change chiefly as it affected other people.

MARY TO SHELLEY.

BATH, *17th December 1816.*

MY BELOVED FRIEND—I waited with the greatest anxiety for your letter. You are well, and that assurance has restored some peace to me.

[Pg 177]How very happy shall I be to possess those darling treasures that are yours. I do not exactly understand what Chancery has to do in this, and wait with impatience for to-morrow, when I shall hear whether they are with you; and then what will you do with them? My heart says, bring them instantly here; but I submit to your prudence. You do not mention Godwin. When I receive your letter to-morrow I shall write to Mrs. Godwin. I hope, yet I fear, that he will show on this occasion some disinterestedness. Poor, dear Fanny, if she had lived until this moment she would have been saved, for my house would then have been a proper asylum for her. Ah! my best love, to you do I owe every joy, every perfection that I may enjoy or boast of. Love me, sweet, for ever. I hardly know what I mean, I am so much agitated. Clare has a very bad cough, but I think she is better to-day. Mr. Carn talks of bleeding if she does not recover quickly, but she is positively resolved not to submit to that. She sends her love. My sweet love, deliver some message from me to your kind friends at Hampstead; tell Mrs. Hunt that I am extremely obliged to her for the little profile she was so kind as to send me, and thank Mr. Hunt for his friendly message which I did not hear.

These Westbrooks! But they have nothing to do with your sweet babes; they are yours, and I do not see the pretence for a suit; but to-morrow I shall know all.

Your box arrived to-day. I shall send soon to the upholsterer, for now I long more than ever that our house should be quickly ready for the reception of those dear children whom I love so tenderly. Then there will be a sweet brother and sister for my William, who will lose his pre-eminence as eldest, and be helped third at table, as Clare is continually reminding him.

Come down to me, sweetest, as soon as you can, for I long to see you and embrace.

As to the event you allude to, be governed by your friends and prudence as to when it ought to take place, but it must be in London.

[Pg 178]Clare has just looked in; she begs you not to stay away long, to be more explicit in your letters, and sends her love.

You tell me to write a long letter, and I would, but that my ideas wander and my hand trembles. Come back to reassure me, my Shelley, and bring with you your darling Ianthe and Charles. Thank your kind friends. I long to hear about Godwin.—Your affectionate

MARY.

Have you called on Hogg? I would hardly advise you. Remember me, sweet, in your sorrows as well as your pleasures; they will, I trust, soften the one and heighten the other feeling. Adieu.

To   Percy   Bysshe   Shelley,
5 Gray's Inn Square, London.

No time was lost in putting things on their legal footing. Shelley took Mary up to town, where the marriage ceremony took place at St. Mildred's Church, Broad Street, in presence of Godwin and Mrs. Godwin. On the previous day he had seen his daughter for the first time since her flight from his house two and a half years before.

Both must have felt a strange emotion which, probably, neither of them allowed to appear.

Mary for a fortnight left a blank in her journal. On her return to Clifton she thus shortly chronicled her days—

I have omitted writing my journal for some time. Shelley goes to London and returns; I go with him; spend the time between Leigh Hunt's and Godwin's. A marriage takes place on the 29th of December 1816. Draw; read Lord Chesterfield and Locke.

Godwin's relief and satisfaction were great[Pg 179] indeed. His letter to his brother in the country, announcing his daughter's recent marriage with a baronet's eldest son, can only be compared for adroit manipulation of facts with a later letter to Mr. Baxter of Dundee, in which he tells of poor Fanny's having been attacked in Wales by an inflammatory fever "which carried her off."

He now surpassed himself "in polished and cautious attentions" both to Shelley and Mary, and appeared to wish to compensate in every way for the red-hot, righteous indignation which, owing to wounded pride rather than to offended moral sense, he had thought it his duty to exhibit in the past.

Shelley's heart yearned towards his two poor little children by Harriet, and to get possession of them was now his feverish anxiety. On this business he was obliged, within a week of his return to Bath, to go up again to London. During his absence, on the 13th of January, Clare's little girl, Byron's daughter, was born. "Four days of idleness," are Mary's only allusion to this event. It was communicated to the absent father by Shelley, in a long letter from London. He quite simply assumes the event to be an occasion of great rejoicing to all concerned, and expects Byron to feel the same. The infant, who afterwards developed into a singularly fascinating and lovely child, was described in enthusiastic terms by Mary[Pg 180] as unusually beautiful and intelligent, even at this early stage. Their first name for her was Alba, or "the Dawn"; a reminiscence of Byron's nickname, "Albé."

Most of this month of January, while Mary had Clare and the infant to look after, was of necessity spent by Shelley in London. Harriet's father, Mr. Westbrook, and his daughter Eliza had filed an appeal to the Court of Chancery, praying that her children might be placed in the custody of guardians to be appointed by the Court, and not in that of their father. On 24th January, poor little William's first birthday, the case was heard before Lord Chancellor Eldon. Mary, expecting that the decision would be known at once, waited in painful suspense to hear the result.

Journal, Friday, January 24.—My little William's birthday. How many changes have occurred during this little year; may the ensuing one be more peaceful, and my William's star be a fortunate one to rule the decision of this day. Alas! I fear it will be put off, and the influence of the star pass away. Read the *Arcadia* and *Amadis*; walk with my sweet babe.

Her fears were realised, for two months were to elapse ere judgment was pronounced.

Saturday, January 25.—An unhappy day. I receive bad news and determine to go up to London. Read the *Arcadia* and *Amadis*. Letter from Mrs. Godwin and William.

Accordingly, next day, Mary went up to join her husband in town, and notes in her diary that[Pg 181] she was met at the inn by Mrs. Godwin and William. Well might Shelley say of the ceremony that it was "magical in its effects."

As it turned out, this was her final departure from Bath: she never returned there. On her arrival in London she was warmly welcomed by Shelley's new friends, the Leigh Hunts, at whose house most of her time was spent, and whose genial, social circle was most refreshing to her. The house at Marlow had been taken, and was now being prepared for her reception. Little William and his nurse, escorted by Clare, joined her at the Hunts on the 18th of February, but Clare herself stayed elsewhere. At the end of the month they all departed for their new home, and were established there early in March.

[Pg 182]

CHAPTER X
MARCH 1817-MARCH 1818

The Shelleys' new abode, although situated in a lovely part of the country, was cold and cheerless, and, at that bleak time of year, must have appeared at its worst. Albion House stood (and, though subdivided and much altered in appearance, still stands) in what is now the main street of Great Marlow, and at a considerable distance from the river. At the back the garden-plot rises gradually from the level of the house, terminating in a kind of artificial mound, overshadowed by a spreading cedar; a delightfully shady lounge in summer, but shutting off sky and sunshine from the house. There are two large, low, old-fashioned rooms; one on the ground floor, somewhat like a farmhouse kitchen; the other above it; both facing towards the garden. In one of these Shelley fitted up a library, little thinking that the dwelling, which he had rashly taken on a more than twenty years' lease, would be his home for only a year. The rest of the house accommodated Mary,[Pg 183] Clare, the children and servants, and left plenty of room for visitors. Shelley was hospitality itself, and though he never was in greater trouble for money than during this year, he entertained a constant succession of guests. First among these was Godwin; next, and most frequent, the genial but needy Leigh Hunt, with all his family. With Mary, as with Shelley, he had quickly established himself on a footing of easy, affectionate friendliness, as may be inferred from Mary's letter, written to him during her first days at Marlow.

MARLOW, *1 o'clock, 5th March 1817.*

MY DEAR HUNT—Although you mistook me in thinking I wished you to write about politics in your letters to me—as such a thought was very far from me,—yet I cannot help mentioning your last week's *Examiner*, as its boldness gave me extreme pleasure. I am very glad to find that you wrote the leading article, which I had doubted, as there was no significant hand. But though I speak of this, do not fear that you will be teased by *me* on these subjects when we enjoy your company at Marlow. When there, you shall never be serious when you wish to be merry, and have as many nuts to crack as there are words in the Petitions to Parliament for Reform—a tremendous promise.

Have you never felt in your succession of nervous feelings one single disagreeable truism gain a painful possession of your mind and keep it for some months? A year ago, I remember, my private hours were all made bitter by reflections on the certainty of death, and now the flight of time has the same power over me. Everything passes, and one is hardly conscious of enjoying the present until it becomes the past. I was reading the other day the letters of Gibbon. He entreats Lord Sheffield to come with all his family to visit him at Lausanne, and dwells on the pleasure such a visit will[Pg 184] occasion. There is a little gap in the date of his letters, and then he complains that this solitude is made more irksome by their having been there and departed. So will it be with us in a few months when you will all have left Marlow. But I will not indulge this gloomy feeling. The sun shines brightly, and we shall be very happy in our garden this summer.—Affectionately yours,

MARINA.

Not only did Shelley keep open house for his friends; his kindliness and benevolence to the distressed poor in Marlow and the surrounding country was unbounded. Nor was he content to give money relief; he visited the cottagers; and made himself personally acquainted with them, their needs, and their sufferings.

In all these labours of love and charity he was heartily and constantly seconded by Mary.

No more alone through the world's wilderness,
Although (he) trod the paths of high intent,
(He) journeyed now.[23]

From the time of her union with him Mary had been his consoler, his cherished love, all the dearer to him for the thought that she was dependent on him and only on him for comfort and support, and enlightenment of mind; but yet she was a child,—a clever child,—sedate and thoughtful beyond her years, and full of true womanly devotion,—but still one whose first and only acquaintance with the world had been made by coming violently into collision with it, a dangerous experience, and hardening, especially if[Pg 185] prolonged. From the time of her marriage a maturer, mellower tone is perceptible throughout her letters and writings, as though, the unnatural strain removed, and, above all, intercourse with her father restored, she glided naturally and imperceptibly into the place Nature intended her to fill, as responsible woman and wife, with social as well as domestic duties to fulfil.

The suffering of the past two or three years had left her wiser if also sadder than before; already she was beginning to look on life with a calm liberal judgment of one who knew both sides of many questions, yet still her mind retained the simplicity and her spirit much of the buoyancy of youth. The unquenchable spring of love and enthusiasm in Shelley's breast, though it led him into errors and brought him grief and disillusionment, was a talisman that saved him from Byronic sarcasm, from the bitterness of recoil and the death of stagnation. He suffered from reaction, as all such natures must suffer, but Mary was by his side to steady and balance and support him, and to bring to him for his consolation the balm she had herself received from him. Well might he write—

Now	has	descended	a	serener	hour,
And,	with	inconstant	fortune,	friends	return;
Though	suffering	leaves	the	knowledge	and the power

Which says: Let scorn be not repaid with scorn.[24]

[Pg 186]And consolation and support were sorely needed. In March Lord Chancellor Eldon pronounced the judgment by which he was deprived, on moral and religious grounds, of the custody of his two elder children. How bitterly he felt, how keenly he resented, this decree all the world knows. The paper which he drew up during this celebrated case, in which he declared, as far as he chose to declare them, his sentiments with regard to his separation from Harriet and his union with Mary, is the nearest approach to self-vindication Shelley ever made. But the decision of the Court cast a slur on his name, and on that of his second wife. The final arrangements about the children dragged on for many months. They were eventually given over to the guardianship of a clergyman, a stranger to their father, who had to set aside £200 a year of his income for their maintenance in exile.

Meanwhile Godwin's exactions were incessant, and his demands, sometimes impossible to grant, were harder than ever to deal with now that they were couched in terms of friendship, almost of affection. On 9th March we find Shelley writing to him—

It gives me pain that I cannot send you the whole of what you want. I enclose a cheque to within a few pounds of my possessions.

On 22d March (Godwin has been begging[Pg 187] again, but this time in behalf of his old assistant and amanuensis, Marshall)—

Marshall's proposal is one in which, however reluctantly, I must refuse to engage. It is that I should grant bills to the amount of his debts, which are to expire in thirty months.

On 15th April Godwin writes on his own behalf—

The fact is I owe £400 on a similar score, beyond the £100 that I owed in the middle of 1815; and without clearing this, my mind will never be perfectly free for intellectual occupations. If this were done, I am in hopes that the produce of *Mandeville*, and the sensible improvement in the commercial transactions of Skinner Street would make me a free man, perhaps, for the rest of my life....

My life wears away in lingering sorrow at the endless delays that attend on this affair.... Once every two or three months I throw myself prostrate beneath the feet of Taylor of Norwich, and my other discounting friends, protesting that this is absolutely for the last time. Shall this ever have an end? Shall I ever be my own man again?

One can imagine how such a letter would work on his daughter's feelings.

Nor was Charles Clairmont backward about putting in his claims, although his modest little requests require, like gems, to be extracted carefully from the discursive raptures, the eloquent flights of fancy and poetic description in which they are embedded. In January he had written from Bagnères de Bigorre, where he was "acquiring the language"—

Sometimes I hardly dare believe, situated as I am, that I ought for a moment to nourish the feelings of which I am[Pg 188] now going to talk to you; at other times I am so thoroughly convinced of their infinite utility with regard to the moral existence of a being with strong sensations, or at all events with regard to mine, that I fly to this subject as to a tranquillising medicine, which has the power of so arranging and calming every violent and illicit sensation of the soul as to spread over the frame a deep and delightful contentment, for such is the effect produced upon me by a contemplation of the perfect state of existence, the perfect state of social domestic happiness which I propose to myself. My life has hitherto been a tissue of irregularity, which I assure you I am little content to reflect upon.... I have been always neglectful of one of the most precious possessions which a young man can hold—of my character.... You will now see the object of this letter.... I desire strongly to marry, and to devote myself to the temperate, rational duties of human life.... I see, I confess, some objections to this step.... I am not forgetful of what I owe to Godwin and my Mother, but we are in a manner entirely separated.... It is true my feelings towards my Mother are cold and inactive, but my attachment and respect for Godwin are unalterable, and will remain to me to the last moment of my existence.... The news of his death would be to me a stroke of the severest affliction; that of my own Mother would be no more than the sorrow occasioned by the loss of a common acquaintance.

... Unless every obstacle on the part of the object of my affection were laid aside, you may suppose I should not speak so decisively. She is perfectly acquainted with every circumstance respecting me, and we feel that we love and are suited to each other; we feel that we should be exquisitely happy in being devoted to each other.

... I feel that I could not offer myself to the family without assuring them of my capability of commanding an annual sufficiency to support a little *ménage*—that is to say, as near as I can obtain information, 2000 francs, or about £80.... Do I dream, my dear Shelley, when a gleam of gay hope gives me reason to doubt of the possibility of my scheme?...[Pg 189] Pray lose no time in writing to me, and be as explicit as possible.

The following extract is from a letter to Mary, written in August (the matrimonial scheme is now quite forgotten)—

I will begin by telling you that I received £10 some days ago, minus the expenses.... I also received your letter, but not till after the money.... I am most extremely vexed that Shelley will not oblige me with a single word. It is now nearly six months that I have expected from him a letter about my future plans.

Do, my dear Mary, persuade him to talk with you about them; and if he always persists in remaining silent, I beg you will write for him, and ask him what he would be inclined to approve.... Had I a little fortune of £200 or £300 a year, nothing should ever tempt me to make an effort to increase this golden sufficiency....

Respecting money matters.... I still owe (on the score of my *pension*) nearly £15, this is all my debt here. Another month will accumulate before I can receive your answer, and you will judge of what will be necessary to me on the road, to whatever place I may be destined. I cannot spend less than 3s. 6d. per day.

If Papa's novel is finished before you write, I wish to God you would send it. I am now absolutely without money, but I have no occasion for any, except for washing and postage, and for such little necessaries I find no difficulty in borrowing a small sum.

If I knew Mamma's address, I should certainly write to her in France. I have no heart to write to Skinner Street, for they will not answer my letters. Perhaps, now that this haughty woman is absent, I should obtain a letter. I think I shall make an effort with Fanny. As for Clare, she has entirely forgotten that she has a brother in the world.... Tell me if Godwin has been to visit you at Marlow; if you see Fanny[Pg 190] often; and all about the two Williams. What is Shelley writing?

Shelley, when this letter arrived, was writing *The Revolt of Islam*. To this poem, in spite of duns, sponges, and law's delays, his thoughts and time were consecrated during his first six months at Marlow; in spite, too, of his constant succession of guests; but society with him was not always a hindrance to poetic creation or intellectual work. Indeed, a congenial presence afforded him a kind of relief, a half-unconscious stimulus which yet was no serious interruption to thought, for it was powerless to recall him from his abstraction.

Mary's life at Marlow was very different from what it had been at Bishopsgate and Bath. Her duties as house-mistress and hostess as well as Shelley's companion and helpmeet left her not much time for reverie. But her regular habits of study and writing stood her in good stead. *Frankenstein* was completed and corrected before the end of May. It was offered to Murray, who, however, declined it, and was eventually published by Lackington.

The negotiations with publishers calling her up to town, she paid a visit to Skinner Street. Shelley accompanied her, but was obliged to return to Marlow almost immediately, and as Mrs. Godwin also appears to have been absent,[Pg 191] Mary stayed alone with her father in her old home. To him this was a pleasure.

"Such a visit," he had written to Shelley, "will tend to bring back years that are passed, and make me young again. It will also operate to render us more familiar and intimate, meeting in this snug and quiet house, for such it appears to me, though I daresay you will lift up your hands, and wonder I can give it that appellation."

To Mary every room in the house must have been fraught with unspeakable associations. Alone with the memories of those who were gone, of others who were alienated; conscious of the complete change in herself and transference of her sphere of sympathy, she must have felt, when Shelley left her, like a solitary wanderer in a land of shadows.

"I am very well here," she wrote, "but so intolerably restless that it is painful to sit still for five minutes. Pray write. I hear so little from Marlow that I can hardly believe that you and Willman live there."

Another train of mingled recollections was awakened by the fact of her chancing, one evening, to read through that third canto of *Childe Harold* which Byron had written during their summer in Switzerland together.

Do you remember, Shelley, when you first read it to me one evening after returning from Diodati. The lake was before us, and the mighty Jura. That time is past, and this will also pass, when I may weep to read these words....[Pg 192] Death will at length come, and in the last moment all will be a dream.

What Mary felt was crystallised into expression by Shelley, not many months later—

The	stream	we	gazed	on	then,	rolled	by,
Its		waves			are		unreturning;
But		we			yet		stand

59

> In a lone land,
> Like tombs to mark the memory
> Of hopes and fears, which fade and flee
> In the light of life's dim morning.

On the last day of May, Mary returned to Marlow, where the Hunts were making a long stay. Externally life went quietly on. The summer was hot and beautiful, and they passed whole days in their boat or their garden, or in the woods. Their studies, as usual, were unremitting. Mary applied herself to the works of Tacitus, Buffon, Rousseau, and Gibbon. Shelley's reading at this time was principally Greek: Homer, Æschylus, and Plato. His poem was approaching completion. Mary, now that *Frankenstein* was off her hands, busied herself in writing out the journal of their first travels. It was published, in December, as *Journal of a Six Weeks' Tour*, together with the descriptive letters from Geneva of 1816.

But her peace and Shelley's was threatened by an undercurrent of ominous disturbance which gained force every day.

Byron remained abroad. But Clare and Clare's[Pg 193] baby remained with the Shelleys. At Bath she had passed as "Mrs." Clairmont, but now resumed her former style, while Alba was said to be the daughter of a friend in London, sent for her health into the country. As time, however, went by, and the infant still formed one of the Marlow household, curiosity, never long dormant, became aroused. Whose was this child? And if, as officious gossip was not slow to suggest, it was Clare's, then who was its father? As month after month passed without bringing any solution of this problem, the vilest reports arose concerning the supposed relations of the inhabitants of Albion House—false rumours that embittered the lives of Alba's generous protectors, but to which Shelley's unconventionality and unorthodox opinions, and the stigma attached to his name by the Chancery decree, gave a certain colour of probability, and which in part, though indirectly, conduced to his leaving England again,—as it proved, for ever.

Again and again did he write to Byron, pointing out with great gentleness and delicacy, but still in the plainest terms, the false situation in which they were placed with regard to friends and even to servants by their effort to keep Clare's secret; suggesting, almost entreating, that, if no permanent decision could be arrived at, some temporary arrangement should at least be made for[Pg 194] Alba's boarding elsewhere. Byron, at this time plunged in dissipation at Venice, shelved or avoided the subject as long as he could. Clare was friendless and penniless, and her chances of ever earning an honest living depended on her power of keeping up appearances and preserving her character before the world. But the child was a remarkably beautiful, intelligent, and engaging creature, and its mother, impulsive, uncontrolled, and reckless, was at no trouble to conceal her devotion to it, regardless of consequences, and of the fact that these consequences had to be endured by others.

Those who had forfeited the world's kindness seemed, as such, to be the natural *protégés* of Shelley; and even Mary, who, not long before, had summed up all her earthly wishes in two items,—"a garden, *et absentia Claire*,"—stood by her now in spite of all. But their letters make it perfectly evident that they were fully alive to the danger that threatened them, and that, though they willingly harboured the child until some safe and fitting asylum should be found for it, they had never contemplated its residing permanently with them.

To Mary Shelley this state of things brought one bitter personal grief and disappointment in the loss of her earliest friend, Isabel or Isobel Baxter, now married to Mr. David Booth, late brewer and subsequently schoolmaster at [Pg 195]Newburgh-on-Tay, a man of shrewd and keen intellect, an immense local reputation for learning, and an estimation of his own gifts second to that of none of his admirers.

The Baxters, as has already been said, were people of independent mind, of broad and liberal views; full of reverence and admiration for the philosophical writings of Godwin. Mary, in her extreme youth and inexperience, had quite expected that Isabel would have upheld her action when she first left her father's house with Shelley. In that she was disappointed, as was, after all, not surprising.

Now, however, her friend, whose heart must have been with her all along, would surely feel justified in following that heart's dictates, and would return to the familiar, affectionate friendship which survives so many differences of opinion. And her hope received an encouragement when, in August, Mr. Baxter, Isabel's father, accepted an invitation to stay at Marlow. He arrived on the 1st of September, full of doubts as to what sort of place he was coming to,—apprehensions which, after a very short intercourse with Shelley, were changed into surprise and delight.

But his visit was cut short by the birth, on the very next day, of Mary's little girl, Clara. He found it expedient to depart for a time, but returned later in the month for a longer stay.

[Pg 196]This second visit more than confirmed his first impression, and he wrote to his daughter in warm, nay, enthusiastic praise of Shelley, against whom Isabel was, not unnaturally, much prejudiced, so much so, it seems, as to blind her even to the merits of his writings.

After a warm panegyric of Shelley as

A being of rare genius and talent, of truly republican frugality and plainness of manners, and of a soundness of principle and delicacy of moral tact that might put to shame (if shame they had) many of his detractors,—and withal so amiable that you have only to be half an hour in his company to convince you that there is not an atom of malevolence in his whole composition.

Mr. Baxter proceeds—

Is there any wonder that I should become attached to such a man, holding out the hand of kindness and friendship towards me? Certainly not. Your praise of his book[25] put me in mind of what Pope says of Addison—

Damn with faint praise; assent with civil leer,
And, without sneering, others teach to sneer.

[You say] "some parts appear to be well written, but the arguments appear to me to be neither new nor very well managed." After Hume such a publication is quite puerile! As to the arguments not being new, it would be a wonder indeed if any new arguments could be adduced in a controversy which has been carried on almost since ever letters were known. As to their not being well managed, I should be happy if you would condescend on the particular instances of their being ill managed; it was the first of Shelley's works I had read. I read it with the notion that it *could* only contain silly, crude, undigested and puerile remarks on a worn-out subject; and yet I was unable to discover any of that want of management which you complain of; but, God help me, I[Pg 197]thought I saw in it everything that was opposite. As to its being puerile to write on such a subject after David Hume, I by no means think that he has exhausted the subject. I think rather that he has only proposed it—thrown it out, as it were, for a matter of discussion to others who might come after him, and write in a less bigoted, more liberal, and more enlightened age than the one he lived in. Think only how many great men's labours we should decree to be puerile if we were to hold everything puerile that has been written on this subject since the days of Hume! Indeed, my dear, the remark altogether savours more of the envy and illiberality of one jealous of his talents than the frankness and candour characteristic of my Isobel. Think, my dear, think for a moment what you would have said of this work had it come from Robert,[26] who is as old as Shelley was when he wrote it, or had it come from me, or even from———O! I must not say David:[27] he, to be sure, is far above any such puerility.

Her father's letter made Isabel waver, but in vain. It had no effect on Mr. Booth, who had been at the trouble of collecting and believing all the scandals about Alba, or "Miss Auburn," as she seems to have been called. He was not one to be biassed by personal feelings or beguiled by fair appearances, in the face of stubborn, unaccountable facts. He preferred to take the facts and draw his own inference—an inference which apparently seemed to him no improbable one.

For a long time nothing decisive was said or done, but while the fate of her early friendship hung in the balances, Mary's anxiety for some settlement about Alba became almost intolerable[Pg 198] to her, weighing on her spirits, and helping, with other depressing causes, to retard her restoration to health.

On the 19th of September she summed up in her journal the heads of the seventeen days after Clara's birth during which she had written nothing.

I am confined Tuesday, 2d. Read *Rhoda*, Pastor's *Fireside*, *Missionary*, *Wild Irish Girl*, *The Anaconda*, *Glenarvon*, first volume of Percy's *Northern Antiquities*. Bargain with Lackington concerning *Frankenstein*.

Letter from Albé (Byron). An unamiable letter from Godwin about Mrs. Godwin's visits. Mr. Baxter returns to town. Thursday, 4th, Shelley writes his poem; his health declines. Friday, 19th, Hunts arrive.

As the autumn advanced it became evident that the sunless house at Marlow was exceedingly cold, and far too dreary a winter residence to be desirable for one of Shelley's feeble constitution, or even for Mary and her infant children. Shelley's health grew worse and worse. His poem was finished and dedicated to Mary in the beautiful lines beginning—

So now my summer-task is ended, Mary,
And I return to thee, mine own heart's home;
As to his Queen some victor Knight of Faëry,
Earning bright spoils for her enchanted dome;
Nor thou disdain, that ere my fame become
A star among the stars of mortal night,
If it indeed may cleave its natal gloom,

Its doubtful promise thus I would unite
With thy beloved name, thou Child of love and light.

But the reaction from the "agony and bloody sweat of intellectual travail," the troubles and griefs of the past year, and the ceaseless worry about money, all told injuriously on his physical state. He had to be constantly away from his home, up in town, on business; and his thoughts turned longingly again towards Italy. Byron had signified his consent to receive and provide for his daughter, subject to certain stringent conditions, chief among which was the child's complete separation from its mother, from the time it passed into his keeping. In writing to him on 24th September, Shelley adverts to his own wish to winter at Pisa, and the possibility in this case of his being himself Alba's escort to Italy.

"Now, dearest, let me talk to you," he writes to Mary. "I think we ought to go to Italy. I think my health might receive a renovation there, for want of which perhaps I should never entirely overcome that state of diseased action which is so painful to my beloved. I think Alba ought to be with her father. This is a thing of incredible importance to the happiness, perhaps, of many human beings. It might be managed without our going there. Yes; but not without an expense which would, in fact, suffice to settle us comfortably in a spot where I might be regaining that health which you consider so valuable. It is valuable to you, my own dearest. I see too plainly that you will never be quite happy till I am well. Of myself I do not speak, for I feel only for you."

He goes on to discuss the practicability of the plan from the financial point of view, calculating what sum they may hope to get by the sale of their lease and furniture, and how much he may be able to borrow, either from his kind friend Horace Smith, or from money-lenders on *post obits*, a ruinous process to which he was, all his life, forced to resort.

Poor Mary in the chilly house at Marlow, with her three-weeks-old baby, her strength far from re-established, and her house full of guests, who made themselves quite at home, was not likely to take the most sanguine view of affairs.

25th September 1817.

You tell me, dearest, to write you long letters, but I do not know whether I can to-day, as I am rather tired. My spirits, however, are much better than they were, and perhaps your absence is the cause. Ah! my love! you cannot guess how wretched it was to see your languor and increasing illness. I now say to myself, perhaps he is better; but then I watched you every moment, and every moment was full of pain both to you and to me. Write, my love, a long account of what Lawrence says; I shall be very anxious until I hear.

I do not see a great deal of our guests; they rise late, and walk all the morning. This is something like a contrary fit of Hunt's, for I meant to walk to-day, and said so; but they left me, and I hardly wish to take my first walk by myself; however, I must to-morrow, if he still shows the same want of *tact*. Peacock dines here every day, *uninvited*, to drink his bottle. I have not seen him; he morally disgusts me; and Marianne says that he is very ill-tempered.

I was much pained last night to hear from Mr. Baxter that Mr. Booth is ill-tempered and jealous towards Isabel; and Mr. Baxter thinks she half regrets her marriage; so she is to be another victim of that ceremony. Mr. Baxter is not at all pleased with his son-in-law; but we can talk of that when we meet.

... A letter came from Godwin to-day, very short. You will see him; tell me how he is. You are loaded with business, the event of most of which I am anxious to learn, and none so much as whether you can do anything for my Father.

MARLOW, *26th September 1817.*

You tell me to decide between Italy and the sea. I think, dearest, if—what you do not seem to doubt, but which I do, a little—our finances are in sufficiently good a state to bear the expense of the journey, our inclination ought to decide. I feel some reluctance at quitting our present settled state, but as we *must* leave Marlow, I do not know that stopping short on this side the Channel would be pleasanter to me than crossing it. At any rate, my love, do not let us encumber ourselves with a lease again.... By the bye, talking of authorship, do get a sketch of Godwin's plan from him. I do not think that I ought to get out of the habit of writing, and I think that the thing he talked of would just suit me. I am glad to hear that Godwin is well.... As to Mrs. Godwin, something very analogous to disgust arises whenever I mention her. That last accusation of Godwin's[28] adds bitterness to every feeling I ever felt against her.... Mr. Baxter thinks that Mr. Booth keeps Isabel from writing to me. He has written to her to-day warmly in praise of us both, and telling her by all means not to let the acquaintance cool, and that in such a case her loss would be much greater than mine. He has taken a prodigious fancy to us, and is continually talking of and praising "Queen Mab," which he vows is the best poem of modern days.

MARLOW, *28th September 1817.*

DEAREST LOVE—Clare arrived yesterday night, and whether it might be that she was in a croaking humour (in ill spirits she certainly was), or whether she represented things[Pg 202] as they really were, I know not, but certainly affairs did not seem to wear a very good face. She talks of Harriet's debts to a large amount, and something about Longdill's having undertaken for them, so that they must be paid. She mentioned also that you were entering into a *post obit* transaction. Now this requires our serious consideration on one account. These things (*post obits*), as you well know, are affairs of wonderful length; and if you must complete one before you settle on going to Italy, Alba's departure ought certainly not to be delayed.... You have not mentioned yet to Godwin your thoughts of Italy; but if you determine soon, I would have you do it, as these things are always better to be talked of some days before they take place. I took my first walk to-day. What a dreadfully cold place this house is! I was shivering over a fire, and the garden looked cold and dismal; but as soon as I got into the road, I found, to my infinite surprise, that the sun was shining, and the air warm and delightful.... I will now tell you something that will make you laugh, if you are not too teased and ill to laugh at anything. Ah! dearest, is it so? You know now how melancholy it makes me sometimes to think how ill and comfortless you may be, and I so far away from you. But to my story. In Elise's last letter to her *chere amie*, Clare put in that Madame Clairmont was very ill, so that her life was in danger, and added, in Elise's person, that she (Elise) was somewhat shocked to perceive that Mademoiselle Clairmont's gaiety was not abated by the *douloureuse* situation of her amiable sister. Jenny replies—

"Mon amie, avec quel chagrin j'apprends la maladie de cette jolie et aimable Madame Clairmont; pauvre chère dame, comme je la plains. Sans doute elle aime tendrement son mari, et en être séparée pour toujours—en avoir la certitude elle sentir—quelle cruelle chose; qu'il doit être un méchant homme pour quitter sa femme. Je ne sais ce qu'il y a, mais cette jeune et jolie femme me tient singulièrement au cœur; je l'avoue que je n'aime point mademoiselle sa sœur. Comment! avoir à craindre pour les jours d'une si charmante[Pg 203] sœur, et n'en pas perdre un grain de gaîté; elle me met en colere."

Here is a noble resentment thrown away! Really I think this *mystification* of Clare's a little wicked, although laughable. I am just now surrounded by babes. Alba is scratching and crowing, William is amusing himself with wrapping a shawl round him, and Miss Clara staring at the fire.... Adieu, dearest love. I want to say again, that you may fully answer me, how very, *very* anxious I am to know the whole extent of your present difficulties and pursuits; and remember also that if this *post obit* is to be a long business, Alba must go before it is finished. Willy is just going to bed. When I ask him where you are, he makes me a long speech that I do not understand. But I know my own one, that you are away, and I wish that you were with me. Come soon, my own only love.—Your affectionate girl,

M. W. S.

P.S.—What of *Frankenstein*? and your own poem—have you fixed on a name? Give my love to Godwin when Mrs. Godwin is not by, or you must give it her, and I do not love her.

5th October 1817.

... How happy I shall be, my own dear love, to see you again. Your last was so very, very short a visit; and after you were gone I thought of so many things I had to say to you, and had no time to say. Come Tuesday, dearest, and let us enjoy some of each other's company; come and see your sweet babes and the little Commodore;[29] she is lively and an uncommonly interesting child. I never see her without thinking of the expressions in my mother's letters concerning Fanny. If a mother's eyes were not partial, she seemed like this Alba. She mentions her intelligent eyes and great vivacity; but this is a melancholy subject.

But Shelley's enforced absences became more and more frequent; brief visits to his home were[Pg 204] all that he could snatch. As the desire to escape grew stronger, the fair prospect only seemed to recede. New complications appeared in the shape of Harriet's creditors, who pressed hard on Shelley for a settlement of their hitherto unknown and unsuspected claims. So perilous with regard to them was his position that Mary herself was fain to caution him to stay away and out of sight for fear of arrest. It was almost more than she could do to keep up the mask of cheerfulness, yet her letters of counsel and encouragement were her husband's mainstay.

"Dearest and best of living beings," he wrote in October, "how much do your letters console me when I am away from you. Your letter to-day gave me the greatest delight; so soothing, so powerful and quiet are your expressions, that it is almost like folding you to my heart.... My own Mary, would it not be better for you to come to London at once? I think we could quite as easily do something with the house if you were in London—that is to say, all of you—as in the country."

The next two letters were written in much depression. She could not get up her strength; she dared not indulge in the hope of going abroad, for she realised, as Shelley could not do, how little money they would have and how much they already owed. Their income, and more, went in supporting and paying for other people, and left them nothing to live on! Clare was unsettled, unhappy, and petulant. Godwin, ignorant[Pg 205] like the rest of the world of her story and her present situation, unaware of Shelley's proposed move, and certain to oppose it with the energy of despair when he heard of it, was an impending visitor.

16th October 1817.

So you do not come to-night love, nor any night; you are always away, and this absence is long and becomes each day more dreary. Poor Curran! so he is dead, and a sod on his breast, as four years ago I heard him prophesy would be the case within that year.

Nothing is done, you say in your letter, and indeed I do not expect anything will be done these many months. This, if you continued well, would not give me so much pain, except on Alba's account. If she were with her father, I could wait patiently, but the thought of what may come "between the cup and the lip"—between now and her arrival at Venice—is a heavy burthen on my soul. He may change his mind, or go to Greece, or to the devil; and then what happens?

My dearest Shelley, be not, I entreat you, too self-negligent; yet what can you do? If you were here, you might retort that question upon me; but when I write to you I indulge false hopes of some miraculous answer springing up in the interval. Does not Longdill[30] treat you ill? he makes out long bills and does nothing. You say nothing of the late arrest, and what may be the consequences, and may they not detain you? and may you not be detained many months? for Godwin must not be left unprovided. All these things make me run over the months, and know not where to put my finger and say—during this year your Italian journey shall commence. Yet when I say that it is on Alba's account that I am anxious, this is only when you are away, and with too much faith I believe you to be well. When I see you, drooping and languid, in pain, and unable to enjoy life, then[Pg 206] on your account I ardently wish for bright skies and Italian sun.

You will have received, I hope, the manuscript that I sent yesterday in a parcel to Hookham. I am glad to hear that the printing goes on well; bring down all that you can with you.

If we were free and had no anxiety, what delight would Godwin's visit give me; as it is, I fear that it will make me dreadfully miserable. Cannot you come with him? By the way you write I hardly expect you this week, but is it really so?

I think Alba's remaining here exceedingly dangerous, yet I do not see what is to be done. Your babes are well. Clara already replies to her nurse's caresses by smiles, and Willy kisses her with great tenderness.—Your affectionate

MARY.

P.S.—I wish you would purchase a gown for Milly,[31] with a little note with it from Marianne,[32] that it may appear to come from her. You can get one, I should think, for 12s. or 14s.; but it must be *stout*; such a kind of one as we gave to the servant at Bath.

Willy has just said good-night to me; he kisses the paper and says good-night to you. Clara is asleep.

MARLOW, *Saturday, 18th October 1817.*

Mr. Wright has called here to-day, my dearest Shelley, and wished to see you. I can hardly have any doubt that his business is of the same nature as that which made him call last week. You will judge, but it appears to me that an arrest on Monday will follow your arrival on Sunday.

My love, you ought not to come down. A long, long week has passed, and when at length I am allowed to expect you, I am obliged to tell you not to come. This is very cruel. You may easily judge that I am not happy; my spirits sink during this continued absence. Godwin, too, will come[Pg 207] down; he will talk as if we meant to stay here; and I must—must I?—tell fifty prevarications or direct *lies*. When I thought that you would be here also, I knew that your presence would lead to general conversation; but Clare will absent herself. We shall be alone, and he will talk of your private affairs. I am sure that I shall never be able to support it.

And when is this to end? Italy appears to me farther off than ever, and the idea of it never enters my mind but Godwin enters also, and makes it lie heavy at my heart. Had you not better speak? you might relieve me from a heavy burden. Surely he cannot be blind to the many heavy reasons that urge us. Your health, the indispensable one, if every other were away. I assure you that if my Father said, "Yes, you must go; do what you can for me; I know that you will do all you can;" I should, far from writing so melancholy a letter, prepare everything with a light heart; arrange our affairs here; and come up to town, to await patiently the effect of your efforts. I know not whether it is early habit or affection, but the idea of his silent quiet disapprobation makes me weep as it did in the days of my childhood.

I shall not see you to-morrow. God knows when I shall see you! Clare is for ever wearying with her idle and childish complaints. Can you not send me some consolation?—Ever your affectionate

MARY.

The fears of an arrest were not realised. Early in November Shelley came for three days to Marlow, after which Mary went up to stay with him in London.

During this fortnight's visit the question of renewed intercourse with Isabel Booth was practically decided, and decided against Mary. She had written on the 4th of November to Mr. Baxter inviting Christy to come on a visit. Subsequently a plan was started for Isabel Booth's[Pg 208] accompanying the Shelleys in their Italian trip,—they little dreaming that when they left England it would be for the last time.

Apparently Mr. Baxter made some effort to bring Mr. Booth round to his way of thinking. The two passed an evening with the Shelleys at their lodgings. But it availed nothing, and in the end poor Mr. Baxter was driven himself to write to Shelley, breaking off the acquaintance. The letter was written much against the grain, and contrary to the convictions of the writer, who seems to have been much put to it to account for his action, the true grounds for which he could not bring himself to give. Shelley, however, was not slow to divine the real instigator in the affair, and wrote back a letter which, by its temperance, simplicity, and dignity, must have pricked Baxter to the heart. Mary added a playful postscript, showing that she still clung to hope—

MY DEAR SIR—You see I prophesied well three months ago, when you were here. I then said that I was sure Mr. Booth was averse to our intercourse, and would find some means to break it off. I wish I had you by the fire here in my little study, and it might be "double, double, toil and trouble," but I could quickly convince you that your girls are not below me in station, and that, in fact, I am the fittest companion for them in the world, but I postpone the argument until I see you, for I know (pardon me) that *viva voce* is all in all with you.

Two or three times more Mary wrote to[Pg 209] Isabel, but the correspondence dropped and the friends met no more for many years.

The preparations for their migration extended over two or three months more. During January Shelley suffered much from the renewal of an attack of ophthalmia, originally caught while visiting the poor people at Marlow. The house there was finally sold, and on the 10th of February they quitted it and went up to London. Their final departure from England did not take place until March. They made the most of their time of waiting, seeing as much of their friends and of objects of interest as circumstances allowed.

Journal, Thursday, February 12 (Mary).—Go to the Indian Library and the Panorama of Rome. On Friday, 13th, spend the morning at the British Museum looking at the Elgin marbles. On Saturday, 14th, go to Hunt's. Clare and Shelley go to the opera. On Sunday, 15th, Mr. Bransen, Peacock, and Hogg dine with us.

Wednesday, February 18.—Spend the day at Hunt's. On Thursday, 19th, dine at Horace Smith's, and copy Shelley's Eclogue. On Friday, 20th, copy Shelley's critique on *Rhododaphne*. Go to the Apollonicon with Shelley. On Saturday, 21st, copy Shelley's critique, and go to the opera in the evening. Spend Sunday at Hunt's. On Monday, 23d February, finish copying Shelley's critique, and go to the play in the evening—*The Bride of Abydos*. On Tuesday go to the opera—*Figaro*. On Wednesday Hunt dines with us. Shelley is not well.

Sunday, March 1.—Read Montaigne. Spend the evening at Hunt's. On Monday, 2d, Shelley calls on Mr. Baxter. Isabel Booth is arrived, but neither comes nor sends. Go to the play in the evening with Hunt and Marianne, and see a[Pg 210] new comedy damned. On Thursday, 5th, Papa calls, and Clare visits Mrs. Godwin. On Sunday, 8th, we dine at Hunt's, and meet Mr. Novello. Music.

Monday, March 9.—Christening the children.

This was doubtless a measure of precaution, lest the omission of any such ceremony might in some future time operate as a civil disadvantage towards the children. They received the names of William, Clara Everina, and Clara Allegra.

Tuesday, March 10.—Packing. Hunt and Marianne spend the day with us. Mary Lamb calls. Papa in the evening. Our adieus.

Wednesday, March 11.—Travel to Dover.

Thursday, March 12.—France. Discussion of whether we should cross. Our passage is rough; a sick lady is frightened and says the Lord's Prayer. We arrive at Calais for the third time.

Mary little thought how long it would be before she saw the English shores again, nor that, when she returned, it would be alone.

CHAPTER XI
MARCH 1818-JUNE 1819

The external events of the four Italian years have been repeatedly told and profusely commented on by Shelley's various biographers. Summed up, they are the history of a long strife between the intellectual and creative stimulus of lovely scenes and immortal works of art on the one hand, and the wearing friction of vexatious outward events and crushing afflictions on the other. For Shelley they were a period of rapid, of exotic, mental growth and development, interspersed with intervals of exhaustion and depression, of restlessness, or unnatural calm. For Mary they were years of courageous effort, of heroic resistance to overpowering odds. She endured, and she overcame; but some victories are obtained at such cost as to be at the time scarcely distinguishable from defeats, and the story of hers survives in no one act or work of her own, but in the *Cenci*, *Prometheus Unbound*, *Epipsychidion*, and *Adonais*.

The travellers proceeded, *via* Lyons and Chambéry, to Milan, whence Shelley and Mary made an expedition to Como in search of a house. After looking at several,—one "beautifully situated, but too small," another "out of repair, with an excellent garden, but full of serpents," a third which seemed promising, but which they failed to get,—they appear to have given up the scheme altogether, and to have returned to Milan. For the next week they were in frequent correspondence with Byron on the subject of Allegra. This had to be carried on entirely by Shelley, as Byron refused all communication with Clare, and undertook to provide for his child on the sole condition that, from the day it left her, its mother entirely relinquished it, and never saw it again.

This appeared to Shelley cruelly and needlessly harsh. His own paternal heart was still bleeding from fresh wounds, and although, as he again pointed out, his interest in the matter was entirely on the opposite side to Clare's, he pleaded her cause with earnestness. He did not touch on the question of Byron's attitude towards Clare herself, he contended only for the mother and child, in letters as remarkable for their simple good sense as for their perfect delicacy and courtesy of expression, and every line of which is inspired with the unselfish ardour of a heart full of love.

Poor Clare herself was dreadfully unhappy. Any illusion she may ever have had about Byron had long been over, but she had possibly not realised before coming to Italy the perfect horror he had of seeing her; an event, as he told his friends the Hoppners, which would make it necessary for him instantly to quit Venice. The reports about his present mode of life, which, even at Milan did not fail to reach them, were, to say the least, not encouraging; and from a later letter of Shelley's it would seem that he warned Clare now, at the last minute, to pause and reflect before she sent Allegra away to such a father. She, however, was determined that till seven years old, at least, the child should be with one or other of its parents, and Byron would only consent to be that one on condition that it grew up in ignorance of its mother. It appears to have been assumed by all parties that, in refusing to hand Allegra altogether over to her father, they would be sacrificing for her the prospect of a brilliant position and fortune. Even supposing that this had been so, it is impossible to think that such a consideration would have weighed, at any rate with the Shelleys, but for the impossibility of keeping Clare's secret if Allegra remained with them, and the constant danger of worse scandal to which her unexplained presence must expose them. Clare, distracted with grief as she was, yet dreaded discovery acutely, and firmly believed she was acting for Allegra's best interests in parting from her.

It ended in the little girl's being sent to Venice on the 28th of April in the care of Elise, the Swiss nurse, with whom Mary Shelley, for Allegra's sake, consented to part, though she valued her very much, but who, not long afterwards, returned to her.

As soon as they had gone, the Shelleys and Clare left Milan; and travelling leisurely through Parma, Modena, Bologna, and Pisa (where a letter from Elise reached them), they arrived on the 9th of May at Leghorn. Here they made the acquaintance of Mr. and Mrs. Gisborne. The lady, formerly Mrs. Reveley, had been an intimate friend of Mary Wollstonecraft's (when Mary Godwin), and had been so warmly admired by Godwin before his first marriage as to arouse some jealousy in Mr. Reveley. Indeed, his admiration had been returned by so warm a feeling of friendship on her part that Godwin was frankly surprised when on his pressing her, shortly after her widowhood, to become his second wife, she refused him point blank, nor, by all his eloquence, was to be persuaded to change her mind. A beautiful girl, and highly accomplished, she had married very young, and had one son of her first marriage, Henry Reveley, a young civil engineer, who was now living in Italy with her and her second husband.

This Mr. Gisborne struck Mary as being the reverse of intelligent, and is described in Shelley's letters in most uncomplimentary terms. His appearance cannot certainly have been in his favour, but that there must have been more in him than met the eye seems also beyond a doubt, as, at a later time, Shelley addressed to him some of his most interesting and most intimate letters.

To Mrs. Gisborne they bore a letter of introduction from Godwin, and it was not long before her acquaintance with Mrs. Shelley ripened into friendship. "Reserved, yet with easy manners;" so Mary described her at their first meeting. On the next day the two had a long conversation about Mary's father and mother. Of her mother, indeed, Mary learned more from Mrs. Gisborne than from any one else. She wrote her father an immediate account of these first interviews, and his answer is unusually demonstrative in expression.

I received last Friday a delightful letter from you. I was extremely gratified by your account of Mrs. Gisborne. I have not seen her, I believe, these twenty years; I think not since she was Mrs. Gisborne; and yet by your description she is still a delightful woman. How inexpressibly pleasing it is to call back the recollection of years long past, and especially when the recollection belongs to a person in whom one deeply interested oneself, as I did in Mrs. Reveley. I can hardly hope for so great a pleasure as it would be to me to see her again.

At the Bagni di Lucca, where they settled themselves for a time, Mary heard from her father of the review of *Frankenstein* in the *Quarterly*. Peacock had reported it to be unfavourable, so it[Pg 216] was probably a relief to find that the reviewers "did not pretend to find anything blasphemous in the story."

They say that the *gentleman* who has written the book is a *man of talents*, but that he employs his powers in a way disagreeable to them.

All this, however, tended to keep Mary's old ardour alive. She never was more strongly impelled to write than at this time; she felt her powers fresh and strong within her; all she wanted was some motive, some suggestion to guide her in the choice of a subject. While at Leghorn Shelley had come upon a manuscript account, which Mary transcribed, of that terrible story of the *Cenci* afterwards dramatised by himself. His first idea was that Mary should take it for the subject of a play. He was convinced that she had dramatic talent as a writer, and that he had none; two erroneous conclusions, as the sequel showed. But such an assurance from such a source could not but be flattering to Mary's ambition, and stimulating to her innate love of literary work. During all the early part of their time in Italy their thoughts were busy with some subject for Mary's tragedy. One proposed and strongly urged by Shelley was *Charles the First*. It was partially carried out by himself before his death, and perhaps occurred to him now in connection with a suggestion of Godwin's[Pg 217] for a book very different in scope and character, and far better suited to Mary's genius than the drama. It would have been a series of *Lives of the Commonwealth's Men*; "our calumniated Republicans," as Shelley calls them.

She was immensely attracted by the idea, but was forced to abandon it at the time, for lack of the necessary books of reference. But Shelley, who believed her powers to be of the highest order, was as eager as she herself could be for her to undertake original work of some kind, and was constantly inciting her to effort in this direction.

More than two months were spent at the Bagni di Lucca—reading, writing, riding, and enjoying to the full the balmy Italian skies. Shelley, in whom the creative mood was more or less dormant, and who "despaired of providing anything original," translated the *Symposium* of Plato, partly as an exercise, partly to "give Mary some idea of the manners and feelings of the Athenians, so different on many subjects from that of any other community that ever existed." Together they studied Italian, and Shelley reported Mary's progress to her father.

Mary has just finished Ariosto with me, and indeed has attained a very competent knowledge of Italian. She is now reading Livy.

She also transcribed his translation of the *Symposium*, and his Eclogue *Rosalind and*[Pg 218] *Helen*, which, begun at Marlow, had been thrown aside till she found it and persuaded him to complete it.

Meanwhile Clare hungered and thirsted for a sight of Allegra, of whom she heard occasionally from Elise, and who was not now under Byron's roof, but living, by his permission, with Mrs. Hoppner, wife of the British Consul at Venice, who had volunteered to take temporary charge of her. Her distress moved Shelley to so much commiseration that he resolved or consented to do what must have been supremely disagreeable to him. He went himself to Venice, hoping by a personal interview to modify in some degree Byron's inexorable resolution. Clare accompanied him, unknown, of course, to Byron. They started on the 17th of August. On that day Mary wrote the following letter to Miss Gisborne—

MRS. SHELLEY TO MRS. GISBORNE.

BAGNI DI LUCCA, *17th August 1818.*

MY DEAR MADAM—It gave me great pleasure to receive your letter after so long a silence, when I had begun to conjecture a thousand reasons for it, and among others illness, in which I was half right. Indeed, I am much concerned to hear of Mr. R.'s attacks, and sincerely hope that nothing will retard his speedy recovery. His illness gives me a slight hope that you might now be induced to come to the baths, if it were even to try the effect of the hot baths. You would find the weather cool; for we already feel in this part of the world that the year is declining, by the cold mornings and evenings.[Pg 219] I have another selfish reason to wish that you would come, which I have a great mind not to mention, yet I will not omit it, as it might induce you. Shelley and Clare are gone; they went to-day to Venice on important business; and I am left to take care of the house. Now, if all of you, or any of you, would come and cheer my solitude, it would be exceedingly kind. I daresay you would find many of your friends here; among the rest there is the Signora Felichi, whom I believe you knew at Pisa. Shelley and I have ridden almost every evening. Clare did the same at first, but she has been unlucky, and once fell from her horse, and hurt her knee so as to knock her up for some time. It is the fashion here for all the English to ride, and it is very pleasant on these fine evenings, when we set out at sunset and are lighted home by Venus, Jupiter, and Diana, who kindly lend us their light after the sleepy Apollo is gone to bed. The road which we frequent is raised somewhat above, and overlooks the river, affording some very fine points of view amongst these woody mountains.

Still, we know no one; we speak to one or two people at the Casino, and that is all; we live in our studious way, going on with Tasso, whom I like, but who, now I have read more than half his poem, I do not know that I like half so well as Ariosto. Shelley translated the *Symposium* in ten days. It is a most beautiful piece of writing. I think you will be delighted with it. It is true that in many particulars it shocks our present manners; but no one can be a reader of the works of antiquity unless they can transport themselves from these to other times, and judge, not by our, but their morality.

Shelley is tolerably well in health; the hot weather has done him good. We have been in high debate—nor have we come to any conclusion—concerning the land or sea journey to Naples. We have been thinking that when we want to go, although the equinox will be past, yet the equinoctial winds will hardly have spent themselves; and I cannot express to you how I fear a storm at sea with two such young children as William and Clara. Do you know the periods when the[Pg 220] Mediterranean is troubled, and when the wintry halcyon days come? However, it may be we shall see you before we proceed southward.

We have been reading Eustace's *Tour through Italy*; I do not wonder the Italians reprinted it. Among other select specimens of his way of thinking, he says that the Romans did not derive their arts and learning from the Greeks; that Italian ladies are chaste, and the lazzaroni honest and industrious; and that, as to assassination and highway robbery in Italy, it is all a calumny—no such things were ever heard of. Italy was the garden of Eden, and all the Italians Adams and Eves, until the blasts of hell (*i.e.* the French—for by that polite name he designates them) came. By the bye, an Italian servant stabbed an English one here—it was thought dangerously at first, but the man is doing better.

I have scribbled a long letter, and I daresay you have long wished to be at the end of it. Well, now you are; so my dear Mrs. Gisborne, with best remembrances, yours, obliged and affectionately,

MARY W. SHELLEY.

From Florence, where he arrived on the 20th, Shelley wrote to Mary, telling her that Clare had changed her intention of going in person to Venice, and had decided on the more politic course of remaining herself at Fusina or Padua, while Shelley went on to see Byron.

"Well, my dearest Mary," he went on, "are you very lonely? Tell me truth, my sweetest, do you ever cry? I shall hear from you once at Venice and once on my return here. If you love me, you will keep up your spirits; and at all events tell me truth about it, for I assure you I am not of a disposition to be flattered by your sorrow, though I should be by your cheerfulness, and above all by seeing such fruits of my absence as was produced when I was at Geneva."

It was during Shelley's absence with Byron on[Pg 221] their voyage round the lake of Geneva that Mary had begun to write *Frankenstein*. But on the day when she received this letter she was very uneasy about her little girl, who was seriously unwell from the heat. On writing to Shelley she told him of this; and, from his answer, one may infer that she had suggested the advisability of taking the child to Venice for medical advice.

PADUA, MEZZOGIORNO.

MY BEST MARY—I found at Mount Selica a favourable opportunity for going to Venice, when I shall try to make some arrangement for you and little Ca to come for some days, and shall meet you, if I do not write anything in the meantime, at Padua on Thursday morning. Clare says she is obliged to come to see the Medico, whom we missed this morning, and who has appointed as the only hour at which he can be at leisure, 8 o'clock in the morning. You must, therefore, arrange matters so that you should come to the Stella d'Oro a little before that hour, a thing only to be accomplished by setting out at half-past 3 in the morning. You will by this means arrive at Venice very early in the day, and avoid the heat, which might be bad for the babe, and take the time when she would at least sleep great part of the time. Clare will return with the return carriage, and I shall meet you, or send to you, at Padua. Meanwhile, remember *Charles the First*, and do you be prepared to bring at least some of *Mirra* translated; bring the book also with you, and the sheets of *Prometheus Unbound*, which you will find numbered from 1 to 26 on the table of the Pavilion. My poor little Clara; how is she to-day? Indeed, I am somewhat uneasy about her; and though I feel secure there is no danger, it would be very comfortable to have some reasonable person's opinion about her. The Medico at Padua is certainly a man in great practice; but I confess he does not satisfy me. Am I not[Pg 222] like a wild swan, to be gone so suddenly? But, in fact, to set off alone to Venice required an exertion. I felt myself capable of making it, and I knew that you desired it.... Adieu, my dearest love. Remember, remember *Charles the First* and *Mirra*. I have been already imagining how you will conduct some scenes. The second volume of *St. Leon* begins with this proud and true sentiment—

"There is nothing which the human mind can conceive which it may not execute." Shakespeare was only a human being. Adieu till Thursday.—Your ever affectionate,

P. B. S.

His next letter, however, announced yet another revolution in Clare's plans. Her heart failed her at the idea of remaining to endure her suspense all alone in a strange place; and so, braving the possible consequences of Byron's discovering her move before he was informed of it, she went on with Shelley to Venice, and, the morning after their arrival, proceeded to Mr. Hoppner's house. Here she was kindly welcomed by him and his wife, a pretty Swiss woman, with a sympathetic motherly heart, who knew all about her and Allegra. They insisted, too, on Shelley's staying with them, and he was nothing loth to accept the offer, for Byron's circle would not have suited him at all.

He was pleased with his hostess, something in whose appearance reminded him of Mary. "She has hazel eyes and sweet looks, rather Maryish," he wrote. And in another letter he described her as

[Pg 223]So good, so beautiful, so angelically mild that, were she wise too, she would be quite a Mary. But she is not very accomplished. Her eyes are like a reflection of yours; her manners are like yours when you know and like a person.

He could enjoy no pleasure without longing for Mary to share it, and from the moment he reached Venice he was planning impatiently for her to follow him, to experience with him the strange emotions aroused by the first sight of the wonderful city, and to make acquaintance with his new friends.

He lost no time in calling on Byron, who gave him a very friendly reception. Shelley's intention on leaving Lucca was to go with his family to Florence, and the plan he urged on Byron was that Allegra should come to spend some time there with her mother. To this Byron objected, as likely to raise comment, and as a reopening of the whole question. He was, however, in an affable mood, and not indisposed to meet Shelley halfway. He had heard of Clare's being at Padua, but nothing of her subsequent change of plan; and, assuming that the whole party were staying there, he offered to send Allegra as far as that, on a week's visit. Finding that things were not as he supposed, and that Mrs. Shelley was likely to come presently to Venice, he proposed to lend them for some time a villa which he rented at Este, and to let Allegra stay with them.[Pg 224] The offer was promptly and gratefully accepted by Shelley. The fact of Clare's presence in Venice had, perforce, to be kept dark; for that there was no help; the great thing was to get her and Allegra away as soon as possible. He sent directions to Mary to pack up at once and travel with the least possible delay to Este. There he would meet her with Clare, Allegra, and Elise, who were to be established, with Mary's little ones, at Byron's villa, Casa Cappucini, while she and he proceeded to Venice.

When the letter came, Mary had the Gisbornes staying with her on a visit. For that reason, and on account of little Clara's indisposition, the summons to depart so suddenly can hardly have been welcome; she obeyed it, however, and left the Bagni di Lucca on the 31st of August. Owing to delays about the passport, her journey took rather longer than they had expected. The intense heat of the weather, added to the fatigue of travelling and probably change of diet, seriously affected the poor baby, who, by the time they got to Este on 5th September, was dangerously ill. Shelley, who had been waiting for them impatiently, was also far from well, and their visit to Venice had to be deferred for more than a fortnight, during which Mary had time to hear enough of Venetian society to horrify and disgust her.

[Pg 225]*Journal. Saturday, September 5.*—Arrive at Este. Poor Clara is dangerously ill. Shelley is very unwell, from taking poison in Italian cakes. He writes his drama of *Prometheus*. Read seven cantos of Dante. Begin to translate *A Cajo Graccho* of Monti, and *Measure for Measure*.

Wednesday, September 16.—Read the *Filippo* of Alfieri. Shelley and Clare go to Padua. He is very ill from the effects of his poison.

To Mrs. Gisborne she wrote as follows—

September 1818.

MY DEAR MRS. GISBORNE—I hasten to write to you to say that we have arrived safe, and yet I can hardly call it safe, since the fatigue has given my poor *Ca* an attack of dysentery; and although she is now somewhat recovered from that disorder, she is still in a frightful state of weakness and fever, and is reduced to be so thin in this short time that you would hardly know her again.

The physician of Este is a stupid fellow; but there is one come from Padua, and who appears clever; so I hope under his care she will soon get well, although we are still in great anxiety concerning her. I found Mr. Shelley very anxious for our non-arrival, for, besides other delays, we were detained a whole day at Florence for a signature to our passport. The house at Este is exceedingly pleasant, with a large garden and quantities of excellent fruit. I have not yet been to Venice, and know not when I shall, since it depends upon the state of Clara's health. I hope Mr. Reveley is quite recovered from his illness, and I am sure the baths did him a great deal of good. So now I suppose all your talk is how you will get to England. Shelley agrees with me that you could live very well for your £200 per annum in Marlow or some such town; and I am sure you would be much happier than in Italy. How all the English dislike it! The Hoppners speak with the greatest acrimony of the Italians, and Mr. Hoppner says that he was actually driven from Italian society by the young[Pg 226] men continually asking him for money. Everything is saleable in Venice, even the wives of the gentry, if you pay well. It appears indeed a most frightful system of society. Well! when shall we see you again? Soon, I daresay. I am so much hurried that you will be kind enough to excuse the abruptness of this letter. I will write soon again, and in the meantime write to me. Shelley and Clare desire the kindest remembrances.—My dear Mrs. Gisborne, affectionately yours,

MARY W. S.

Casa   Capuccini,   Este.

Send our letters to this direction.

No more of the journal was written till the 24th, and in the meantime great trouble had fallen on the writers. Shelley was impatient for Clara to be within reach of better medical advice, and anxious to get Mary to Venice. He went forward himself on the 22d, returning next day as far as Padua to meet Mary and Clara, with Clare, who, however, only came over to Padua to see the Medico. The baby was very ill, and was getting worse every hour, but they judged it best to press on. In their hurry they had forgotten their passport, and had some difficulty in getting past the *dogana* in consequence. Shelley's impetuosity carried all obstacles before it, and the soldiers on duty had to give way. On reaching Venice Mary went straight with her sick child to the inn, while Shelley hurried for the doctor. It was too late. When he got back (without the medical man) he found Mary well-nigh beside herself with distress. Another doctor had already[Pg 227] been summoned, but little Clara was dying, and in an hour all was over.

This blow reduced Mary to "a kind of despair";—the expression is Shelley's. Mr. Hoppner, on hearing what had happened, insisted on taking them away at once from the inn to his house. Four days she spent in Venice after that, the first of which was a blank; of the second she merely records—

An idle day. Go to the Lido and see Albé there.

After that she roused herself. There was Shelley to be comforted and supported, there was Byron to be interviewed. One of her objects in coming had been to try and persuade him after all to let Allegra stay. So she nerved herself to pay this visit, and to go about and see something of Venice with Shelley.

Sunday, September 27.—Read fourth canto of *Childe Harold*. It rains. Go to the Doge's Palace, Ponte dei Sospiri, etc. Go to the Academy with Mr. and Mrs. Hoppner, and see some fine pictures. Call at Lord Byron's and see the *Farmaretta*.

Monday, September 28.—Go with Mrs. Hoppner and Cavaliere Mengaldo to the Library. Shopping. In the evening Lord Byron calls.

Tuesday, September 29.—Leave Venice, and arrive at Este at night. Clare is gone with the children to Padua.

Wednesday, September 30.—The chicks return. Transcribe *Mazeppa*. Go to the opera in the evening.

A quiet, sad fortnight at Este followed. An idle one it was not, for Shelley not only wrote[Pg 228] *Julian and Maddalo*, but worked on portions of his drama of *Prometheus Unbound*, the idea of which had haunted him ever since he came to Italy. Clare, for the time, was happy with her child. Mary read several plays of Shakespeare and the lives of Alfieri and Tasso in Italian.

On the 12th of October she arrived once more at Venice with Shelley. She passed the greater part of her time there with the Hoppners, who were exceedingly friendly. Shelley visited Byron several times, probably trying to get an extension of leave for Allegra. In this, however, he must have failed, as on the 24th he went to Este to fetch her, returning with her on the 29th. Having restored the poor little girl to the Hoppners' care, he and Mary went once more to Este, but this time only to prepare for departure. On the 5th of November the whole party, including Elise (who was not retained for Allegra's service), left the Villa Capuccini and travelled by slow stages to Rome.

No further allusion to her recent bereavement is to be found in Mary's journal. She attempted to behave like the Stoic her father had wished her to be.[33]She had written to him of her affliction, and received the following answer from the philosopher—

[Pg 229]SKINNER STREET, *27th October 1818.*

MY DEAR MARY—I sincerely sympathise with you in the affliction which forms the subject of your letter, and which I may consider as the first severe trial of your constancy and the firmness of your temper that has occurred to you in the course of your life; you should, however, recollect that it is only persons of a very ordinary sort, and of a pusillanimous disposition, that sink long under a calamity of this nature. I assure you such a recollection will be of great use to you. We seldom indulge long in depression and mourning except when we think secretly that there is something very refined in it, and that it does us honour.

Such a homily, at such a time, must have made Mary feel like a person of a very ordinary sort indeed. But she strove, only too hard, to carry out her father's principles; for, by doing violence to her sensitive nature, she might crush but could not kill it. The passionate impulses of her mother were curiously mated in her with her father's reflective temperament; and the noble courage which she inherited from Mary Wollstonecraft went hand in hand with somewhat of Godwin's constitutional shrinking from any manifestation of emotion. And the effect of determinate, excessive self-restraint on a heart like hers was to render the crushed feelings morbid in their acuteness, and to throw on her spirits a load of endurance which was borne, indeed, but at ruinous cost, and operated largely, among other causes, to make her seem cold when she was really suffering.

[Pg 230]At such times it was not altogether well for her that she was Shelley's companion. For, when his health and spirits were good, he craved and demanded companionship,—personal, intellectual, playful,—companionship of all sorts; but when they ebbed, when his vitality was low, when the simultaneous exaltation of conception and labour of realisation—a tremendous expenditure of force—was over, and left him shattered, shaken, surprised at himself like one who in a dream falls from a height and awakens with the shock,—tired, and yet dull,—then the one panacea for him was animal spirits in some congenial acquaintance; whether a friend or a previous stranger mattered little, provided the personality was congenial and the spirits buoyant. Mary did her best, bravely and nobly. But the loss of a child was one thing to Shelley, another thing to her. She strove to overcome the low spirits from which she suffered. But endurance, though more heroic than spontaneous cheerfulness, is not to be compared with it in its benign effect on other people; nay, it may even have a depressing effect when a yielding to emotion "of the ordinary sort" may not. All these truths, however, do not become evident at once; like other life-experience they have to be spelled out by slow and painful degrees.

To seek for respite from grief or care in [Pg 231]intellectual culture and the acquisition of knowledge was instinctive and habitual both in Shelley and in Mary. They visited Ferrara and Bologna, then travelled by a winding road among the Apennines to Terni, where they saw the celebrated waterfall—

It put me in mind of Sappho leaping from a rock, and her form vanishing as in the shape of a swan in the distance.

Friday, November 20.—We travel all day the Campagna di Roma—a perfect solitude, yet picturesque, and relieved by shady dells. We see an immense hawk sailing in the air for prey. Enter Rome. A rainy evening. Doganas and cheating innkeepers. We at length get settled in a comfortable hotel.

After one week in Rome, during which they visited as many of the wonders of the Eternal City as the time allowed, they journeyed on to Naples, reading Montaigne by the way.

At Naples they remained for three months. Of their life there Mary's journal gives no account; she confines herself almost entirely to noting down the books they read, and one or two excursions. They lived in very great seclusion, greater than was good for them, but Shelley suffered much from ill-health, and not a little from its treatment by an unskilful physician. They read incessantly,—Livy, Dante, Sismondi, Winkelmann, the Georgics and Plutarch's*Lives, Gil Blas,* and *Corinne.* They left no beautiful or interesting scene unvisited; they ascended [Pg 232]Vesuvius, and made excursions to Pompeii, Herculaneum, and Paestum.

71

On the 8th of December Mary records—

Go on the sea with Shelley. Visit Capo Miseno, the Elysian Fields, Avernus, Solfatara. The Bay of Baiae is beautiful, but we are disappointed by the various places we visit.

The impression of the scene, however, remained after the temporary disappointment had been forgotten, and she sketched it from memory many years later in the fanciful introduction to her romance of *The Last Man*, the story of which purports to be a tale deciphered from sibylline leaves, picked up in the caverns.

Shelley, however, suffered from extreme depression, which, out of solicitous consideration for Mary, he disguised as much as possible under a mask of cheerfulness, insomuch that she never fully realised what he endured at this time until she read the mournful poems written at Naples, after he who wrote them had passed for ever out of sight.

She blamed herself then for what seemed to her her blindness,—for having perhaps let slip opportunities of cheering him which she would have sold her soul to recall when it was too late. That *he*, at the time, felt in her no such want of sympathy or help is shown by his concluding words in the advertisement of *Rosalind and*[Pg 233] *Helen*, and *Lines written among the Euganean Hills*, dated Naples, 20th December, where he says of certain lines "which image forth the sudden relief of a state of deep despondency by the radiant visions disclosed by the sudden burst of an Italian sunrise in autumn on the highest peak of those delightful mountains," that, if they were not erased, it was "at the request of a dear friend, with whom added years of intercourse only add to my apprehension of its value, and who would have had more right than any one to complain that she has not been able to extinguish in me the very power of delineating sadness."

Much of this sadness was due to physical suffering, but external causes of anxiety and vexation were not wanting. One was the discovery of grave misconduct on the part of their Italian servant, Paolo. An engagement had been talked of between him and the Swiss nurse Elise, but the Shelleys, who thought highly of Elise and by no means highly of Paolo, tried to dissuade her from the idea. An illness of Elise's revealed the fact that an illicit connection had been formed. The Shelleys, greatly distressed, took the view that it would not do to throw Elise on the world without in some degree binding Paolo to do his duty towards her, and they had them married. How far this step was well-judged may be a[Pg 234] matter of opinion. Elise was already a mother when she entered the Shelleys service. Whether a woman already a mother was likely to do better for being bound for life to a man whom they "knew to be a rascal" may reasonably be doubted even by those who hold the marriage-tie, as such, in higher honour than the Shelleys did. But whether the action was mistaken or not, it was prompted by the sincerest solicitude for Elise's welfare, a solicitude to be repaid, at no distant date, by the basest ingratitude. Meanwhile Mary lost her nurse, and, it may be assumed, a valuable one; for any one who studies the history of this and the preceding years must see all three of the poor doomed children throve as long as Elise was in charge of them.

Clare was ailing, and anxious too; how could it be otherwise? Just before Allegra's third birthday, Mary received a letter from Mrs. Hoppner which was anything but reassuring. It gave an unsatisfactory account of the child, who did not thrive in the climate of Venice, and a still more unsatisfactory account of Byron.

Il faut espérer qu'elle se changera pour son mieux quand il ne sera plus si froid; mais je crois toujours que c'est très malheureux que Miss Clairmont oblige cette enfant de vivre à Venise, dont le climat est nuisible en tout au physique de la petite, et vraiment, pour ce que fera son père, je le trouve un[Pg 235] peu triste d'y sacrifier l'enfant. My Lord continue de vivre dans une débauche affreuse qui tôt ou tard le menera a sà ruine....

Quant à moi, je voudrois faire tout ce qui est en mon pouvoir pour cette enfant, que je voudrois bien volontiers rendre aussi heureuse que possible le temps qu'elle restera avec nous; car je crains qu'après elle devra toujours vivre avec des étrangers, indifferents à son sort. My Lord bien certainement ne la rendra jamais plus à sa mère; ainsi il n'y a rien de bon à espérer pour cette chère petite.

This letter, if she saw it, may well have made Clare curse the day when she let Allegra go. Still, after they returned to Rome at the beginning of March, a brighter time set in.

Journal, Friday, March 5.—After passing over the beautiful hills of Albano, and traversing the Campagna, we arrive at the Holy City again, and see the Coliseum again.

All that Athens ever brought forth wise,
All that Afric ever brought forth strange,
All that which Asia ever had of prize,
Was here to see. Oh, marvellous great change!
Rome living was the world's sole ornament;
And dead, is now the world's sole monument.

Sunday, March 7.—Move to our lodgings. A rainy day. Visit the Coliseum. Read the Bible.

Monday, March 8.—Visit the Museum of the Vatican. Read the Bible.

Tuesday, March 9.—Shelley and I go to the Villa Borghese. Drive about Rome. Visit the Pantheon. Visit it again by moonlight, and see the yellow rays fall through the roof upon the floor of the temple. Visit the Coliseum.

[Pg 236]*Wednesday, March 10.*—Visit the Capitol, and see the most divine statues.

Not one of the party but was revived and invigorated by the beauty and overpowering interest of the surrounding scenes, and the delight of a lovely Italian spring. To Shelley it was life itself.

"The charm of the Roman climate," says Mrs. Shelley, "helped to clothe his thoughts in greater beauty than they had ever worn before. And as he wandered among the ruins, made one with nature in their decay, or gazed on the Praxitelean shapes that throng the Vatican, the Capitol, and the palaces of Rome, his soul imbibed forms of loveliness which became a portion of itself."

The visionary drama of *Prometheus Unbound*, which had haunted, yet eluded him so long, suddenly took life and shape, and stood before him, a vivid reality. During his first month at Rome he completed it in its original three-act form. The fourth act was an afterthought, and was added at a later date.

For a short, enchanted time—his health renewed, the deadening years forgotten, his susceptibilities sharpened, not paralysed, by recent grief—he gave himself up to the vision of the realisation of his life-dream; the disappearance of evil from the earth.

"He believed," wrote Mary Shelley, "that mankind had only to will that there should be no evil, and there would be[Pg 237] none.... That man should be so perfectionised as to be able to expel evil from his own nature, and from the greater part of the creation was the cardinal point of his system. And the subject he loved best to dwell on, was the image of one warring with the Evil Principle, oppressed not only by it, but by all, even the good, who were deluded into considering evil a necessary portion of humanity. A victim full of fortitude and hope, and the spirit of triumph emanating from a reliance in the ultimate omnipotence of good."

"This poem," he himself says, "was chiefly written upon the mountainous ruins of the Baths of Caracalla, among the flowers, glades, and thickets of odoriferous blossoming trees, which are extended in ever winding labyrinths upon its immense platforms and dizzy arches suspended in the air. The bright blue sky of Rome, and the effect of the vigorous awakening of spring in that divinest climate, and the new life with which it drenches the spirits even to intoxication, were the inspiration of this drama."[34]

And while he wrought and wove the radiant web of his poem, Mary, excited to greatest enthusiasm by the treasures of sculpture at Rome, and infected by the atmosphere of art around her, took up again her favourite pursuit of drawing, which she had discontinued since going to Marlow, and worked at it many hours a day, sometimes all day. She was writing, too; a thoroughly congenial occupation, at once soothing and stimulating to her. She studied the Bible, with the keen fresh interest of one who comes new to it, and she read Livy and Montaigne.

Little William was thriving, and growing more[Pg 238] interesting every day. His beauty and promise and angelic sweetness made him the pet and darling of all who knew him, while to his parents he was a perpetual source of ever fresh and increasing delight. And his mother looked forward to the birth in autumn of another little one who might, in some measure, fill the place of her lost Clara.

Clare, who, also, was in better health, was not behindhand in energy or industry. Music was her favourite pursuit; she took singing-lessons from a good master and worked hard.

They led a somewhat less secluded life than at Naples, and at the house of Signora Dionizi, a Roman painter and authoress (described by Mary Shelley as "very old, very miserly, and very mean"), Mary and Clare, at any rate, saw a little of Italian society. For this, however, Shelley did not care, nor was he attracted by any of the few English with whom he came in contact. Yet he felt his solitude. In April, when the strain of his work was over, his spirits drooped, as usual; and he longed then for some *congenial distraction*, some human help to bear the burden of life till the moment of weakness should have passed. But the fount of inspiration, the source of temporary elation and strength, had not been exhausted by *Prometheus*.

On the 22d of April Mary notes—

[Pg 239]Visit the Palazzo Corunna, and see the picture of Beatrice Cenci.

The interest in the old idea was revived in him; he became engrossed in the subject, and soon after his "lyrical drama" was done, he transferred himself to this other, completely different work. There was no talk, now, of passing it on to Mary, and indeed she may well have recoiled from the unmitigated horrors of the tale. But, though he dealt with it himself, Shelley still felt on unfamiliar ground, and, as he proceeded, he submitted what he wrote to Mary for her judgment and criticism; the only occasion on which he consulted her about any work of his during its progress towards completion.

Late in April they made the acquaintance of one English (or rather, Irish) lady, who will always be gratefully remembered in connection with the Shelleys.

This was Miss Curran, a daughter of the late Irish orator, who had been a friend of Godwin's, and to whose death Mary refers in one of her letters from Marlow.[35]

Mary may, perhaps, have met her in Skinner Street; in any case, the old association was one link between them, and another was afforded by similarity in their present interests and occupations. Mary was very keen about her drawing[Pg 240] and painting. Miss Curran had taste, and some skill, and was vigorously prosecuting her art-studies in Rome. Portrait painting was her especial line, and each of the Shelley party, at different times, sat to her; so that during the month of May they met almost daily, and became well acquainted.

This new interest, together with the unwillingness to bring to an end a time at once so peaceful and so fruitful, caused them once and again to postpone their departure, originally fixed for the beginning of May. They stayed on longer than it is safe for English people to remain in Rome. Ah! why could no presentiment warn them of impending calamity? Could they, like the Scottish witch in the ballad, have seen the fatal winding-sheet creeping and clinging ever higher and higher round the wraith of their doomed child, they would have fled from the face of Death. But they had no such foreboding.

Not a fortnight after his portrait had been taken by Miss Curran, William showed signs of illness. How it was that, knowing him to be so delicate,—having learned by bitterest experience the danger of southern heat to an English-born infant,—having, as early as April, suspected the Roman air of causing "weakness and depression, and even fever" to Shelley himself, how, after all[Pg 241] this, they risked staying in Rome through May is hard to imagine.

They were to pay for their delay with the best part of their lives. William sickened on the 25th, but had so far recovered by the 30th that his parents, though they saw they ought to leave Rome as soon as he was fit to travel, were in no immediate anxiety about him, and were making their summer plans quite in a leisurely way; Mary writing to ask Mrs. Gisborne to help them with some domestic arrangements, begging her to inquire about houses at Lucca or the Baths of Pisa, and to engage a servant for her.

The journal for this and the following days runs—

Sunday, May 30.—Read Livy, and *Persiles and Sigismunda*. Draw. Spend the evening at Miss Curran's.

Monday, May 31.—Read Livy, and *Persiles and Sigismunda*. Draw. Walk in the evening.

Tuesday, June 1.—Drawing lesson. Read Livy. Walk by the Tiber. Spend the evening with Miss Curran.

Wednesday, June 2.—See Mr. Vogel's pictures. William becomes very ill in the evening.

Thursday, June 3.—William is very ill, but gets better towards the evening. Miss Curran calls.

Mary took this opportunity of begging her friend to write for her to Mrs. Gisborne, telling her of the inevitable delay in their journey.

ROME, *Thursday, 3d June 1819.*

DEAR MRS. GISBORNE—Mary tells me to write for her, for she is very unwell, and also afflicted. Our poor little William[Pg 242] is at present very ill, and it will be impossible to quit Rome so soon as we intended. She begs you, therefore, to forward the letters here, and still to look for a servant for her, as she certainly intends coming to Pisa. She will write to you a day or two before we set out.

William has a complaint of the stomach; but fortunately he is attended by Mr. Bell, who is reckoned even in London one of the first English surgeons.

I know you will be glad to hear that both Mary and Mr. Shelley would be well in health were it not for the dreadful anxiety they now suffer.

EMELIA CURRAN.

Two days after, Mary herself wrote a few lines to Mrs. Gisborne.

5th June 1819.

William is in the greatest danger. We do not quite despair, yet we have the least possible reason to hope.

I will write as soon as any change takes place. The misery of these hours is beyond calculation. The hopes of my life are bound up in him.—Ever yours affectionately,

M. W. S.

I am well, and so is Shelley, although he is more exhausted by watching than I am. William is in a high fever.

Sixty death-like hours did Shelley watch, without closing his eyes. Clare, her own troubles forgotten in this moment of mortal suspense, was a devoted nurse.

As for Mary, her very life ebbed with William's, but as yet she bore up. There was no real hope from the first moment of the attack, but the poor child made a hard struggle for life. Two more days and nights of anguish and terror and deadly sinking of heart,—and then, in the blank page[Pg 243] following *June 4*, the last date entered in the diary, are the words—

The journal ends here.—P. B. S.

On Monday, the 7th of June, at noonday, William died.

[Pg 244]
CHAPTER XII
JUNE 1819-SEPTEMBER 1820

It was not fifteen months since they had all left England; Shelley and Mary with the sweet, blue-eyed "Willmouse," and the pretty baby, Clara, so like her father; Clare and the "bluff, bright-eyed little Commodore," Allegra; the Swiss nurse and English nursemaid; a large and lively party, in spite of cares and anxieties and sorrows to come. In one short, spiritless paragraph Mary, on the 4th of August, summed up such history as there was of the sad two months following on the blow which had left her childless.

Journal, Wednesday, August 4, 1819, Leghorn (Mary).—I begin my journal on Shelley's birthday. We have now lived five years together; and if all the events of the five years were blotted out, I might be happy; but to have won and then cruelly to have lost, the associations of four years, is not an accident to which the human mind can bend without much suffering.

Since I left home I have read several books of Livy, *Clarissa Harlowe*, the *Spectator*, a few novels, and am now reading the Bible, and Lucan's *Pharsalia*, and Dante. Shelley is to-day twenty-seven years of age. Write; read Lucan[Pg 245] and the Bible. Shelley writes the *Cenci*, and reads Plutarch's *Lives*. The Gisbornes call in the evening. Shelley reads *Paradise Lost* to me. Read two cantos of the *Purgatorio*.

Three days after William's death, Shelley, Mary, and Clare had left Rome for Leghorn. Once more they were alone together—how different now from the three heedless young things who, just five years before, had set out to walk through France with a donkey!

Shelley, then, a creature of feelings and theories, full of unbalanced impulses, vague aspirations and undeveloped powers; inexperienced in everything but uncomprehended pain and the dim consciousness of half-realised mistakes. Mary, the fair, quiet, thoughtful girl, earnest and impassioned, calm and resolute, as ignorant of practical life as precocious in intellect; with all her mind worshipping the same high ideals as Shelley's, and with all her heart worshipping him as the incarnation of them. Clare her very opposite; excitable and enthusiastic, demonstrative and capricious, clever, but silly; with a mind in which a smattering of speculative philosophy, picked up in Godwin's house, contended for the mastery with such social wisdom as she had picked up in a boarding school. Both of them mere children in years. Now poor Clare was older without being much wiser, saddened yet not sobered; suffering bitterly from her ambiguous position, yet unable[Pg 246] or unwilling to put an end to it; the worse by her one great error, which had brought her to dire grief; the better by one great affection—for her child,—the source of much sorrow, it is true, but also of truest joy of self-devotion, and the only instrument of such discipline that ever she had.

Shelley had found what he wanted, the faithful heart which to his own afforded peace and stability and the balance which, then, he so much needed; a kindred mind, worthy of the best his had to give; knowing and expecting that best, too, and satisfied with nothing short of it. And his best had responded. In these few years he had realised powers the extent of which could not have been foretold, and which might, without that steady sympathy and support, have remained unfulfilled possibilities for ever. In spite of the far-reaching consequences of his errors, in spite of torturing memories, in spite of ill-health, anxiety, poverty, vexation, and strife, the Shelley of *Queen Mab* had become the Shelley of *Prometheus Unbound* and the *Cenci*.

Of this development he himself was conscious enough. In so far as he was known to his contemporaries, it was only by his so-called atheistic opinions, and his departures theoretical and actual, from conventional social morality; and even these owed their notoriety, not to his genius, but to the fact that they were such strange vagaries in the[Pg 247] heir to a baronetcy. In his new life he had, indeed, known the deepest grief as well as the purest love, but those griefs which are memorial shrines of love did not paralyse him. They were rather among the influences which elicited the utmost possibilities of his nature; his lost children, as lovely ideals, were only half lost to him.

75

But with Mary it was otherwise. Her occupation was gone. When after the death of her first poor little baby, she wrote: "Whenever I am left alone to my own thoughts, and do not read to divert them, they always come back to the same point—that I was a mother, and am so no longer;" a new sense was dawning in her which never had waned, and which, since William's birth, had asserted itself as the key to her nature.

She had known very little of the realities of life when she left her father's house with Shelley, and he, her first reality, belonged in many ways more to the ideal than to the real world. But for her children, her association with him, while immeasurably expanding her mental powers, might have tended to develop these at the expense of her emotional nature, and to starve or to stifle her human sympathies. In her children she found the link which united her ideal love with the universal heart of mankind, and it was as a mother that she learned the sweet charities of human nature. This maternal love deepened her feelings[Pg 248] towards her own father, it gave her sympathy with Clare and helped towards patience with her, it saved her from overmuch literary abstraction, and prevented her from pining when Shelley was buried in dreams or engrossed in work, and she loved these children with the unconscious passionate gratitude of a reserved nature towards anything that constrains from it the natural expression of that fund of tenderness and devotion so often hidden away under a perversely undemonstrative manner. Now, in one short year, all this was gone, and she sank under the blow of William's loss. She could not even find comfort in the thought of the baby to be born in autumn, for, after the repeated rending asunder of beloved ties, she looked forward to new ones with fear and trembling, rather than with hope. The physical reaction after the strain of long suspense and watching had told seriously on her health, never strong at these times; the efforts she had made at Naples were no longer possible to her. Even Clare with all her misery was, in one sense, better off than she, for Allegra *lived*. She tried to rise above her affliction, but her care for everything was gone; the whole world seemed dull and indifferent. Poor Shelley, only too liable to depression at all times, and suffering bitterly himself from the loss of his beloved child, tried to keep up his spirits for Mary's sake.

[Pg 249]Thou sittest on the hearth of pale Despair,
Where,
For thine own sake, I cannot follow thee.

Perhaps the effort he thus made for her sake had a bracing effect on himself, but the old Mary seemed gone,—lost,—and even he was powerless to bring her back; she could not follow him; any approach of seeming forgetfulness in others increased her depression and gloom.

The letter to Miss Curran, which follows, was written within three weeks of William's death.

LEGHORN, *27th June 1819.*

MY DEAR MISS CURRAN—I wrote to you twice on our journey, and again from this place, but I found the other day that Shelley had forgotten to send the letter; and I have been so unwell with a cold these last two or three days that I have not been able to write. We have taken an airy house here, in the vicinity of Leghorn, for three months, and we have not found it yet too hot. The country around us is pretty, so that I daresay we shall do very well. I am going to write another stupid letter to you, yet what can I do? I no sooner take up my pen than my thoughts run away with me, and I cannot guide it except about *one* subject, and that I must avoid. So I entreat you to join this to your many other kindnesses, and to excuse me. I have received the two letters forwarded from Rome. My father's lawsuit is put off until July. It will never be terminated. I hear that you have quitted the pestilential air of Rome, and have gained a little health in the country. Pray let us hear from you, for both Shelley and I are very anxious—more than I can express—to know how you are. Let us hear also, if you please, anything you may have done about the tomb, near which I shall lie one day, and care not, for my own sake, how soon. I never shall recover that blow; I feel it more than at Rome; the thought never leaves me for a[Pg 250] single moment; everything on earth has lost its interest to me. You see I told you that I could only write to you on one subject; how can I, since, do all I can (and I endeavour very sincerely) I can think of no other, so I will leave off. Shelley is tolerably well, and desires his kindest remembrances.—Most affectionately yours,

MARY W. SHELLEY.

Their sympathetic friend, Leigh Hunt, grieved at the tone of her letters and at Shelley's account of her, tried to convey to her a little kindly advice and encouragement.

8 YORK BUILDINGS, NEW ROAD.
July 1819.

MY DEAR MARY—I was just about to write to you, as you will see by my letter to Shelley, when I received yours. I need not say how it grieves me to see you so dispirited. Not that I wonder at it under such sufferings; but I know, at least I have often suspected, that you have a tendency, partly constitutional perhaps, and partly owing to the turn of your philosophy, to look over-intensely at the dark side of human things; and they must present double dreariness through such tears as you are now shedding. Pray consent to take care of your health, as the ground of comfort; and cultivate your laurels on the strength of it. I wish you would strike your pen into some more genial subject (more obviously so than your last), and bring up a fountain of gentle tears for us. That exquisite passage about the cottagers shows what you could do.[36]

Mary received his counsels submissively, and would have carried them out if she could. But her nervous prostration was beyond her own power to cure or remove, and it was hard for others and impossible for herself to know how far her dejected state was due to mental and how far to physical causes.

[Pg 251]Shelley was not, and dared not be, idle. He worked at his Tragedy and finished it; many of the Fragments, too, belong to this time. They are the speech of pain, but those who can teach in song what they learn in suffering have much, very much to be thankful for. Mary persisted in study; she even tried to write. But the spring of invention was low.

She exerted herself to send to Mrs. Hunt an account of their present life and surroundings.

LEGHORN, *28th August 1819.*

MY DEAR MARIANNE—We are very dull at Leghorn, and I can therefore write nothing to amuse you. We live in a little country house at the end of a green lane, surrounded by a *podere*. These *poderi* are just the things Hunt would like. They are like our kitchen-gardens, with the difference only that the beautiful fertility of the country gives them. A large bed of cabbages is very unpicturesque in England, but here the furrows are alternated with rows of grapes festooned on their supporters, and the hedges are of myrtle, which have just ceased to flower; their flower has the sweetest faint smell in the world, like some delicious spice. Green grassy walks lead you through the vines. The people are always busy, and it is pleasant to see three or four of them transform in one day a bed of Indian corn to one of celery. They work this hot weather in their shirts, or smock-frocks (but their breasts are bare), their brown legs nearly the colour, only with a rich tinge of red in it, of the earth they turn up. They sing, not very melodiously, but very loud, Rossini's music, "Mi rivedrai, ti rivedrò," and they are accompanied by the *cicala*, a kind of little beetle, that makes a noise with its tail as loud as Johnny can sing; they live on trees; and three or four together are enough to deafen you. It is to the *cicala* that[Pg 252] Anacreon has addressed an ode which they call "To a Grasshopper" in the English translations.

Well, here we live. I never am in good spirits—often in very bad; and Hunt's portrait has already seen me shed so many tears that, if it had his heart as well as his eyes, he would weep too in pity. But no more of this, or a tear will come now, and there is no use for that.

By the bye, a hint Hunt gave about portraits. The Italian painters are very bad; they might make a nose like Shelley's, and perhaps a mouth, but I doubt it; but there would be no expression about it. They have no notion of anything except copying again and again their Old Masters; and somehow mere copying, however divine the original, does a great deal more harm than good.

Shelley has written a good deal, and I have done very little since I have been in Italy. I have had so much to see, and so many vexations, independently of those which God has kindly sent to wean me from the world if I were too fond of it. Shelley has not had good health by any means, and, when getting better, fate has ever contrived something to pull him back. He never was better than the last month of his stay in Rome, except the last week—then he watched sixty miserable death-like hours without closing his eyes; and you may think what good that did him.

We see the *Examiners* regularly now, four together, just two months after the publication of the last. These are very delightful to us. I have a word to say to Hunt concerning what he says concerning Italian dancing. The Italians dance very badly. They dress for their dances in the ugliest manner; the men in little doublets, with a hat and feather; they are very stiff; nothing but their legs move; and they twirl and jump with as little grace as may be. It is not for their dancing, but their pantomime, that the Italians are famous. You remember what we told you of the ballet of *Othello*. They tell a story by action, so that words appear perfectly superfluous things for them. In that they are graceful, agile, impressive, and very affecting; so that I delight in nothing[Pg 253] so much as a deep tragic ballet. But the dancing, unless, as they sometimes do, they dance as common people (for instance, the dance of joy of the Venetian citizens on the return of Othello), is very bad indeed.

I am very much obliged to you for all your kind offers and wishes. Hunt would do Shelley a great deal of good, but that we may not think of; his spirits are tolerably good. But you do not tell me how you get on; how Bessy is, and where she is. Remember me to her. Clare is learning thorough bass and singing. We pay four crowns a month for her master, lessons three times a week; cheap work this, is it not? At Rome we paid three shillings a lesson and the master stayed two hours. The one we have now is the best in Leghorn.

I write in the morning, read Latin till 2, when we dine; then I read some English book, and two cantos of Dante with Shelley. In the evening our friends the Gisbornes come, so we are not perfectly alone. I like Mrs. Gisborne very much indeed, but her husband is most dreadfully dull; and as he is always with her, we have not so much pleasure in her company as we otherwise should....

The neighbourhood of Mrs. Gisborne, "charming from her frank and affectionate nature," and full of intellectual sympathy with the Shelleys, was a boon indeed at this melancholy time. Through her Shelley was led to the study of Spanish, and the appearance on the scene of Charles Clairmont, who had just passed a year in Spain, was an additional stimulus in this direction. Together they read several of Calderon's plays, from which Shelley derived the greatest delight, and which enabled him for a time to forget everyday life and its troubles. Another[Pg 254] diversion to his thoughts was the scheme of a steamboat which should ply between Leghorn and Marseilles, to be constructed by Henry Reveley, mainly at Shelley's expense. He was elated at promoting a project which he conceived to be of great public usefulness and importance, and happy at being able to do a friend a good turn. He followed every stage of the steamer's construction with keen interest, and was much disappointed when the idea was given up, as, after some months, it was; not, however, until much time, labour, and money had been expended on it.

Mary, though she endeavoured to fill the blanks in her existence by assiduous reading, could not escape care. Clare was in perpetual thirst for news of her Allegra, and Godwin spared them none of his usual complaints. He, too, was much concerned at the depressed tone of Mary's letters, which seemed to him quite disproportionate to the occasion, and thought it his duty to convince her, by reasoning, that she was not so unhappy as she thought herself to be.

SKINNER STREET, *9th September 1819.*

MY DEAR MARY—Your letter of 19th August is very grievous to me, inasmuch as you represent me as increasing the degree of your uneasiness and depression.

You must, however, allow me the privilege of a father and a philosopher in expostulating with you on this depression. I[Pg 255] cannot but consider it as lowering your character in a memorable degree, and putting you quite among the commonalty and mob of your sex, when I had thought I saw in you symptoms entitling you to be ranked among those noble spirits that do honour to our nature. What a falling off is here! How bitterly is so inglorious a change to be deplored!

What is it you want that you have not? You have the husband of your choice, to whom you seem to be unalterably attached, a man of high intellectual attainments, whatever I and some other persons may think of his morality, and the defects under this last head, if they be not (as you seem to think) imaginary, at least do not operate as towards you. You have all the goods of fortune, all the means of being useful to others, and shining in your proper sphere. But you have lost a child: and all the rest of the world, all that is beautiful, and all that has a claim upon your kindness, is nothing, because a child of two years old is dead.

The human species may be divided into two great classes: those who lean on others for support, and those who are qualified to support. Of these last, some have one, some five, and some ten talents. Some can support a husband, a child, a small but respectable circle of friends and dependents, and some can support a world, contributing by their energies to advance their whole species one or more degrees in the scale of perfectibility. The former class sit with their arms crossed, a prey to apathy and languor, of no use to any earthly creature, and ready to fall from their stools if some kind soul, who might compassionate, but who cannot respect them, did not come from moment to moment and endeavour to set them up again. You were formed by nature to belong to the best of these classes, but you seem to be shrinking away, and voluntarily enrolling yourself among the worst.

Above all things, I entreat you, do not put the miserable delusion on yourself, to think there is something fine, and beautiful, and delicate, in giving yourself up, and agreeing to be nothing. Remember too, though at first your nearest connections may pity you in this state, yet that when they see you[Pg 256] fixed in selfishness and ill humour, and regardless of the happiness of every one else, they will finally cease to love you, and scarcely learn to endure you.

The other parts of your letter afford me much satisfaction. Depend upon it, there is no maxim more true or more important than this; Frankness of communication takes off bitterness. True philosophy invites all communication, and withholds none.

Such a letter tended rather to check frankness of communication than to bind up a broken heart. Poor Mary's feelings appear in her letter to Miss Curran, with whom she was in correspondence about a monumental stone for the tomb in Rome.

The most pressing entreaties on my part, as well as Clare's, cannot draw a single line from Venice. It is now six months since we have heard, even in an indirect manner, from there. God knows what has happened, or what has not! I suppose Shelley must go to see what has become of the little thing; yet how or when I know not, for he has never recovered from his fatigue at Rome, and continually frightens me by the approaches of a dysentery. Besides, we must remove. My lying-in and winter are coming on, so we are wound up in an inextricable dilemma. This is very hard upon us; and I have no consolation in any quarter, for my misfortune has not altered the tone of my Father's letters, so that I gain care every day. And can you wonder that my spirits suffer terribly? that time is a weight to me? And I see no end to this. Well, to talk of something more interesting, Shelley has finished his tragedy, and it is sent to London to be presented to the managers. It is still a *deep secret*, and only one person, Peacock (who presents it), knows anything about it in England. With Shelley's public and private enemies, it would certainly fall if known to be his; his sister-in-law alone would hire[Pg 257] enough people to damn it. It is written with great care, and we are in hopes that its story is sufficiently polished not to shock the audience. We shall see. Continue to direct to us at Leghorn, for if we should be gone, they will be faithfully forwarded to us. And when you return to Rome just have the kindness to inquire if there should be any stray letter for us at the post-office. I hope the country air will do you real good. You must take care of yourself. Remember that one day you will return to England, and that you may be happier there.—Affectionately yours,

M. W. S.

At the end of September they removed to Florence, where they had engaged pleasant lodgings for six months. The time of Mary's confinement was now approaching, an event, in Shelley's words, "more likely than any other to retrieve her from some part of her present melancholy depression."

They travelled by short, easy stages; stopping for a day at Pisa to pay a visit to a lady with whom from this time their intercourse was frequent and familiar. This was Lady Mountcashel, who had, when a young girl, been Mary Wollstonecraft's pupil, and between whom and her teacher so warm an attachment had existed as to arouse the jealousy and dislike of her mother, Lady Kingsborough. She had long since been separated from Lord Mountcashel, and lived in Italy with a Mr. Tighe, and their two daughters, Laura and Nerina. As Lady Mountcashel she had entertained Godwin at her house during his visit to Ireland after his first wife's death. She[Pg 258] is described by him as a remarkable person, "a republican and a democrat in all their sternness, yet with no ordinary portion either of understanding or good nature." In dress and appearance she was somewhat singular, and had that disregard for public opinion on such matters which is habitually implied in the much abused term "strong-minded." In this respect she had now considerably toned down. Her views on the relations of the sexes were those of William Godwin, and she had put them into practice. But she and the gentleman with whom she lived in permanent, though irregular, union had succeeded in constraining, by their otherwise exemplary life, the general respect and esteem. They were known as "Mr. and Mrs. Mason," and had so far lived down criticism that their actual position had come to be ignored or forgotten by those around them. Mr. Tighe, or "Tatty," as he was familiarly called by his few intimates, was of a retiring disposition, a lover of books and of solitude. Mrs. Mason was as remarkable for her strong practical common sense as for her talents and cultivation and the liberality of her views. She had a considerable knowledge of the world, and was looked up to as a model of good breeding, and an oracle on matters of deportment and propriety.

She had kept up correspondence with Godwin,[Pg 259] and her acquaintance with the Shelleys was half made before she saw them. She conceived an immediate affection for Mary, as well for her own as for her mother's sake, and was to prove a constant and valuable friend, not to her only, but to Shelley, and most especially to Clare.

After a week in Florence, Mary's journal was resumed.

Saturday, October 9.—Arrive at Florence. Read Massinger. Shelley begins Clarendon; reads Massinger, and Plato's *Republic*. Clare has her first singing lesson on Saturday. Go to the opera and see a beautiful ballet

Monday, October 11.—Read Horace; work. Go to the Gallery. Shelley finishes the first volume of Clarendon. Read the *Little Thief*.

Wednesday, October 20.—Finish the First Book of Horace's Odes. Work, walk, read, etc. On Saturday letters are sent to England. On Tuesday one to Venice. Shelley visits the Galleries. Reads Spenser and Clarendon aloud.

Thursday, October 28.—Work; read; copy *Peter Bell*. Monday night a great fright with Charles Clairmont. Shelley reads Clarendon aloud and *Plato's Republic*. Walk. On Thursday the protest from the Bankers. Shelley writes to them, and to Peacock, Longdill, and H. Smith.

Tuesday, November 9.—Read Madame de Sevigné. Bad news from London. Shelley reads Clarendon aloud, and Plato. He writes to Papa.

On the 12th of November a son was born to the Shelleys, and brought the first true balm of consolation to his poor mother's heart.

"You may imagine," wrote Shelley to Leigh Hunt, "that this is a great relief and a great comfort to me amongst all[Pg 260] my misfortunes.... Poor Mary begins (for the first time) to look a little consoled; for we have spent, as you may imagine, a miserable five months."

The child was healthy and pretty, and very like William. Neither Mary's strength nor her spirits were altogether re-established for some time, but the birth of "Percy Florence" was, none the less, the beginning of a new life for her. She turned, with the renewed energy of hope, to her literary work and studies. One of her first tasks was to transcribe the just written fourth act of *Prometheus Unbound*. She had work of her own on hand too; a historical novel,*Castruccio, Prince of Lucca* (afterwards published as *Valperga*), a laborious but very congenial task, which occupied her for many months.

And indeed all the solace of new and tender ties, all the animating interest of intellectual pursuits, was sorely needed to counteract the wearing effect of harassing cares and threatening calamities. Godwin was now being pressed for the accumulated unpaid house-rent of many years; so many that, when the call came, it was unexpected by him, and he challenged its justice. He had engaged in a law-suit on the matter, which he eventually lost. The only point which appeared to admit of no reasonable doubt was that Shelley would shortly be called upon to find a large sum of money for him, and this at a time when he was[Pg 261] himself in unexpected pecuniary straits, owing to the non-arrival of his own remittances from England—a circumstance rendered doubly vexatious by the fact that a large portion of the money was pledged to Henry Reveley for the furtherance of his steamboat. A draft for £200, destined for this purpose, was returned, protested by Shelley's bankers. And though the money was ultimately recovered, its temporary loss caused no small alarm. Meanwhile every mail brought letters from Godwin of the most harrowing nature; the philosophy which he inculcated in a case of bereavement was null and void where impending bankruptcy was concerned. He well knew how to work on his daughter's feelings, and he did not spare her. Poor Shelley was at his wits' end.

"Mary is well," he wrote (in December) to the Gisbornes; "but for this affair in London I think her spirits would be good. What shall I, what can I, what ought I to do? You cannot picture to yourself my perplexity."

It appeared not unlikely that he might even have to go to England, a journey for which his present state of health quite unfitted him, and which he could not but be conscious would be no permanent remedy, but only a temporary alleviation, of Godwin's thoroughly unsound circumstances. Mary, in her grief for her father, began to think that the best thing for him might be to[Pg 262] leave England altogether and settle abroad; an idea from which Mrs. Mason, with her strong sagacity, earnestly dissuaded her.

Her views on the point were expressed in a letter to Shelley Mary had written asking her if she could give Charles Clairmont any introductions at Vienna, where he had now gone to seek his fortune as a teacher of languages; and also begging for such assistance as she might be able to lend in the matter of obtaining access to historical documents or other MS. bearing on the subjects of Mary's projected novel.

MRS. MASON TO SHELLEY.

MY DEAR SIR—I deferred answering your letter till this post in hopes of being able to send some recommendations for your friend at Vienna, in which I have been disappointed; and I have now also a letter from my dear Mary; so I will answer both together. It gives me great pleasure to hear such a good account of the little boy and his mother.... I am sorry to perceive that your visit to Pisa will be so much retarded; but I admire Mary's courage and industry. I sincerely regret that it is not in my power to be of service to her in this undertaking.... All I can say is, that when you have got all you can there (where I suppose the manuscript documents are chiefly to be found) and that you come to this place, I have scarcely any doubt of being able to obtain for you many books on the subject which interests you. Probably everything in print which relates to it is as easy to be had here as at Florence.... I am very sorry indeed to think that Mr. Godwin's affairs are in such a bad way, and think he would be much happier if he had nothing to do with trade; but I am afraid he would not be comfortable out of England.[Pg 263] You who are young do not mind the thousand little wants that men of his age are not habituated to; and I, who have been so many years a vagabond on the face of the earth, have long since forgotten them; but I have seen people of my age much discomposed at the absence of long-accustomed trifles; and though philosophy supports in great matters, it seldom vanquishes the small everydayisms of life. I say this that Mary may not urge her father too much to leave England. It may sound odd, but I can't help thinking that Mrs. Godwin would enjoy a tour in foreign countries more than he would. The physical inferiority of women sometimes teaches them to support or overlook little inconveniences better than men.

"I am very sorry," she writes to Mary in another letter, "to find you still suffer from low spirits. I was in hopes the little boy would have been the best remedy for that. Words of consolation are but empty sounds, for to time alone it belongs to wear out the tears of affliction. However, a woman who gives milk should make every exertion to be cheerful on account of the child she nourishes."

Whether the plan for Godwin's expatriation was ever seriously proposed to him or not, it was, at any rate, never carried out. But none the less for this did the Shelleys live in the shadow of his gloom, which co-operated with their own pecuniary strait, previously alluded to, and with the nipping effects of an unwontedly severe winter, to make life still difficult and dreary for them.

"Shelley Calderonised on the late weather," wrote Mary to Mrs. Gisborne; "he called it an epic of rain with an episode of frost, and a few similes concerning fine weather. We have heard from England, although not from the Bankers; but Peacock's letter renders the affair darker than ever. Ah! my dear friend, you, in your slow and sure way of proceeding,[Pg 264] ought hardly to have united yourself to our eccentric star. I am afraid that you will repent it, and it grieves us both more than you can imagine that all should have gone so ill; but I think we may rest assured that this is delay, and not loss; it can be nothing else. I write in haste—a carriage at the door to take me out, and *Percy* asleep on my knee. Adieu. Charles is at Vienna by this time."...

They had intended remaining six months at Florence, but the place suited Shelley so ill that they took advantage of the first favourable change in the weather, at the end of January, to remove to Pisa, where the climate was milder, and where they now had pleasant friends in the Masons at "Casa Silva." They wished, too, to consult the celebrated Italian surgeon, Vaccà, on the subject of Shelley's health. Vaccà's advice took the shape of an earnest exhortation to him to abstain from drugs and remedies, to live a healthy life, and to leave his complaint, as far as possible, to nature. And, though he continued liable to attacks of pain and illness, and on one occasion had a severe nervous attack, the climate of Pisa proved in the end more suitable to him than any other, and for more than two years he remained there or in the immediate neighbourhood. He and Mary were never more industrious than at this time; reading extensively, and working together on a translation of Spinoza they had begun at Florence, and which occupied them, at intervals, for many months. Little Percy, a most healthy[Pg 265] and satisfactory infant, had in March an attack of measles, but so slight as to cause no anxiety. Once, however, during the summer they had a fright about him, when an unusually alarming letter from her father upset Mary so much as to cause in her nursling, through her, symptoms of an illness similar to that which had destroyed little Clara. On this occasion she authorised Shelley, at his earnest request, to intercept future letters of the kind, an authority of which he had to avail himself at no distant date, telling Godwin that his domestic peace, Mary's health and happiness, and his child's life, could no longer be entirely at his mercy.

No wonder that his own nervous ailments kept their hold of him. And to make matters better for him and for Mary, Paolo, the rascally Italian servant whom they had dismissed at Naples, now concocted a plot for extorting money from Shelley by accusing him of frightful crimes. Legal aid had to be called in to silence him. To this end they employed an attorney of Leghorn, named Del Rosso, and, for convenience of communication, they occupied for a few weeks Casa Ricci, the Gisbornes' house there, the owners being absent in England. Shelley made Henry Reveley's workshop his study. Hence he addressed his poetical "Letter to Maria Gisborne," and here too it was that "on a beautiful summer evening[Pg 266] while wandering among the lanes, whose myrtle hedges were the bowers of the fireflies (they) heard the carolling of the skylark, which inspired one of the most beautiful of his poems."[37]

If external surroundings could have made them happy they might have been so now, but Shelley, though in better health, was very nervous. Paolo's scandal and the legal affair embittered his life, to an extent difficult indeed to estimate, for it is certain that for some one else's sake, though *whose* sake has never transpired, he had accepted when at Naples responsibilities at once delicate and compromising. Paolo had knowledge of the matter, and used this knowledge partly to revenge himself on Shelley for dismissing him from his service, partly to try and extort money from him by intimidation. The Shelleys hoped they had "crushed him" with Del Rosso's help, but they could not be certain, because, as Mary wrote to Miss Curran, they "could only guess at his accomplices." With Shelley in a state of extreme nervous irritability, with Mary deprived of repose by her anguish on her father's account and her feverish anxiety to help him, with Clare unsettled and miserable about Allegra, venting her misery by writing to Byron letters unreasonable and provoking, though excusable, and then regretting[Pg 267] having sent them, they were not likely to be the most cheerful or harmonious of trios.

The weather became intolerably hot by the end of August, and they migrated to Casa Prinni, at the Baths of S. Giuliano di Pisa. The beauty of this place, and the delightful climate, refreshed and invigorated them all. They spent two or three days in seeing Lucca and the country around, when Shelley wrote the *Witch of Atlas*. Exquisite poem as it is, it was, in Mary's mood of the moment, a disappointment to her. Ever since the *Cenci* she had been strongly impressed with the conviction that if he could but write on subjects of universal *human* interest, instead of indulging in those airy creations of fancy which demand in the reader a sympathetic, but rare, quality of imagination, he would put himself more in touch with his contemporaries, who so greatly misunderstood him, and that, once he had elicited a responsive feeling in other men, this would be a source of profound happiness and of fresh and healthy inspiration to himself. "I still think I was right," she says, woman-like, in the *Notes to the Poems of 1820*, written long after Shelley's death. So from one point of view she undoubtedly was, but there are some things which cannot be constrained. Shelley was Shelley, and at the moment when he was moved to write a poem like the *Witch of Atlas*,[Pg 268] it was useless to wish that it had been something quite different.

His next poem was to be inspired by a human subject, and perhaps then poor Mary would have preferred a second Witch of Atlas.

[Pg 269]
CHAPTER XIII
SEPTEMBER 1820-AUGUST 1821

The baths were of great use to Shelley in allaying his nervous irritability. Such an improvement in him could not be without a corresponding beneficial effect on Mary. In the study of Greek, which she had begun with him at Leghorn, she found a new and wellnigh inexhaustible fund of intellectual pleasure. Their life, though very quiet, was somewhat more varied than it had been at Leghorn, partly owing to their being within easy reach of Pisa and of their friends at Casa Silva.

The Gisbornes had returned from England, and, during a short absence of Clare's, Mary tried, but ineffectually, to persuade Mrs. Gisborne to come and occupy her room for a time. Some circumstance had arisen which led shortly after to a misunderstanding between the two families, soon over, but painful while it lasted. It was probably connected with the abandonment of the projected steamboat; Henry Reveley, while in[Pg 270] England, having changed his mind and reconsidered his future plans.

In October a curiously wet season set in.

Journal. Wednesday, October 18.—Rain till 1 o'clock. At sunset the arch of cloud over the west clears away; a few black islands float in the serene; the moon rises; the clouds spot the sky, but the depth of heaven is clear. The nights are uncommonly warm. Write. Shelley reads *Hyperion* aloud. Read Greek.

My thoughts arise and fade in solitude;
The verse that would invest them melts away
Like moonlight in the heaven of spreading day.
How beautiful they were, how firm they stood,
Flecking the starry sky like woven pearl.

Friday, October 20.—Shelley goes to Florence. Write. Read Greek. Wind N.W., but more cloudy than yesterday, yet sometimes the sun shines out; the wind high. Read Villani.

Saturday, October 21.—Rain in the night and morning; very cloudy; not an air stirring; the leaves of the trees quite still. After a showery morning it clears up somewhat, and the sun shines. Read Villani, and ride to Pisa.

Sunday, October 22.—Rainy night and rainy morning; as bad weather as is possible in Italy. A little patience and we shall have St. Martin's summer. At sunset the arch of clear sky appears where it sets, becoming larger and larger, until at 7 o'clock the dark clouds are alone over Monte Nero; Venus shines bright in the clear azure, and the trunks of the trees are tinged with the silvery light of the rising moon. Write, and read Villani. Shelley returns with Medwin. Read *Sismondi*.

Of Tom Medwin, Shelley's cousin and great admirer, who now for the first time appeared on the scene, they were to see, if anything, more than they wished.

He was a lieutenant on half-pay, late of the 8th[Pg 271] Dragoons; much addicted to literature, and with no mean opinion of his own powers in that line.

Journal. Tuesday, October 24.—Rainy night and morning; it does not rain in the afternoon. Shelley and Medwin go to Pisa. Walk; write.

Wednesday, October 25.—Rain all night. The banks of the Serchio break, and by dark all the baths are overflowed. Water four feet deep in our house. "The weather fine."

This flood brought their stay at the Baths to a sudden end. As soon as they could get lodgings they returned to Pisa. Here, not long after, Medwin fell ill, and was six weeks invalided in their house. They showed him the greatest kindness; Shelley nursing him like a brother. His society was, for a time, a tolerably pleasant change; he knew Spanish, and read with Shelley a great deal in that language, but he had no depth or breadth of mind, and his literary vanity and egotism made him at last what Mary Shelley described as a *seccatura*, for which the nearest English equivalent is, a bore.

Journal, Sunday, November 12.—Percy's birthday. A divine day; sunny and cloudless; somewhat cold in the evening. It would be pleasant enough living in Pisa if one had a carriage and could escape from one's house to the country without mingling with the inhabitants, but the Pisans and the Scolari, in short, the whole population, are such that it would sound strange to an English person if I attempted to express what I feel concerning them—crawling and crab-like through their sapping streets. Read *Corinne*. Write.

Monday, November 13.—Finish *Corinne*. Write. My eyes keep me from all study; this is very provoking.

Tuesday, November 14.—Write. Read Homer, Targione, and Spanish. A rainy day. Shelley reads Calderon.

Thursday, November 23.—Write. Read Greek and Spanish. Medwin ill. Play at chess.

Friday, November 24.—Read Greek, Villani, and Spanish with M.... Pacchiani in the evening. A rainy and cloudy day.

Friday, December 1.—Read Greek, *Don Quixote*, Calderon, and Villani. Pacchiani comes in the evening. Visit La Viviani. Walk. Sgricci is introduced. Go to a *funzione* on the death of a student.

Saturday, December 2.—Write an Italian letter to Hunt. Read *Œdipus*, *Don Quixote*, and Calderon. Pacchiani and a Greek prince call—Prince Mavrocordato.

In these few entries occur four new and remarkable names. Pacchiani, who had been, if he was not still, a university professor, but who was none the less an adventurer and an impostor; in orders, moreover, which only served as a cloak for his hypocrisy; clever withal, and eloquent; well knowing where, and how, to ingratiate himself. He amused, but did not please the Shelleys. He was, however, one of those people who know everybody, and through him they made several acquaintances; among them the celebrated Improvisatore, Sgricci, and the young Greek statesman and patriot, Prince Alexander Mavrocordato. With the improvisations of Sgricci, his eloquence, his *entrain*, both Mary and Clare were fairly carried away with excitement. Older, experienced folk looked with a more critical eye on his performances, but to these English girls the exhibition was an absolute novelty, and seemed inspired. Sgricci was during this winter a frequent visitor at "Casa Galetti."

Prince Mavrocordato proved deeply interesting, both to Mary and Shelley. He "was warmed by those aspirations for the independence of his country which filled the hearts of many of his countrymen," and in the revolution which, shortly afterwards, broke out there, he was to play an important part, as one of the foremost of modern Greek statesmen. To him, at a somewhat later date, was dedicated Shelley's lyrical drama of *Hellas*; "as an imperfect token of admiration, sympathy, and friendship."

This new acquaintance came to Mary just when her interest in the Greek language and literature was most keen. Before long the prince had volunteered to help her in her studies, and came often to give her Greek lessons, receiving instruction in English in return.

"Do you not envy my luck," she wrote to Mrs. Gisborne, "that having begun Greek, an amiable, young, agreeable, and learned Greek prince comes every morning to give me a lesson of an hour and a half. This is the result of an acquaintance with Pacchiani. So you see, even the Devil has his use."

The acquaintance with Pacchiani had already had another and a yet more memorable result, which affected Mary none the less that it did so indirectly. Through him they had come to know Emilia Viviani, the noble and beautiful Italian girl, immured by her father in a convent at Pisa until such time as a husband could be found for her who would take a wife without a dowry. Shelley's acquaintance with Emilia was an episode, which at one time looked like an era, in his existence. An era in his poetry it undoubtedly was, since it is to her that the *Epipsychidion* is addressed.

Mary and Clare were the first to see the lovely captive, and were struck with astonishment and admiration. But on Shelley the impression she made was overwhelming, and took possession of his whole nature. Her extraordinary beauty and grace, her powers of mind and conversation, warmed by that glow of genius so exclusively southern, another variety of which had captivated them all in Sgricci, and which to northern minds seems something phenomenal and inspired,—

these were enough to subdue any man, and, when added to the halo of interest shed around her by her misfortunes and her misery, made her, to Shelley, irresistible.

All his sentiments, when aroused, were passions; he pitied, he sympathised, he admired and venerated passionately; he scorned, hated, and condemned passionately too. But he never was swayed by any love that did not excite his imagination: his attachments were ever in [Pg 275]proportion to the power of idealisation evoked in him by their objects. And never, surely, was there a subject for idealisation like Emilia; the Spirit of Intellectual Beauty in the form of a goddess; the captive maiden waiting for her Deliverer; the perfect embodiment of immortal Truth and Loveliness, held in chains by the powers of cruelty, tyranny, and hypocrisy.

She was no goddess, poor Emilia, as indeed he soon found out; only a lovely young creature of vivid intelligence and a temperament in which Italian ardour was mingled with Italian subtlety; every germ of sentiment magnified and intensified in outward effect by fervour of manner and natural eloquence; the very reverse of human nature in the north, where depth of feeling is apt to be in proportion to its inveterate dislike of discovery, where warmth can rarely shake off self-consciousness, and where many of the best men and women are so much afraid of seeming a whit better than they really are, that they take pains to appear worse. Rightly balanced, the whole sum of Emilia's gifts and graces would have weighed little against Mary's nobleness of heart and unselfish devotion; her talents might not even have borne serious comparison with Clare's vivacious intellect. But to Shelley, haunted by a vision of perfection, and ever apt to recognise in a mortal image "the likeness of[Pg 276] that which is, perhaps, eternal,"[38] she seemed a revelation, and, like all revelations, supreme, unique, superseding for the time every other possibility. It was a brief madness, a trance of inspiration, and its duration was counted only by days. They met for the first time early in December. By the 10th she was corresponding with him as her *diletto fratello*. Before the month was over *Epipsychidion* had been written.

Before the middle of January he could write of her—

My conception of Emilia's talents augments every day. Her moral nature is fine, but not above circumstances; yet I think her tender and true, which is always something. How many are only one of these things at a time!...

There is no reason that you should fear any admixture of that which you call *love*....

This was written to Clare. She had very quickly become intimate and confidential with Emilia, and estimated her to a nicety at her real worth, admiring her without idealising her or caring to do so. She knew Shelley pretty intimately too, and, being personally unconcerned in the matter, could afford at once to be sympathetic and to speak her mind fearlessly; the consequence being that Shelley was unconstrained in communication with her.

That *Mary* should be his most sympathetic confidant at this juncture was not in the nature[Pg 277] of things. She, too, had begun by idealising Emilia, but her affection and enthusiastic admiration were soon outdone and might well have been quenched by Shelley's rapt devotion. She did not misunderstand him, she knew him too well for that, but the better she understood him the less it was possible for her to feel with him; nor could it have been otherwise unless she had been really as cold as she sometimes appeared. Loyal herself, she never doubted Shelley's loyalty, but she suffered, though she did not choose to show it: her love, like a woman's,—perhaps even more than most women's—was exclusive; Shelley's, like a man's,—like many of the best of men's,—inclusive.

She did not allow her feelings to interfere with her actions. She continued to show all possible sympathy and kindness to Emilia, who in return would style her her dearest, loveliest friend and sister. No wonder, however, if at times Mary could not quite overcome a slight constraint of manner, or if this was increased when her dearest sister, with sweet unconsciousness, would openly probe the wound her pride would fain have hidden from herself; when Emilia, for instance, wrote to Shelley—

Mary does not write to me. Is it possible that she loves me less than the others do? I should indeed be inconsolable at that.

[Pg 278]Or to be informed in a letter to herself that this constraint of manner had been talked over by Emilia with Shelley, who had assured her that Mary's apparent coldness was only "the ash which covered an affectionate heart."

He was right, indeed, and his words were the faithful echo of his own true heart. He might have added, of himself, that his transient enthusiasms resembled the soaring blaze of sparks struck by a hammer from a glowing mass of molten metal.

But, in everyday prose, the situation was a trying one for Mary, and surely no wife of two and twenty could have met it more bravely and simply than she did.

"It is grievous," she wrote to Leigh Hunt, "to see this beautiful girl wearing out the best years of her life in an odious convent, where both mind and body are sick from want of the appropriate exercise for each. I think she has great talent, if not genius; or if not an internal fountain, how could she have acquired the mastery she has of her own language, which she writes so beautifully, or those ideas which lift her so far above the rest of the Italians? She has not studied much, and now, hopeless from a five years' confinement, everything disgusts her, and she looks with hatred and distaste even on the alleviations of her situation. Her only hope is in a marriage which her parents tell her is concluded, although she has never seen the person intended for her. Nor do I think the change of situation will be much for the better, for he is a younger brother, and will live in the house with his mother, who they say is *molto seccante*. Yet she may then have the free use of her limbs; she may then be able to walk out among the fields,[Pg 279] vineyards, and woods of her country, and see the mountains and the sky, and not as now, a dozen steps to the right, and then back to the left another dozen, which is the longest walk her convent garden affords, and that, you may be sure, she is very seldom tempted to take."

By the middle of February Shelley was sending his poem for publication, speaking of it as the production of "a part of himself already dead." He continued, however, to take an almost painful interest in Emilia's fate; she, poor girl, though not the sublime creature he had thought her, was infinitely to be pitied. Before their acquaintance ended, she was turning it to practical account, after the fashion of most of Shelley's friends, by begging for and obtaining considerable sums of money.

If Mary then indulged in a little retrospective sarcasm to her friend, Mrs. Gisborne, it is hardly wonderful. Indeed, later allusions are not wanting to show that this time was felt by her to be one of annoyance and bitterness.

Two circumstances were in her favour. She was well, and, therefore, physically able to look at things in their true light; and, during a great part of the time, Clare was away. In the previous October, during their stay at the Baths, she had at last resolved on trying to make out some sort of life for herself, and had taken a situation as governess in a Florentine family. She had come back to the Shelleys for the month of December[Pg 280] (when it was that she became acquainted with Emilia Vivani), but had returned to Florence at Christmas.

She had been persuaded to this step by the judicious Mrs. Mason, who had soon perceived the strained relations existing between Mary and Clare, and had seen, too, that the disunion was only the natural and inevitable result of circumstances. It was not only that the two girls were of opposite and jarring temperament; there was also the fact that half the suspicious mistrust with Shelley was regarded by those who did not personally know him, and the shadow of which rested on Mary too, was caused by Clare's continued presence among them. As things were now, it might have passed without remark, but for the scandalous reports which dated back to the Marlow days, and which had recently been revived by the slanders of Paolo, although the extent of these slanders had not yet transpired. Shelley had been alive enough to the danger at one time, but had now got accustomed and indifferent to it. He had a great affection and a great compassion for Clare; her vivacity enlivened him; he said himself that he liked her although she teased him, and he certainly missed her teasing when she was away. But Mary, to whom Clare's perpetual society was neither a solace nor a change, and who, as the mother of[Pg 281]children, could no longer look at things from a purely egotistic point of view, must have felt it positively unjust and wrong to allow their father's reputation to be sacrificed—to say nothing of her own—to what was in no wise a necessity. Shelley loved solitude—a mitigated solitude that is;—he certainly did not pine for general society. Yet many of his letters bear unmistakable evidence to the pain and resentment he felt at being universally shunned by his own countrymen, as if he were an enemy of the human race. But Mary, a woman, and only twenty-two, must have been self-sufficient indeed if, with all her mental resources, she had not required the renovation of change and contrast and varied intercourse, to keep her mind and spirit fresh and bright, and to fit her for being a companion and a resource to Shelley. That she and he were condemned to protracted isolation was partly due to Clare, and when Mary was weak and dejected, her consciousness of this became painful, and her feeling towards the sprightly, restless Miss Clairmont was touched with positive antipathy. Shelley, considering Clare the weaker party, supported her, in the main, and certainly showed no desire to have her away. He might have seen that to impose her presence on Mary in such circumstances was, in fact, as great a piece of tyranny as he had suffered from when Eliza[Pg 282] Westbrook was imposed on him. But of this he was, and he remained, perfectly unconscious. Clare ought to have retired from the field, but her dependent condition, and her wretched anxiety about Allegra, were her excuse for clinging to the only friends she had.

All this was evident to Mrs. Mason, and it was soon shown that she had judged rightly, as the relations between Mary and Clare became cordial and natural once they were relieved from the intolerable friction of daily companionship.

During this time of excitement and unrest one new acquaintance had, however, begun, which circumstances were to develop into a close and intimate companionship.

In January there had arrived at Pisa a young couple of the name of Williams; mainly attracted by the desire to see and to know Shelley, of whose gifts and virtues and sufferings they had heard much from Tom Medwin, their neighbour in Switzerland the year before. Lieutenant Edward Elliker Williams had been, first, in the Navy, then in the Army; had met his wife in India, and, returning with her to England, had sold his commission and retired on half-pay. He was young, of a frank straightforward disposition and most amiable temper, modest and unpretentious, with some literary taste, and no strong prejudices. Jane Williams was young and pretty, gentle and graceful, neither[Pg 283] very cultivated nor particularly clever, but with a comfortable absence of angles in her disposition, and an abundance of that feminine tact which prevents intellectual shortcomings from being painfully felt, and which is, in its way, a manifestation of genius. Not an uncommon type of woman, but quite new in the Shelleys' experience. At first they thought her rather wanting in animation, and Shelley was conscious of her lack of literary refinement, but these were more and more compensated for, as time went on, by her natural grace and her taste for music. "Ned" was something of an artist, and Mary Shelley sat more than once to him for her portrait. There was, in short, no lack of subjects in common, and the two young couples found a mutual pleasure in each other's society which increased in measure as they became better acquainted.

In March poor Clare received with bitter grief the intelligence that her child had been placed by Byron in a convent, at Bagnacavallo, not far from Ravenna, where he now lived. Under the sway of the Countess Guiccioli, whose father and brother were domesticated in his house, he was leading what, in comparison with his Venetian existence, was a life of respectability and virtue. His action with regard to Allegra was considered by the Shelleys as, probably, inevitable in the circumstances, but to Clare it was a terrible blow. She[Pg 284] felt more hopelessly separated from her child than ever, and she had seen enough of Italian convent education and its results to convince her that it meant moral and intellectual degradation and death. Her despairing representations to this effect were, of course, unanswered by Byron, who contented himself with a Mephistophelian sneer in showing her letter to the Hoppners.

With the true "malignity of those who turn sweet food into poison, transforming all they touch to the malignity of their own natures,"[39] he had no hesitation in giving credit to the reports about Clare's life in the Shelleys' family, nor in openly implying his own belief in their probable truth.

But for this, and for one great alarm caused by the sudden and unaccountable stoppage of Shelley's income (through a mistake which happily was discovered and speedily rectified by his good friend, Horace Smith), the spring was, for Mary, peaceful and bright. She was assiduous in her Greek studies, and keenly interested in the contemporary European politics of that stirring time; as full of sympathy as Shelley himself could be with the numerous insurrectionary outbreaks in favour of liberty. And when the revolution in Greece broke out, and one bright April morning Prince Mavrocordato rushed in to announce to her[Pg 285] the proclamation of Prince Hypsilantes, her elation and joy almost equalled his own.

In companionship with the Williams', aided and abetted by Henry Reveley, Shelley's old passion for boating revived. In the little ten-foot long boat procured for him for a few pauls, and then fitted up by Mr. Reveley, they performed many a voyage, on the Arno, on the canal between Pisa and Leghorn, and even on the sea. Their first trip was marked by an accident—Williams contriving to overturn the boat. Nothing daunted, Shelley declared next day that his ducking had added fire to, instead of quenching, the nautical ardour which produced it, and that he considered it a good omen to any enterprise that it began in evil, as making it more likely that it would end in good.

All these events are touched on in the few specimen extracts from Mary's journal and letters which follow—

Wednesday, January 31.—Read Greek. Call on Emilia Viviani. Shelley reads the *Vita Nuova* aloud to me in the evening.

Friday, February 2.—Read Greek. Write. Emilia Viviani walks out with Shelley. The Opera, with the Williams' (*Il Matrimonio Segreto*).

Tuesday, February 6.—Read Greek. Sit to Williams. Call on Emilia Viviani. Prince Mavrocordato in the evening. A long metaphysical argument.

Wednesday, February 7.—Read Greek. Sit to Williams. In the evening the Williams', Prince Mavrocordato, and Mr. Taafe.

[Pg 286]*Monday, February 12.*—Read Greek (no lesson). Finish the *Vita Nuova*. In the afternoon call on Emilia Viviani. Walk. Mr. Taafe calls.

Thursday, February 27.—Read Greek. The Williams to dine with us. Walk with them. Il Diavolo Pacchiani calls. Shelley reads "The Ancient Mariner" aloud.

Saturday, March 4.—Read Greek (no lesson). Walk with the Williams'. Read Horace with Shelley in the evening. A delightful day.

Sunday, March 5.—Read Greek. Write letters. The Williams' to dine with us. Walk with them. Williams relates his history. They spend the evening with us, with Prince Mavrocordato and Mr. Taafe.

Thursday, March 8.—Read Greek (no lesson). Call on Emilia Viviani. E. Williams calls. Shelley reads *The Case is Altered* of Ben Jonson aloud in the evening. A mizzling day and rainy night.... March winds and rains are begun, the last puff of winter's breath,—the eldest tears of a coming spring; she ever comes in weeping and goes out smiling.

Monday, March 12.—Read Greek (no lesson). Finish the *Defence of Poetry*. Copy for Shelley; he reads to me the *Tale of a Tub*. A delightful day after a misty morning.

Wednesday, March 14.—Read Greek (no lesson). Copy for Shelley. Walk with Williams. Prince Mavrocordato in the evening. I have an interesting conversation with him concerning Greece. The second bulletin of the Austrians published. A sirocco, but a pleasant evening,

Friday, March 16.—Read Greek. Copy for Shelley. Walk with Williams. Mrs. Williams confined. News of the Revolution of Piedmont, and the taking of the citadel of Candia by the Greeks. A beautiful day, but not hot.

Sunday, March 18.—Read Greek. Copy for Shelley. A sirocco and mizzle. Bad news from Naples. Walk with Williams. Prince Mavrocordato in the evening.

Monday, March 26.—Read Greek. Alex. Mavrocordato. Finish the *Antigone*. A mizzling day. Spend the evening at the Williams'.

[Pg 287]*Wednesday, March 28.*—Read Greek. Alex. Mavrocordato. Call on Emilia Viviani. Walk with Williams. Mr. Taafe in the evening. A fine day, though changeful as to clouds and wind. The State of Massa declares the Constitution. The Piedmontese troops are at Sarzana.

Sunday, April 1.—Read Greek. Alex. Mavrocordato calls with news about Greece. He is as gay as a caged eagle just free. Call on Emilia Viviani. Walk with Williams; he spends the evening with us.

Monday, April 2.—Read Greek. Alex. Mavrocordato calls with the proclamation of Ipsilanti. Write to him. Ride with Shelley into the Cascini. A divine day, with a north-west wind. The theatre in the evening. Tachinardi.

Wednesday, April 11.—Read Greek, and *Osservatore Fiorentino*. A letter that overturns us.[40] Walk with Shelley. In the evening Williams and Alex. Mavrocordato.

Friday, April 13.—Read Greek. Alex. Mavrocordato calls. *Osservatore Fiorentino*. Walk with the Williams'. Shelley at Casa Silva in the evening. An explanation of our difficulty.

Monday, April 16.—Write. Targioni. Read Greek. Mrs. Williams to dinner. In the evening Mr. Taafe. A wet morning: in the afternoon a fierce maestrale. Shelley, Williams, and Henry Reveley try to come up the canal to Pisa; miss their way, are capsized, and sleep at a contadino's.

Tuesday, April 24.—Read Greek. Alex. Mavrocordato. Hume. Villani. Walk with the Williams'. Alex. M. calls in the evening, with good news from Greece. The Morea free.

They now migrated once more to the beautiful neighbourhood of the Baths of San Giuliano di Pisa; the Williams' established themselves at Pugnano, only four miles off: the canal fed by the Serchio ran between the two places, and the little boat was in constant requisition.

[Pg 288]Our boat is asleep on Serchio's stream,
Its sails are folded like thoughts in a dream,
The helm sways idly, hither and thither;
Dominic, the boatman, has brought the mast,
And the oars, and the sails; but 'tis sleeping fast,
Like a beast, unconscious of its tether.[41]

The canal which, fed by the Serchio, was, though an artificial, a full and picturesque stream, making its way under verdant banks, sheltered by trees that dipped their boughs into the murmuring waters. By day, multitudes of ephemera darted to and fro on the surface; at night, the fireflies came out among the shrubs on the banks; the *cicale*, at noonday, kept up their hum; the aziola cooed in the quiet evening. It was a pleasant summer, bright in all but Shelley's health and inconstant spirits; yet he enjoyed himself greatly, and became more and more attached to the part of the country where chance appeared to cast us. Sometimes he projected taking a farm, situated on the height of one of the near hills, surrounded by chestnut and pine woods and overlooking a wide extent of country; or of settling still further in the maritime Apennines, at Massa. Several of his slighter and unfinished poems were inspired by these scenes, and by the companions around us. It is the nature of that poetry, however, which overflows from the soul, oftener to express sorrow and regret than joy; for it is when oppressed by the weight of life and away from those he loves, that the poet has recourse to the solace of expression in verse.[42]

87

Journal. Thursday, May 3.—Read Villani. Go out in boat; call on Emilia Viviani. Walk with Shelley. In the evening Alex. Mavrocordato, Henry Reveley, Dancelli, and Mr. Taafe.

Friday, May 4.—Read Greek. (Alex. M.) Read Villani. Shelley goes to Leghorn by sea with Henry Reveley.

[Pg 289]*Tuesday, May 8.*—Packing. Read Greek (Alex. Mavrocordato). Shelley goes to Leghorn. In the evening walk with Alex. M. to Pugnano. See the Williams; return to the Baths. Shelley and Henry Reveley come. The weather quite April; rain and sunshine, and by no means warm.

Saturday, June 23.—Abominably cold weather—rain, wind, and cloud—quite an Italian November or a Scotch May. Shelley and Williams go to Leghorn. Write. Read and finish Malthus. Begin the answer.[43] Jane (Williams) spends the day here, and Edward returns in the evening. Read Greek.

Sunday, June 24.—Write. Read the *Answer to Malthus*. Finish it. Shelley at Leghorn.

Monday, June 25.—Little babe not well. Shelley returns. The Williams call. Read old plays. Vaccà calls.

Tuesday, June 26.—Babe well. Write. Read Greek. Shelley not well. Mr. Taafe and Granger dine with us. Walk with Shelley. Vaccà calls. Alex. Mavrocordato sails.

Thursday, June 28.—Write. Read Greek. Read Mackenzie's works. Go to Pugnano in the boat. The warmest day this month. Fireflies in the evening.

They were near enough to Pisa to go over there from time to time to see Emilia and other friends, and for Prince Mavrocordato to come frequently and give them the latest political news: the Greek lessons had been voluntarily abjured by Mary when it seemed probable that the Prince might be summoned at any moment to play an active part in the affairs of his country, as actually happened in June. Shelley was still tormented by the pain in his side, but his health and spirits were insensibly improving, as he himself [Pg 290]afterwards admitted. He was occupied in writing *Hellas*, his elegy on Keats's death, *Adonais* also belongs to this time. Ned Williams, infected by the surrounding atmosphere of literature, had tried his 'prentice hand on a drama. In the words of his own journal—

Went in the summer to Pugnano—passed the first three months in writing a play entitled *The Promise, or a year, a month, and a day*. S. tells me if they accept it he has great hopes of its success before an audience, and his hopes always enliven mine.

Mary was straining every nerve to finish *Valperga*, in the hope of being able to send it to England by the Gisbornes, who were preparing to leave Italy,—a hope, however, which was not fulfilled.

MARY TO MRS. GISBORNE.

BATHS OF S. GIULIANO,
30th June 1821.

MY DEAR MRS. GISBORNE—Well, how do you get on? Mr. Gisborne says nothing of that in the note which he wrote yesterday, and it is that in which I am most interested.

I pity you exceedingly in all the disagreeable details to which you are obliged to sacrifice your time and attention. I can conceive no employment more tedious; but now I hope it is nearly over, and that as the fruit of its conclusion you will soon come to see us. Shelley is far from well; he suffers from his side and nervous irritation. The day on which he returned from Leghorn he found little Percy ill of a fever produced by teething. He got well the next day, but it was so strong while it lasted that it frightened us greatly. You know how much reason we have to fear the deceitful appearance of[Pg 291] perfect health. You see that this, your last summer in Italy, is manufactured on purpose to accustom you to the English seasons.

It is warmer now, but we still enjoy the delight of cloudy skies. The "Creator" has not yet made himself heard. I get on with my occupation, and hope to finish the rough transcript this month. I shall then give about a month to corrections, and then I shall transcribe it. It has indeed been a child of mighty slow growth since I first thought of it in our library at Marlow. I then wanted the body in which I might embody my spirit. The materials for this I found at Naples, but I wanted other books. Nor did I begin it till a year afterwards at Pisa; it was again suspended during our stay at your house, and continued again at the Baths. All the winter I did not touch it, but now it is in a state of great forwardness, since I am at page 71 of the third volume. It has indeed been a work of some labour, since I have read and consulted a great many books. I shall be very glad to read the first volume to you, that you may give me your opinion as to the conduct and interest of the story. June is now at its last gasp. You talked of going in August, I hope therefore that we may soon expect you. Have you heard anything concerning the inhabitants of Skinner Street? It is now many months since I received a letter, and I begin to grow alarmed. Adieu.—Ever sincerely yours,

MARY W. S.

On the 26th of July the Gisbornes came to pay their friends a short farewell visit; on the 29th they started for England; Shelley going with them as far as Florence, where he and Mary thought again of settling for the winter, and where he wished to make inquiries about houses. During his few days' absence the Williams' were almost constantly with Mary. Edward Williams was busy painting a portrait of her in miniature, [Pg 292]intended by her as a surprise for Shelley on his birthday, the 4th of August. But when that day arrived Shelley was unavoidably absent. On his return to the Baths he had found a letter from Lord Byron, with a pressing invitation to visit him at Ravenna, whence Byron was on the point of departing to join Countess Guiccioli and her family, who had been exiled from the Roman States for Carbonarism, and who, for the present, had taken refuge at Florence.

Shelley's thoughts turned at once, as they could not but do, to poor little Allegra, in her convent of Bagnacavallo. What was to become of her? Where would or could she be sent? or was she to be conveniently forgotten and left behind? He was off next day, the 3d; paid a flying visit to Clare, who was staying for her health at Leghorn, and arrived at Ravenna on the 6th.

The miniature was finished and ready for him on his birthday. Mary, alone on that anniversary, was fain to look back over the past eventful seven years,—their joys, their sorrows, their many changes. Not long before, she had said, in a letter to Clare, "One is not gay, at least I am not, but peaceful, and at peace with all the world." The same tone characterises the entry in her journal for 4th August.

Shelley's birthday. Seven years are now gone; what changes! what a life! We now appear tranquil, yet who[Pg 293] knows what wind——but I will not prognosticate evil; we have had enough of it. When Shelley came to Italy I said, all is well, if it were permanent; it was more passing than an Italian twilight. I now say the same. May it be a Polar day, yet that, too, has an end.

[Pg 294]
CHAPTER XIV
AUGUST-NOVEMBER 1821

From Bologna Shelley wrote to Mary an amusing account of his journey, so far. But this letter was speedily followed by another, written within a few hours of his arrival at Ravenna; a letter, this second one, to make Mary's blood run cold, although it is expressed with all the calmness and temperance that Shelley could command.

RAVENNA, *7th August 1821*.

MY DEAREST MARY—I arrived last night at 10 o'clock, and sate up talking with Lord Byron until 5 this morning. I then went to sleep, and now awake at 11, and having despatched my breakfast as quick as possible, mean to devote the interval until 12, when the post departs, to you.

Lord Byron is very well, and was delighted to see me. He has, in fact, completely recovered his health, and lives a life totally the reverse of that which he led at Venice. He has a permanent sort of *liaison* with Contessa Guiccioli, who is now at Florence, and seems from her letters to be a very amiable woman. She is waiting there until something shall be decided as to their emigration to Switzerland or stay in Italy, which is yet undetermined on either side. She was compelled to escape from the Papal territory in great haste, as measures had already been taken to place her in a convent, where she[Pg 295] would have been unrelentingly confined for life. The oppression of the marriage contract, as existing in the laws and opinions of Italy, though less frequently exercised, is far severer than that of England. I tremble to think of what poor Emilia is destined to.

Lord Byron had almost destroyed himself in Venice; his state of debility was such that he was unable to digest any food; he was consumed by hectic fever, and would speedily have perished, but for this attachment, which has reclaimed him from the excesses into which he threw himself, from carelessness rather than taste. Poor fellow! he is now quite well, and immersed in politics and literature. He has given me a number of the most interesting details on the former subject, but we will not speak of them in a letter. Fletcher is here, and as if, like a shadow, he waxed and waned with the substance of his master, Fletcher also has recovered his good looks, and from amidst the unseasonable gray hairs a fresh harvest of flaxen locks has put forth.

We talked a great deal of poetry and such matters last night, and, as usual, differed, and I think more than ever. He affects to patronise a system of criticism fit for the production of mediocrity, and, although all his fine poems and passages have been produced in defiance of this system, yet I recognise the pernicious effects of it in the *Doge of Venice*, and it will cramp and limit his future efforts, however great they may be, unless he gets rid of it. I have read only parts of it, or rather, he himself read them to me, and gave me the plan of the whole.

Allegra, he says, is grown very beautiful, but he complains that her temper is violent and imperious. He has no intention of leaving her in Italy; indeed, the thing is too improper in itself not to carry condemnation along with it. Contessa Guiccioli, he says, is very fond of her; indeed, I cannot see why she should not take care of it, if she is to live as his ostensible mistress. All this I shall know more of soon.

Lord Byron has also told me of a circumstance that shocks me exceedingly, because it exhibits a degree of desperate and wicked malice, for which I am at a loss to account. When [Pg 296]I hear such things my patience and my philosophy are put to a severe proof, whilst I refrain from seeking out some obscure hiding-place, where the countenance of man may never meet me more. It seems that *Elise*, actuated either by some inconceivable malice for our dismissing her, or bribed by my enemies, has persuaded the Hoppners of a story so monstrous and incredible that they must have been prone to believe any evil to have believed such assertions upon such evidence. Mr. Hoppner wrote to Lord Byron to state this story as the reason why he declined any further communications with us, and why he advised him to do the same. Elise says that Claire was my mistress; that is very well, and so far there is nothing new; all the world has heard so much, and people may believe or not believe as they think good. She then proceeds further to say that Claire was with child by me; that I gave her the most violent medicine to procure abortion; that this not succeeding she was brought to bed, and that I immediately tore the child from her and sent it to the Foundling Hospital,—I quote Mr. Hoppner's words,—and this is stated to have taken place in the winter after we left Este. In addition, she says that both Claire and I treated you in the most shameful manner; that I neglected and beat you, and that Claire never let a day pass without offering you insults of the most violent kind, in which she was abetted by me.

As to what Reviews and the world say, I do not care a jot, but when persons who have known me are capable of conceiving of me—not that I have fallen into a great error, as would have been the living with Claire as my mistress—but that I have committed such unutterable crimes as destroying or abandoning a child, and that my own! Imagine my despair of good! Imagine how it is possible that one of so weak and sensitive a nature as mine can run further the gauntlet through this hellish society of men! *You* should write to the Hoppners a letter refuting the charge, in case you believe and know, and can prove that it is false, stating the grounds and proof of your belief. I need not dictate what you should say, nor, I hope, inspire you with warmth to rebut a charge which you[Pg 297] only can effectually rebut. If you will send the letter to me here, I will forward it to the Hoppners. Lord Byron is not up. I do not know the Hoppners' address, and I am anxious not to lose a post.

P. B. S.

Mary's feelings on the perusal of this letter may be faintly imagined by those who read it now, and who know what manner of woman she actually was. They are expressed, as far as they could be expressed, in the letter which, in accordance with Shelley's desire, and while still smarting under the first shock of grief and profound indignation, she wrote off to Mrs. Hoppner, and enclosed in a note to Shelley himself.

MARY TO SHELLEY.

MY DEAR SHELLEY—Shocked beyond all measure as I was, I instantly wrote the enclosed. If the task be not too dreadful, pray copy it for me; I cannot.

Read that part of your letter that contains the accusation. I tried, but I could not write it. I think I could as soon have died. I send also Elise's last letter: enclose it or not, as you think best.

I wrote to you with far different feelings last night, beloved friend, our barque is indeed "tempest tost," but love me as you have ever done, and God preserve my child to me, and our enemies shall not be too much for us. Consider well if Florence be a fit residence for us. I love, I own, to face danger, but I would not be imprudent.

Pray get my letter to Mrs. Hoppner copied for a thousand reasons. Adieu, dearest! Take care of yourself—all yet is well. The shock for me is over, and I now despise the slander; but it must not pass uncontradicted. I sincerely thank Lord Byron for his kind unbelief.—Affectionately yours,

M. W. S.

[Pg 298]Do not think me imprudent in mentioning E.'s[44] illness at Naples. It is well to meet facts. They are as cunning as wicked. I have read over my letter; it is written in haste, but it were as well that the first burst of feeling should be expressed.

PISA, *10th August 1821.*

My dear Mrs. Hoppner—After a silence of nearly two years I address you again, and most bitterly do I regret the occasion on which I now write. Pardon me that I do not write in French; you understand English well, and I am too much impressed to shackle myself in a foreign language; even in my own my thoughts far outrun my pen, so that I can hardly form the letters. I write to defend him to whom I have the happiness to be united, whom I love and esteem beyond all living creatures, from the foulest calumnies; and to you I write this, who were so kind, and to Mr. Hoppner, to both of whom I indulged the pleasing idea that I have every reason to feel gratitude. This is indeed a painful task. Shelley is at present on a visit to Lord Byron at Ravenna, and I received a letter from him to-day, containing accounts that make my hand tremble so much that I can hardly hold the pen. It tells me that Elise wrote to you, relating the most hideous stories against him, and that you have believed them. Before I speak of these falsehoods, permit me to say a few words concerning this miserable girl. You well know that she formed an attachment with Paolo when we proceeded to Rome, and at Naples their marriage was talked of. We all tried to dissuade her; we knew Paolo to be a rascal, and we thought so well of her. An accident led me to the knowledge that without marrying they had formed a connection. She was ill; we sent for a doctor, who said there was danger of a miscarriage, I would not throw the girl on the world without in some degree binding her to this man. We had them married at Sir R. A. Court's. She left us, turned Catholic at Rome, married him, and then went to Florence. After the disastrous death of my[Pg 299] child we came to Tuscany. We have seen little of them, but we have had knowledge that Paolo has formed a scheme of extorting money from Shelley by false accusations. He has written him threatening letters, saying that he would be the ruin of him, etc. We placed them in the hands of a celebrated lawyer here, who has done what he can to silence him. Elise has never interfered in this, and indeed the other day I received a letter from her, entreating, with great professions of love, that I would send her money. I took no notice of this, but although I know her to be in evil hands, I would not believe that she was wicked enough to join in his plans without proof. And now I come to her accusations, and I must indeed summon all my courage whilst I transcribe them, for tears will force their way, and how can it be otherwise?

You know Shelley, you saw his face, and could you believe them? Believe them only on the testimony of a girl whom you despised? I had hoped that such a thing was impossible, and that although strangers might believe the calumnies that this man propagated, none who had ever seen my husband could for a moment credit them.

He says Claire was Shelley's mistress, that—upon my word I solemnly assure you that I cannot write the words. I send you a part of Shelley's letter that you may see what I am now about to refute, but I had rather die than copy anything so vilely, so wickedly false, so beyond all imagination fiendish.

But that you should believe it! That my beloved Shelley should stand thus slandered in your minds—he, the gentlest and most humane of creatures—is more painful to me, oh! far more painful than words can express. Need I say that the union between my husband and myself has ever been undisturbed? Love caused our first imprudence—love, which, improved by esteem, a perfect trust one in the other, a confidence and affection which, visited as we have been by severe calamities (have we not lost two children?), has increased daily and knows no bounds. I will add that Claire has been separated from us for about a year. She lives with a respectable German family at Florence. The reasons for this[Pg 300] were obvious: her connection with us made her manifest as the Miss Clairmont, the mother of Allegra; besides we live much alone, she enters much into society there, and, solely occupied with the idea of the welfare of her child, she wished to appear such that she may not be thought in after times to be unworthy of fulfilling the maternal duties. You ought to have paused before you tried to convince the father of her child of such unheard-of atrocities on her part. If his generosity and knowledge of the world had not made him reject the slander with the ridicule it deserved, what irretrievable mischief you would have occasioned her. Those who know me well believe my simple word—it is not long ago that my father said in a letter to me that he had never known me utter a falsehood,—but you, easy as you have been to credit evil, who may be more deaf to truth—to you I swear by all that I hold sacred upon heaven and earth, by a vow which I should die to write if I affirmed a falsehood,—I swear by the life of my child, by my blessed, beloved child, that I know the accusations to be false. But I have said enough to convince you, and are you not convinced? Are not my words the words of truth? Repair, I conjure you, the evil you have done by retracting your confidence in one so vile as Elise, and by writing to me that you now reject as false every circumstance of her infamous tale.

You were kind to us, and I will never forget it; now I require justice. You must believe me, and do me, I solemnly entreat you, the justice to confess you do so.

Mary W. Shelley.

I send this letter to Shelley at Ravenna, that he may see it, for although I ought, the subject is too odious to me to copy it. I wish also that Lord Byron should see it; he gave no credit to the tale, but it is as well that he should see how entirely fabulous it is.

Shelley, meanwhile, never far from her in thought, and knowing only too well how acutely she would suffer from all this, was writing to her again.

[Pg 301]SHELLEY TO MARY.

MY DEAREST MARY—I wrote to you yesterday, and I begin another letter to-day without knowing exactly when I can send it, as I am told the post only goes once a week. I daresay the subject of the latter half of my letter gave you pain, but it was necessary to look the affair in the face, and the only satisfactory answer to the calumny must be given by you, and could be given by you alone. This is evidently the source of the violent denunciations of the *Literary Gazette*, in themselves contemptible enough, and only to be regarded as effects which show us their cause, which, until we put off our mortal nature, we never despise—that is, the belief of persons who have known and seen you that you are guilty of crimes. A certain degree and a certain kind of infamy is to be borne, and, in fact, is the best compliment which an exalted nature can receive from a filthy world, of which it is its hell to be a part, but this sort of thing exceeds the measure, and even if it were only for the sake of our dear Percy, I would take some pains to suppress it. In fact it shall be suppressed, even if I am driven to the disagreeable necessity of prosecuting him before the Tuscan tribunals....

....

Write to me at Florence, where I shall remain a day at least, and send me letters, or news of letters. How is my little darling? and how are you, and how do you get on with your book? Be severe in your corrections, and expect severity from me, your sincere admirer. I flatter myself you have composed something unequalled in its kind, and that, not content with the honours of your birth and your hereditary aristocracy, you will add still higher renown to your name. Expect me at the end of my appointed time. I do not think I shall be detained. Is Claire with you? or is she coming? Have you heard anything of my poor Emilia, from whom I got a letter the day of my departure, saying that her marriage was deferred for a very short time, on account of the illness[Pg 302] of her Sposo? How are the Williams', and Williams especially? Give my very kindest love to them.

Lord Byron has here splendid apartments in the house of his mistress's husband, who is one of the richest men in Italy. *She* is divorced, with an allowance of 1200 crowns a year—a miserable pittance from a man who has 120,000 a year. Here are two monkeys, five cats, eight dogs, and ten horses, all of whom (except the horses) walk about the house like the masters of it. Tita, the Venetian, is here, and operates as my valet; a fine fellow, with a prodigious black beard, and who has stabbed two or three people, and is one of the most good-natured-looking fellows I ever saw.

We have good rumours of the Greeks here, and a Russian war. I hardly wish the Russians to take any part in it. My maxim is with Æschylus: τὸ δυσσεβές—μετὰ μὲν πλείονα τίκτει, σφετέρᾳ δ᾿ εἰκότα γέννᾳ.

....

There is a Greek exercise for you. How should slaves produce anything but tyranny, even as the seed produces the plant? Adieu, dear Mary.—Yours affectionately,

S.

At Ravenna there was only a weekly post. Shelley had to wait a long time for Mary's answer, and before it could reach him he was writing to her yet a third time. His mind was now full of Allegra. She was not to be left alone in Italy. Shelley, enlightened by Emilia Viviani, had been able to give Byron, on the subject of convents, such information as to "shake his faith in the purity of these receptacles." But no conclusions of any sort had been arrived at as to her future; and Shelley entreated Mary to rack her brains, to inquire of all her friends, to leave no stone unturned, if by any possibility she could find some[Pg 303]fitting asylum, some safe home for the lovely child. He had been to see the little girl at her convent, and all readers of his letters know the description of the fairy creature, who, with her "contemplative seriousness, mixed with excessive vivacity, seemed a thing of a higher and a finer order" than the children around her; happy and well cared for, as far as he could judge; pale, but lovelier and livelier than ever, and full of childish glee and fun.

At this point of his letter Mary's budget arrived, and Shelley continued as follows—

RAVENNA, *Thursday*.

I have received your letter with that to Mrs. Hoppner. I do not wonder, my dearest friend, that you should have been moved. I was at first, but speedily regained the indifference which the opinion of anything or anybody, except our own consciousness, amply merits, and day by day shall more receive from me. I have not recopied your letter, such a measure would destroy its authenticity, but have given it to Lord Byron, who has engaged to send it with his own comments to the Hoppners. People do not hesitate, it seems, to make themselves panders and accomplices to slander, for the Hoppners had exacted from Lord Byron that these accusations should be concealed from *me*. Lord Byron is not a man to keep a secret, good or bad, but in openly confessing that he has not done so he must observe a certain delicacy, and therefore wished to send the letter himself, and, indeed, this adds weight to your representations. Have you seen the article in the *Literary Gazette* on me? They evidently allude to some story of this kind. However cautious the Hoppners have been in preventing the calumniated person from asserting his justification, you know too much of the world not to be certain that this was the utmost limit of their caution. So much for nothing.

[Pg 304]Lord Byron is immediately coming to Pisa. He will set off the moment I can get him a house. Who would have imagined this?... What think you of remaining at Pisa? The Williams' would probably be induced to stay there if we did; Hunt would certainly stay, at least this winter, near us, should he emigrate at all; Lord Byron and his Italian friends would remain quietly there; and Lord Byron has certainly a very great regard for us. The regard of such a man is worth some of the tribute we must pay to the base passions of humanity in any intercourse with those within their circle; he is better worth it than those on whom we bestow it from mere custom.

The Masons are there, and, as far as solid affairs are concerned, are my friends. I allow this is an argument for Florence. Mrs. Mason's perversity is very annoying to me, especially as Mr. Tighe is seriously my friend. This circumstance makes me averse from that intimate continuation of intercourse which, once having begun, I can no longer avoid.

At Pisa I need not distil my water, if I *can* distil it anywhere. Last winter I suffered less from my painful disorder than the winter I spent in Florence. The arguments for Florence you know, and they are very weighty; judge (*I know you like the job*) which scale is overbalanced. My greatest content would be utterly to desert all human society. I would retire with you and our child to a solitary island in the sea, would build a boat, and shut upon my retreat the flood-gates of the world. I would read no reviews and talk with no authors. If I dared trust my imagination, it would tell me that there are one or two chosen companions besides yourself whom I should desire. But to this I would not listen. Where two or three are gathered together the devil is among them, and good far more than evil impulses, love far more than hatred, has been to me, except as you have been its object, the source of all sorts of mischief. So on this plan I would be *alone*, and would devote either to oblivion or to future generations the overflowings of a mind which, timely withdrawn from the contagion, should be kept fit for no baser[Pg 305] object. But this it does not appear that we shall do. The other side of the alternative (for a medium ought not to be adopted) is to form for ourselves a society of our own class, as much as possible, in intellect or in feelings, and to connect ourselves with the interests of that society. Our roots never struck so deeply as at Pisa, and the transplanted tree flourishes not. People who lead the lives which we led until last winter are like a family of Wahabee Arabs pitching their tent in the midst of London. We must do one thing or the other,—for yourself, for our child, for our existence. The calumnies, the sources of which are probably deeper than we perceive, have ultimately for object the depriving us of the means of security and subsistence. You will easily perceive the gradations by which calumny proceeds to pretext, pretext to persecution, and persecution to the ban of fire and water. It is for this, and not because this or that fool, or the whole court of fools, curse and rail, that calumny is worth refuting or chastising.

P. B. S.

"So much for nothing," indeed. When Byron made himself responsible for Mary's letter, it was, probably, without any definite intention of withholding it from those to whom it was addressed. He may well have wished to add to this glowing denial of his own insinuations some palliating personal explanation. When, in the previous March, Clare had protested against an Italian convent education for Allegra, he had sent her letter to the Hoppners with a sneer at the "excellent grace" with which these representations came from a woman of the writer's character and present way of life. And yet he knew Shelley,—knew him as the Hoppners could not do; he[Pg 306] knew what Shelley had done for him, for Clare, and Allegra; and to how much slander and misrepresentation he had voluntarily submitted that they might go scot-free. Byron was,—and he knew it,—the last person who should have accepted or allowed others to accept this fresh scandal without proof and without inquiry. He was ashamed of the part he had played, and reluctant to confess to the Hoppners that he had been wrong, and that his words, as often happened, had been far in advance of his knowledge or his solid convictions; but his intentions were to do the best he could. And, satisfying himself with good intentions, he put off the unwelcome day until the occasion was past, and till, finally, the friend whose honour had been entrusted to his keeping was beyond his power to help or to harm. Shelley was dead; and how then explain to the Hoppners why the letter had not been sent before? It was "not worth while," probably, to revive the subject in order to vindicate a mere memory, nor yet to remove an unjust and cruel stigma from the character of those who survived. However it may have been, one thing is undoubted. Mary Shelley never received any answer to her letter of protest, which, after Byron's death, was found safe among his papers.

One more note Shelley sent to Mary from Ravenna on the subject of the promised portrait. It would not seem that the miniature was actually[Pg 307] despatched now, but as his return was so long delayed, the birthday plot had to be divulged.

RAVENNA, *Tuesday, 15th August 1821.*

MY DEAREST LOVE—I accept your kind present of your picture, and wish you would get it prettily framed for me. I will wear, for your sake, upon my heart this image which is ever present to my mind.

I have only two minutes to write; the post is just setting off. I shall leave the place on Thursday or Friday morning. You would forgive me for my longer stay if you knew the fighting I have had to make it so short. I need not say where my own feelings impel me.

It still remains fixed that Lord Byron should come to Tuscany, and, if possible, Pisa; but more of that to-morrow.—Your faithful and affectionate

S.

The foregoing painful episode was enough to fill Mary's mind during the fortnight she was alone. It was well for her that she was within easy reach of cheerful friends, yet, even as it was, she could not altogether escape from bitter thoughts. Clare was at Leghorn, and had to be told of everything. Mary could not but think of the relief it would be to them all if she were to marry; a remote possibility to which she probably alludes in the following letter, written at this time to Miss Curran—

MARY SHELLEY TO MISS CURRAN.

SAN GIULIANO, *17th August.*

MY DEAR MISS CURRAN—It gives me great pain to hear of your ill-health. Will this hot summer conduce to a better state or not? I hope anxiously, when I hear from you again,[Pg 308] to learn that you are better, having recovered from your weakness, and that you have no return of your disorder. I should have answered your letter before, but we have been in the confusion of moving. We are now settled in an agreeable house at the Baths of San Giuliano, about four miles from Pisa, under the shadow of mountains, and with delightful scenery within a walk. We go on in our old manner, with no change. I have had many changes for the worse; one might be for the better, but that is nearly impossible. Our child is well and thriving, which is a great comfort, and the Italian sky gives Shelley health, which is to him a rare and substantial enjoyment. I did [not] receive the letter you mention to have written in March, and you also have missed one of our letters in which Shelley acknowledged the receipt of the drawings you mention, and requested that the largest pyramid might be erected if they could case it with white marble for £25. However, the whole had better stand as I mentioned in my last; for, without the most rigorous inspection, great cheating would take place, and no female could detect them. When we visit Rome, we can do that which we wish. Many thanks for your kindness, which has been very great. I would send you on the books I mentioned, but we live out of the world, and I know of no conveyance. Mr. Purniance says that he sent the life of your father by sea to Rome, directed to you; so, doubtless, it is in the custom-house there.

How enraged all our mighty rulers are at the quiet revolutions which have taken place; it is said that some one said to the Grand Duke here: "Ma richiedono una constituzione qui?" "Ebene, la darò subito" was the reply; but he is not his own master, and Austria would take care that that should not be the case; they say Austrian troops are coming here, and the Tuscan ones will be sent to Germany. We take in *Galignani*, and would send them to you if you liked. I do not know what the expense would be, but I should think slight. If you recommence painting, do not forget Beatrice. I wish very much for a copy of that; you would oblige us greatly by making one. Pray let me hear of your health.[Pg 309] God knows when we shall be in Rome; circumstances must direct, and they dance about like will-o'-the-wisps, enticing and then deserting us. We must take care not to be left in a bog. Adieu, take care of yourself. Believe in Shelley's sincere wishes for your health, and in kind remembrances, and in my being ever sincerely yours,

M. W. SHELLEY.

Clare desires (not remembrances, if they are not pleasant), however she sends a proper message, and says she would be obliged to you, if you let her have her picture, if you could find a mode of conveying it....

Do you know we lose many letters, having spies (not Government ones) about us in plenty; they made a desperate push to do us a desperate mischief lately, but succeeded no further than to blacken us among the English; so if you receive a fresh batch (or green bag) of scandal against us, I assure you it is all a *lie*. Poor souls! we live innocently, as you well know; if we did not, ten to one God would take pity on us, and we should not be so unfortunate.

Shelley's absence, though eventful, was, after all, a short one. In about a fortnight he was back again at the Bagni, and for a few weeks life was quiet.

On the 18th of September Mary records—

Picnic on the Pugnano Mountains; music in the evening. Sleep there.

On another occasion, wishing to find some tolerably cool seaside place where they might spend the next summer, they went,—the Shelleys and Clare,—on a two or three days' expedition of discovery to Spezzia, and were enchanted with the beauty of the bay. Clare had, shortly after, to return to her situation at Florence, but the Shelleys decided to winter at Pisa. They took a top flat in the "Tre[Pg 310] Palazzi di Chiesa," on the Lung' Arno, and spent part of October in furnishing it. They took possession about the 25th; the Williams' coming, not many days later, to occupy a lower flat in the same house. At Lord Byron's request, the Shelleys had taken for him Casa Lanfranchi, the finest palace in the Lung' Arno, just opposite the house where they themselves were established. This close juxtaposition of abodes was likely to prove somewhat inconvenient, in case of Clare's occasional presence at Tre Palazzi. Her first visit, however, to which the following characteristic letter refers, was to the Masons at Casa Silva, and it came to an end just before Byron's arrival in Pisa. Clare had been staying with the Williams' at Pugnano.

CLARE TO MARY.

MY DEAR MARY—I arrived last night—won't you come and see me to-day? The Williams' wish you to forward them Mr. Webb's answer, if possible, to reach them by 2 o'clock afternoon to-day. If Mr. Webb says yes (you will open his note), send Dominico with it to them, and he passing by the Baths must order Pancani to be at Pugnano by 5 o'clock in the afternoon. If there comes no letter from Mr. Webb, they will equally come to you, and I wish you could also in that case contrive to get Pancani ordered for them, for we forgot to arrange how that could be done; if not, they will be there expecting, and perhaps get involved for the next month. I wish you to be so good as to send me immediately my large box and the clothes from the Busati, indeed all that you have of mine, for I must arrange my boxes to get them *bollate* immediately. Don't delay, and my band-box too. If you[Pg 311] could of your great bounty give me a sponge, I should be infinitely obliged to you. Then, when it is dark, and the Williams' arrived, will you ask Mr. Williams to be so good as to come and knock at Casa Silva, and I will return to spend the evening with you? Shelley won't do to fetch me, because he looks singular in the streets. But I wish he would come now to give me some money, as I want to write to Livorno and arrange everything. Later will be inconvenient for me. Kiss the chick for me, and believe me, yours affectionately,

CLARE.

Journal.—All October is left out, it seems.—We are at the Baths, occupied with furnishing our house, copying my novel, etc. etc.

Mary's intention was to devote any profits which might proceed from this work to the relief of her father's necessities, and the hope of being able to help him had stimulated her industry and energy while it eased her heart. She aimed at selling the copyright for £400, and Shelley opened negotiations to this effect with Ollier the publisher. His letter on the subject bears such striking testimony to the estimate he had formed of Mary's powers, and gives, besides, so complete a sketch of the novel itself, that it cannot be omitted here.

SHELLEY TO MR. OLLIER.

PISA, *25th September 1822*.

DEAR SIR—It will give me great pleasure if I can arrange the affair of Mrs. Shelley's novel with you to her and your satisfaction. She has a specific purpose in the sum which she instructed me to require, and, although this purpose could not be answered without ready money, yet I should find means to answer her wishes in that point if you could make it [Pg 312]convenient to pay one-third at Christmas, and give bills for the other two-thirds at twelve and eighteen months. It would give me peculiar satisfaction that you, rather than any other person, should be the publisher of this work; it is the product of no slight labour, and I flatter myself, of no common talent, I doubt not it will give no less credit than it will receive from your names. I trust you know me too well to believe that my judgment deliberately given in testimony of the value of any production is influenced by motives of interest or partiality.

The romance is called *Castruccio, Prince of Lucca*, and is founded, not upon the novel of Machiavelli under that name, which substitutes a childish fiction for the far more romantic truth of history, but upon the actual story of his life. He was a person who, from an exile and an adventurer, after having served in the wars of England and Flanders in the reign of our Edward the Second, returned to his native city, and liberating it from its tyrants, became himself its tyrant, and died in the full splendour of his dominion, which he had extended over the half of Tuscany. He was a little Napoleon, and with a dukedom instead of an empire for his theatre, brought upon the same all the passions and errors of his antitype. The chief interest of the romance rests upon Euthanasia, his betrothed bride, whose love for him is only equalled by her enthusiasm for the liberty of the Republic of Florence, which is in some sort her country, and for that of Italy, to which Castruccio is a devoted enemy, being an ally of the party of the Emperor. This character is a masterpiece; and the keystone of the drama, which is built up with admirable art, is the conflict between these passions and these principles. Euthanasia, the last survivor of a noble house, is a feudal countess, and her castle is the scene of the exhibition of the knightly manners of the time. The character of Beatrice, the prophetess, can only be done justice to in the very language of the author. I know nothing in Walter Scott's novels which at all approaches to the beauty and the sublimity of this—creation, I may say, for it is perfectly original; and, although founded upon the ideas and manners of the age which is represented, is wholly without[Pg 313] a similitude in any fiction I ever read. Beatrice is in love with Castruccio, and dies; for the romance, although interspersed with much lighter matter, is deeply tragic, and the shades darken and gather as the catastrophe approaches. All the manners, customs of the age, are introduced; the superstitions, the heresies, and the religious persecutions are displayed; the minutest circumstance of Italian manners in that age is not omitted; and the whole seems to me to constitute a living and moving picture of an age almost forgotten. The author visited the scenery which she describes in person; and one or two of the inferior characters are drawn from her own observation of the Italians, for the national character shows itself still in certain instances under the same forms as it wore in the time of Dante. The novel consists, as I told you before, of three volumes, each at least equal to one of the *Tales of my Landlord*, and they will be very soon ready to be sent.

No arrangement, however, was come to at this time, and early in January Mary wrote to her father, offering the work to him, and asking him, if he accepted it, to make a bargain concerning it with a publisher.

Godwin accepted the offer, and undertook the responsibility, in a letter from which the following is an extract—

31st January 1822.

I am much gratified by your letter of the 11th, which reached me on Saturday last; it is truly generous of you to desire that I would make use of the produce of your novel. But what can I say to it? It is against the course of nature, unless, indeed, you were actually in possession of a fortune.

………

I said in the preface to *Mandeville* there were two or three works further that I should be glad to finish before I died. If I make use of the money from you in the way you suggest, that may enable me to complete my present work.

[Pg 314]The MS. was, accordingly, despatched to England, but was not published till many months later.

Valperga (as it was afterwards called) was a book of much power and more promise; very remarkable when the author's age is taken into consideration. Apart from local colouring, the interest of the tale turns on the development of the character—naturally powerful and disposed to good, but spoilt by popularity and success, and unguided by principle—of Castruccio himself; and on the contrast between him and Euthanasia, the noble and beautiful woman who sacrifices her possessions, her hopes, and her affections to the cause of fidelity and patriotism.

Beatrice, the prophetess, is one of those gifted but fated souls, who, under the persuasion that they are supernaturally inspired, mistake the ordinary impulses of human nature for Divine commands, and, finding their mistake, yet encourage themselves in what they know to be delusion till the end,—a tragic end.

There are some remarkable descriptive passages, especially one where the wandering Beatrice comes suddenly upon a house in a dreary landscape which she knows, although she has never seen it before except in a haunting dream; every detail of it is horribly familiar, and she is paralysed by the sense of imminent calamity, which, in fact, bursts upon her directly afterwards.

Euthanasia dies at sea, and the account of the[Pg 315] running down and wreck of her ship is a curious, almost prophetic, foreshadowing of the calamity by which, all too soon, Shelley was to lose his life.

The wind changed to a more northerly direction during the night, and the land-breeze of the morning filled their sails, so that, although slowly, they dropt down southward. About noon they met a Pisan vessel, who bade them beware of a Genoese squadron, which was cruising off Corsica; so they bore in nearer to the shore. At sunset that day a fierce sirocco arose, accompanied by thunder and lightning, such as is seldom seen during the winter season. Presently they saw huge dark columns descending from heaven, and meeting the sea, which boiled beneath;

they were borne on by the storm, and scattered by the wind. The rain came down in sheets, and the hail clattered, as it fell to its grave in the ocean; the ocean was lashed into such waves that, many miles inland, during the pauses of the wind, the hoarse and constant murmurs of the far-off sea made the well-housed landsman mutter one more prayer for those exposed to its fury.

Such was the storm, as it was seen from shore. Nothing more was ever known of the Sicilian vessel which bore Euthanasia. It never reached its destined port, nor were any of those on board ever after seen. The sentinels who watched near Vado, a town on the sea-beach of the Maremma, found on the following day that the waves had washed on shore some of the wrecks of a vessel; they picked up a few planks and a broken mast, round which, tangled with some of its cordage, was a white silk handkerchief, such a one as had bound the tresses of Euthanasia the night that she had embarked; and in its knot were a few golden hairs.

....

To follow the fate of Mary's novel, it has been necessary somewhat to anticipate the history, which is resumed in the next chapter, with the journal and letters of the latter part of 1821.

[Pg 316]

CHAPTER XV
NOVEMBER 1821-APRIL 1822

Journal, Thursday, November 1.—Go to Florence. Copy. Ride with the Guiccioli. Albé arrives.

Sunday, November 4.—The Williams' arrive. Copy. Call on the Guiccioli.

Thursday, November 15.—Copy. Read *Caleb Williams* to Jane. Ride with the Guiccioli. Shelley goes on translating Spinoza with Edward. Medwin arrives. Taafe calls. Argyropulo calls. Good news from the Greeks.

Tuesday, November 28.—Ride with the Guiccioli. Suffer much with rheumatism in my head.

Wednesday, November 29.—I mark this day because I begin my Greek again, and that is a study that ever delights me. I do not feel the bore of it, as in learning another language, although it be so difficult, it so richly repays one; yet I read little, for I am not well. Shelley and the Williams go to Leghorn; they dine with us afterwards with Medwin. Write to Clare.

Thursday, November 30.—Correct the novel. Read a little Greek. Not well. Ride with the Guiccioli. The Count Pietro (Gamba) in the evening.

MRS. SHELLEY TO MRS. GISBORNE.

PISA, *30th November 1821.*

MY DEAR MRS. GISBORNE—Although having much to do be a bad excuse for not writing to you, yet you must in some [Pg 317] sort admit this plea on my part. Here we are in Pisa, having furnished very nice apartments for ourselves, and what is more, paid for the furniture out of the fruits of two years' economy, we are at the top of the Tre Palazzi di Chiesa. I daresay you know the house, next door to La Scoto's house on the north side of Lung' Arno; but the rooms we inhabit are south, and look over the whole country towards the sea, so that we are entirely out of the bustle and disagreeable *puzzi*, etc., of the town, and hardly know that we are so enveloped until we descend into the street. The Williams' have been less lucky, though they have followed our example in furnishing their own house, but, renting it of Mr. Webb, they have been treated scurvily. So here we live, Lord Byron just opposite to us in Casa Lanfranchi (the late Signora Felichi's house). So Pisa, you see, has become a little nest of singing birds. You will be both surprised and delighted at the work just about to be published by him; his *Cain*, which is in the highest style of imaginative poetry. It made a great impression upon me, and appears almost a revelation, from its power and beauty. Shelley rides with him; I, of course, see little of him. The lady *whom he serves* is a nice pretty girl without pretensions, good hearted and amiable; her relations were banished Romagna for Carbonarism.

What do you know of Hunt? About two months ago he wrote to say that on 21st October he should quit England, and we have heard nothing more of him in any way; I expect some day he and six children will drop in from the clouds, trusting that God will temper the wind to the shorn lamb. Pray when you write, tell us everything you know concerning him. Do you get any intelligence of the Greeks? Our worthy countrymen take part against them in every possible way, yet such is the spirit of freedom, and such the hatred of these poor people for their oppressors, that I have the warmest hopes—μάντις εἰμ᾽ ἐσθλῶν ἀγωνῶν. Mavrocordato is there, justly revered for the sacrifice he has made of his whole fortune to the cause, and besides for his firmness and talents. If Greece be free, Shelley and I have vowed to go, perhaps to settle there, in one of those beautiful islands where earth, ocean, and sky form the paradise. You will, I hope, tell us all the news of our friends when you write. I see no one that you know. We live in our usual retired way, with few friends and no acquaintances. Clare is returned to her usual residence, and our tranquillity is unbroken in upon, except by those winds, sirocco or tramontana, which now and then will sweep over the ocean of one's mind and disturb or cloud its surface. Since this must be a double letter, I save myself the trouble of copying the enclosed, which was a part of a letter written to you a month ago, but which I did not send. Will you attend to my requests? Every day increases my anxiety concerning the desk. Do have the goodness to pack it off as soon as you can.

Shelley was at your hive yesterday; it is as dirty and busy as ever, so people live in the same narrow circle of space and thought, while time goes on, not as a racehorse, but a "six inside dilly," and puts them down softly at their journey's end; while they have slept and ate, and *ecco tutto*. With this piece of morality, dear Mrs. Gisborne, I end. Shelley begs every remembrance of his to be joined with mine to Mr. Gisborne and Henry.—Ever yours,

MARY W. S.

And now, my dear Mrs. Gisborne, I have a great favour to ask of you. Ollier writes to say that he has placed our two desks in the hands of a merchant of the city, and that they are to come—God knows when! Now, as we sent for them two years ago, and are tired of waiting, will you do us the favour to get them out of his hands, and to send them without delay? If they can be sent without being opened, send them *in statu quo*; if they must be opened, do not send the smallest but get a key (being a patent lock a key will cost half a guinea) made for the largest and send it, and return the other to Peacock. If you send the desk, will you send with it the following things?—A few copies of all Shelley's works, particularly of the second edition of the *Cenci*, my mother's posthumous works, and *Letters from Norway* from Peacock, if you can, but do not delay the box for them.

Journal, Sunday, December 2.—Read the *History of Shipwrecks*. Read Herodotus with Shelley. Ride with La Guiccioli. Pietro and her in the evening.

Monday, December 3.—Write letters. Read Herodotus with Shelley. Finish *Caleb Williams* to Jane. Taafe calls. He says that his Turk is a very moral man, for that when he began a scandalous story he interrupted him immediately, saying, "Ah! we must never speak thus of our neighbours!" Taafe would do well to take the hint.

Thursday, December 6.—Read Homer. Walk with Williams. Spend the evening with them. Call on T. Guiccioli with Jane, while Taafe amuses Shelley and Edward. Read Tacitus. A dismal day.

Friday, December 7.—Letter from Hunt and Bessy. Walk with Shelley. Buy furniture for them, etc. Walk with Edward and Jane to the garden, and return with T. Guiccioli in the carriage. Edward reads the *Shipwreck of the Wager* to us in the evening.

Saturday, December 8.—Get up late and talk with Shelley. The Williams and Medwin to dinner. Walk with Edward and Jane in the garden. Return with T. Guiccioli. T. G. and Pietro in the evening. Write to Clare. Read Tacitus.

Sunday, December 9.—Go to church at Dr. Nott's. Walk with Edward and Jane in the garden. In the evening first Pietro and Teresa, afterwards go to the Williams'.

Monday, December 10.—Out shopping. Walk with the Williams and T. Guiccioli to the garden. Medwin at tea. Afterwards we are alone, and after reading a little Herodotus, Shelley reads Chaucer's *Flower and the Leaf*, and then Chaucer's *Dream* to me. A divine, cold, tramontana day.

Monday, January 14.—Read *Emile*. Call on T. Guiccioli and see Lord Byron. Trelawny arrives.

Edward John Trelawny, whose subsequent history was to be closely bound up with that of Shelley and of Mrs. Shelley, was of good Cornish family, and had led a wandering life, full of romantic adventure. He had become acquainted with Williams and Medwin in Switzerland a year before, since which he had been in Paris and London. Tired of a town life and of society, and in order to "maintain the just equilibrium between the body and the brain," he had determined to pass the next winter hunting and shooting in the wilds of the Maremma, with a Captain Roberts and Lieutenant Williams. For the exercise of his brain, he proposed passing the summer with Shelley and Byron, boating in the Mediterranean, as he had heard that they proposed doing. Neither of the poets were as yet personally known to him, but he had lost no time in seeking their acquaintance. On the very evening of his arrival in Pisa he repaired to the Tre Palazzi, where, in the Williams' room, he first saw Shelley, and was struck speechless with astonishment.

Was it possible this mild-looking beardless boy could be the veritable monster at war with all the world? Excommunicated by the Fathers of the Church, deprived of his civil rights by the fiat of a grim Lord Chancellor, discarded by every member of his family, and denounced by the rival sages of our literature as the founder of a Satanic school? I could not believe it; it must be a hoax.

But presently, when Shelley was led to talk on a theme that interested him—the works of Calderon,—his marvellous powers of mind and command of language held Trelawny spellbound: "After this[Pg 321] touch of his quality," he says, "I no longer doubted his identity."

Mrs. Shelley appeared soon after, and the visitor looked with lively curiosity at the daughter of William Godwin and Mary Wollstonecraft.

Such a rare pedigree of genius was enough to interest me in her, irrespective of her own merits as an authoress. The most striking feature in her face was her calm, gray eyes; she was rather under the English standard of woman's height, very fair and light-haired; witty, social, and animated in the society of friends, though mournful in solitude; like Shelley, though in a minor degree, she had the power of expressing her thoughts in varied and appropriate words, derived from familiarity with the works of our vigorous old writers. Neither of them used obsolete or foreign words. This command of our language struck me the more as contrasted with the scanty vocabulary used by ladies in society, in which a score of poor hackneyed phrases suffice to express all that is felt or considered proper to reveal.[45]

Mary's impressions of the new-comer may be gathered from her journal and her subsequent letter to Mrs. Gisborne.

Journal, Saturday, January 19.—Copy. Walk with Jane. The Opera in the evening. Trelawny is extravagant—*un giovane stravagante*,—partly natural, and partly, perhaps, put on, but it suits him well, and if his abrupt but not unpolished manners be assumed, they are nevertheless in unison with his Moorish face (for he looks Oriental yet not Asiatic), his dark hair, his Herculean form; and then there is an air of extreme good nature which pervades his whole countenance, especially when he smiles, which assures me that his heart is good. He tells strange stories of himself, horrific ones, so that they harrow one up, while with his emphatic but unmodulated voice, his simple[Pg 322] yet strong language, he portrays the most frightful situations; then all these adventures took place between the ages of thirteen and twenty.

I believe them now I see the man, and, tired with the everyday sleepiness of human intercourse, I am glad to meet with one who, among other valuable qualities, has the rare merit of interesting my imagination. The *crew* and Medwin dine with us.

Sunday, January 27.—Read Homer. Walk. Dine at the Williams'. The Opera in the evening. Ride with T. Guiccioli.

Monday, January 28.—The Williams breakfast with us. Go down Bocca d'Arno in the boat with Shelley and Jane. Edward and E. Trelawny meet us there; return in the gig; they dine with us; very tired.

Tuesday, January 29.—Read Homer and Tacitus. Ride with T. Guiccioli. E. Trelawny and Medwin to dinner. The Baron Lutzerode in the evening.

But as the torrent widens towards the ocean, We ponder deeply on each past emotion.

Read the first volume of the *Pirate*.

Sunday, February 3.—Read Homer. Walk to the garden with Jane. Return with Medwin to dinner. Trelawny in the evening. A wild day and night, some clouds in the sky in the morning, but they clear away. A north wind.

Monday, February 4.—Breakfast with the Williams'. Edward, Jane, and Trelawny go to Leghorn. Walk with Jane. Southey's letter concerning Lord Byron. Write to Clare. In the evening the Gambas and Taafe.

Thursday, February 7.—Read Homer, Tacitus, and *Emile*. Shelley and Edward depart for La Spezzia. Walk with Jane, and to the Opera with her in the evening. With E. Trelawny afterwards to Mrs. Beauclerc's ball. During a long, long evening in mixed society how often do one's sensations change, and, swiftly as the west wind drives the shadows of clouds across the sunny hill or the waving corn, so swift do sensations pass, painting—yet, oh! not disfiguring—the[Pg 323] serenity of the mind. It is then that life seems to weigh itself, and hosts of memories and imaginations, thrown into one scale, make the other kick the beam. You remember what you have felt, what you have dreamt; yet you dwell on the shadowy side, and lost hopes and death, such as you have seen it, seem to cover all things with a funeral pall.

The time that was, is, and will be, presses upon you, and, standing the centre of a moving circle, you "slide giddily as the world reels." You look to heaven, and would demand of the everlasting stars that the thoughts and passions which are your life may be as ever-living as they. You would demand of the blue empyrean that your mind might be as clear as it, and that the tears which gather in your eyes might be the shower that would drain from its profoundest depths the springs of weakness and sorrow. But where are the stars? Where the blue empyrean? A ceiling clouds that, and a thousand swift consuming lights supply the place of the eternal ones of heaven. The enthusiast suppresses her tears, crushes her opening thoughts, and.... But all is changed; some word, some look excite the lagging blood, laughter dances in the eyes, and the spirits rise proportionably high.

The Queen is all for revels, her light heart, Unladen from the heaviness of state, Bestows itself upon delightfulness.

Friday, February 8.—Sometimes I awaken from my visionary monotony, and my thoughts flow until, as it is exquisite pain to stop the flowing of the blood, so is it painful to check expression and make the overflowing mind return to its usual channel. I feel a kind of tenderness to those, whoever they may be (even though strangers), who awaken the train and touch a chord so full of harmony and thrilling music, when I would tear the veil from this strange world, and pierce with eagle eyes beyond the sun; when every idea, strange and changeful, is another step in the ladder by which I would climb....

Read *Emile*. Jane dines with me, walk with her. E. Trelawny and Jane in the evening. Trelawny tells us a[Pg 324] number of amusing stories of his early life. Read third canto of *L'Inferno*.

They say that Providence is shown by the extraction that may be ever made of good from evil, that we draw our virtues from our faults. So I am to thank God for making me weak. I might say, "Thy will be done," but I cannot applaud the permitter of self-degradation, though dignity and superior wisdom arise from its bitter and burning ashes.

Saturday, February 9.—Read *Emile*. Walk with Jane, and ride with T. Guiccioli. Dine with Jane. Taafe and T. Medwin call. I retire with E. Trelawny, who amuses me as usual by the endless variety of his adventures and conversation.

MARY TO MRS. GISBORNE.

PISA, *9th February 1822.*

MY DEAR MRS. GISBORNE—Not having heard from you, I am anxious about my desk. It would have been a great convenience to me if I could have received it at the beginning of the winter, but now I should like it as soon as possible. I hope that it is out of Ollier's hands. I have before said what I would have done with it. If both desks can be sent without being opened, let them be sent; if not, give the small one back to Peacock. Get a key made for the larger, and send it, I entreat you, by the very next vessel. This key will cost half a guinea, and Ollier will not give you the money, but give me credit for it, I entreat you. I pray now let me have the desk as soon as possible. Shelley is now gone to Spezzia to get houses for our colony for the summer.

It will be a large one, too large, I am afraid, for unity; yet I hope not. There will be Lord Byron, who will have a large and beautiful boat built on purpose by some English navy officers at Genoa. There will be the Countess Guiccioli and her brother; the Williams', whom you know; Trelawny, a kind of half-Arab Englishman, whose life has been as changeful as that of Anastasius, and who recounts the adventures as[Pg 325] eloquently and as well as the imagined Greek. He is clever; for his moral qualities I am yet in the dark; he is a strange web which I am endeavouring to unravel. I would fain learn if generosity is united to impetuousness, probity of spirit to his assumption of singularity and independence. He is 6 feet high, raven black hair, which curls thickly and shortly, like a Moor's, dark gray expressive eyes, overhanging brows, upturned lips, and a smile which expresses good nature and kindheartedness. His shoulders are high, like an Oriental's, his voice is monotonous, yet emphatic, and his language, as he relates the events of his life, energetic and simple, whether the tale be one of blood and horror, or of irresistible comedy. His company is delightful, for he excites me to think, and if any evil shade the intercourse, that time will unveil—the sun will rise or night darken all. There will be, besides, a Captain Roberts, whom I do not know, a very rough subject, I fancy,—a famous angler, etc. We are to have a small boat, and now that those first divine spring days are come (you know them well), the sky clear, the sun hot, the hedges budding, we sitting without a fire and the windows open, I begin to long for the sparkling waves, the olive-coloured hills and vine-shaded pergolas of Spezzia. However, it would be madness to go yet. Yet as *ceppo* was bad, we hope for a good *pasqua*, and if April prove fine, we shall fly with the swallows. The Opera here has been detestable. The English Sinclair is the *primo tenore*, and acquits himself excellently, but the Italians, after the first, have enviously selected such operas as give him little or nothing to do. We have English here, and some English balls and parties, to which I (*mirabile dictu*) go sometimes. We have Taafe, who bores us out of our senses when he comes, telling a young lady that her eyes shed flowers——why therefore should he send her any? I have sent my novel to Papa. I long to hear some news of it, as, with an author's vanity, I want to see it in print, and hear the praises of my friends. I should like, as I said when you went away, a copy of *Matilda*. It might come out with the desk. I hope as the town fills to hear better news of your plans, we long to[Pg 326] hear from you. What does Henry do? How many times has he been in love?—Ever yours,

M. W. S.

Shelley would like to see the review of the *Prometheus* in the *Quarterly*.

Thursday, February 14.—Read Homer and *Anastasius*. Walk with the Williams' in the evening.... "Nothing of us but what must suffer a sea-change."

This entry marks the day to which Mary referred in a letter written more than a year later, where she says—

A year ago Trelawny came one afternoon in high spirits with news concerning the building of the boat, saying, "Oh! we must all embark, all live aboard; we will all 'suffer a sea-change.'" And dearest Shelley was delighted with the quotation, saying that he would have it for the motto for his boat.

Little did they think, in their lightness of spirit, that in another year the motto of the boat would serve for the inscription on Shelley's tomb.

Journal, Monday, February 18.—Read Homer. Walk with the Williams'. Jane, Trelawny, and Medwin in the evening.[46]

Monday, February 25.—What a mart this world is? Feelings, sentiments,—more invaluable than gold or precious stones is the coin, and what is bought? Contempt, discontent, and disappointment, unless, indeed, the mind be loaded with drearier memories. And what say the worldly to this? Use Spartan coin, pay away iron and lead alone, and store up your[Pg 327] precious metal. But alas! from nothing, nothing comes, or, as all things seem to degenerate, give lead and you will receive clay,—the most contemptible of all lives is where you live in the world, and none of your passions or affections are brought into action. I am convinced I could not live thus, and as Sterne says that in solitude he would worship a tree, so in the world I should attach myself to those who bore the semblance of those qualities which I admire. But it is not this that I want; let me love the trees, the skies, and the ocean, and that all-encompassing spirit of which I may soon become a part,—let me in my fellow-creature love that which is, and not fix my affection on a fair form endued with imaginary attributes; where goodness, kindness, and talent are, let me love and admire them at their just rate, neither adorning nor diminishing, and above all, let me fearlessly descend into the remotest caverns of my own mind; carry the torch of self-knowledge into its dimmest recesses; but too happy if I dislodge any evil spirit, or enshrine a new deity in some hitherto uninhabited nook.

Read *Wrongs of Women* and Homer. Clare departs. Walk with Jane and ride with T. Guiccioli. T. G. dines with us.

Thursday, February 28.—Take leave of the Argyropolis. Walk with Shelley. Ride with T. Guiccioli. Read letters. Spend the evening at the Williams'. Trelawny there.

Friday, March 1.—An embassy. Walk. My first Greek lesson. Walk with Edward. In the evening work.

Sunday, March 3.—A note to, and a visit from, Dr. Nott. Go to church. Walk. The Williams' and Trelawny to dinner.

Mary's experiments in the way of church-going, so new a thing in her experience, and so little in accordance with Shelley's habits of thought and action, excited some surprise and comment. Hogg, Shelley's early friend, who heard of it from Mrs.[Pg 328] Gisborne, now in England, was especially shocked. In a letter to Mary, Mrs. Gisborne remarked, "Your friend Hogg is *molto scandalizzato* to hear of your weekly visits to the *piano di sotto*" (the services were held on the ground floor of the Tre Palazzi).

The same letter asks for news of Emilia Viviani. Mrs. Gisborne had heard that she was married, and feared she had been sacrificed to a man whom she describes as "that insipid, sickening Italian mortal, Danieli the lawyer." She proceeds to say—

We invited Varley one evening to meet Hogg, who was curious to see a man really believing in astrology in the nineteenth century. Varley, as usual, was not sparing of his predictions. We talked of Shelley without mentioning his name; Varley was curious, and being informed by Hogg of his exact age, but describing his person as short and corpulent, and himself as a *bon vivant*, Varley amused us with the following remarks: "Your friend suffered from ill-fortune in May or June 1815. Vexatious affairs on the 2d and 14th of June, or perhaps latter end of May 1820. The following year, disturbance about a lady. Again, last April, at 10 at night, or at noon, disturbance about a bouncing stout lady, and others. At six years of age, noticed by ladies and gentlemen for learning. In July 1799, beginning of charges made against him. In September 1800, at noon, or dusk, very violent charges. Scrape at fourteen years of age. Eternal warfare against parents and public opinion, and a great blow-up every seven years till death," etc. etc. *Is all this true?*

Not a little amused, Mary answered her friend as follows—

[Pg 329]PISA, *7th March 1822.*

MY DEAR MRS. GISBORNE—I am very sorry that you have had so much trouble with my commissions, and vainly, too! *ma che vuole?*Ollier will not give you the money, and we are, to tell you the truth, too poor at present to send you a cheque upon our banker; two or three circumstances having caused

That climax of all human ills,
The inflammation of our weekly bills.

But far more than that, we have not touched a quattrino of our Christmas quarter, since debts in England and other calls swallowed it entirely up. For the present, therefore, we must dispense with those things I asked you for. As for the desk, we received last post from Ollier (without a line) the bill of lading that he talks of, and, *si Dio vuole*, we shall receive it safe; the vessel in which they were shipped is not yet arrived. The worst of keeping on with Ollier (though it is the best, I believe, after all) is that you will never be able to make anything of his accounts, until you can compare the number of copies in hand with his account of their sale. As for my novel, I shipped it off long ago to my father, telling him to make the best of it; and by the way in which he answered my letter, I fancy he thinks he can make something of it. This is much better than Ollier, for I should never have got a penny from him; and, moreover, he is a very bad bookseller to publish with—*ma basta poi*, with all these *seccaturas*.

Poor dear Hunt, you will have heard by this time of the disastrous conclusion of his third embarkment; he is to try a third time in April, and if he does not succeed then, we must say that the sea is *un vero precipizio*, and let him try land. By the bye, why not consult Varley on the result? I have tried the *Sors Homeri* and the *Sors Virgilii*; the first says (I will write this Greek better, but I thought that Mr. Gisborne could read the Romaic writing, and I now quite forget what it was)—

Ἡλώμην, τείως μοι ἀδελφεὸν ἄλλος ἔπεφνεν.
ὡς δ᾽ ὁπότ᾽ Ἰασίωνι εὐπλόκαμος Δημήτηρ.
Δουράτεον μέγαν ἵππον, ὅθ᾽ εἵατο πάντες ἄριστοι.

[Pg 330]Which first seems to say that he will come, though his brother may be prosecuted for a libel. Of the second, I can make neither head nor tail; and the third is as oracularly obscure as one could wish, for who these great people are who sat in a wooden horse,*chi lo sa?* Virgil, except the first line, which is unfavourable, is as enigmatical as Homer—

Fulgores nunc horrificos, sonitumque, metumque
Tum leves calamos, et rasæ hastilia virgæ
Connexosque angues, ipsamque in pectore divæ.

But to speak of predictions or anteductions, some of Varley's are curious enough: "Ill-fortune in May or June 1815." No; it was then that he arranged his income; there was no ill except health, *al solito*, at that time. The particular days of the 2d and 14th of June 1820 were not ill, but the whole time was disastrous. It was then we were alarmed by Paolo's attack and disturbance. About a lady in the winter of last year, enough, God knows! Nothing particular about a fat bouncing lady at 10 at night: and indeed things got more quiet in April. In July 1799 Shelley was only seven years of age. "A great blow-up every seven years." Shelley is not at home; when he returns I will ask him what happened when he was fourteen. In his twenty-second year we made our *scappatura*; at twenty-eight and twenty-nine, a good deal of discomfort on a certain point, but it hardly amounted to a blow-up. Pray ask Varley also about me.

So Hogg is shocked that, for good neighbourhood's sake, I visited the *piano di sotto*; let him reassure himself, since instead of a weekly, it was only a monthly visit; in fact, after going three times I stayed away until I heard he was going away. He preached against atheism, and, they said, against Shelley. As he invited me himself to come, this appeared to me very impertinent; so I wrote to him, to ask him whether he intended any personal allusion, but he denied the charge most entirely. This affair, as you may guess, among the English at Pisa made a great noise; the gossip here is of course out of all bounds, and some people have given them something to talk about. I have seen little of it all; but that[Pg 331] which I have seen makes me long most eagerly for some sea-girt isle, where with Shelley, my babe, and books and horses, we may give the rest to the winds; this we shall not have for the present. Shelley is entangled with Lord Byron, who is in a terrible fright lest he should desert him. We shall have boats, and go somewhere on the sea-coast, where, I daresay, we shall spend our time agreeably enough, for I like the Williams' exceedingly, though there my list begins and ends.

Emilia married Biondi; we hear that she leads him and his mother (to use a vulgarism) a devil of a life. The conclusion of our friendship (*a la Italiana*) puts me in mind of a nursery rhyme, which runs thus—

> As I was going down Cranbourne lane,
> Cranbourne lane was dirty,
> And there I met a pretty maid,
> Who dropt to me a curtsey;
>
> I gave her cakes, I gave her wine,
> I gave her sugar-candy,
> But oh! the little naughty girl,
> She asked me for some brandy.

Now turn "Cranbourne Lane" into Pisan acquaintances, which I am sure are dirty enough, and "brandy" into that wherewithal to buy brandy (and that no small sum *però*), and you have the whole story of Shelley's Italian Platonics. We now know, indeed, few of those whom we knew last year. Pacchiani is at Prato; Mavrocordato in Greece; the Argyropolis in Florence; and so the world slides. Taafe is still here—the butt of Lord Byron's quizzing, and the poet laureate of Pisa. On the occasion of a young lady's birthday he wrote—

> Eyes that shed a thousand flowers!
> Why should flowers be sent to you?
> Sweetest flowers of heavenly bowers,
> Love and friendship, are what are due.

....

After some divine *Italian* weather, we are now enjoying some fine English weather; *cioè*, it does not rain, but not a ray can pierce the web aloft.—Most truly yours,

MARY W. S.

[Pg 332]

MARY SHELLEY TO MRS. HUNT.

5th March 1822.

MY DEAREST MARIANNE—I hope that this letter will find you quite well, recovering from your severe attack, and looking towards your haven Italy with best hopes. I do indeed believe that you will find a relief here from your many English cares, and that the winds which waft you will sing the requiem to all your ills. It was indeed unfortunate that you encountered such weather on the very threshold of your journey, and as the wind howled through the long night, how often did I think of you! At length it seemed as if we should never, never meet; but I will not give way to such a presentiment. We enjoy here divine weather. The sun hot, too hot, with a freshness and clearness in the breeze that bears with it all the delights of spring. The hedges are budding, and you should see me and my friend Mrs. Williams poking about for violets by the sides of dry ditches; she being herself—

> A violet by a mossy stone
> Half hidden from the eye.

Yesterday a countryman seeing our dilemma, since the ditch was not quite dry, insisted on gathering them for us, and when we resisted, saying that we had no *quattrini* (*i.e.* farthings, being the generic name for all money), he indignantly exclaimed, *Oh! se lo faccio per interesse!* How I wish you were with us in our rambles! Our good cavaliers flock together, and as they do not like *fetching a walk with the absurd womankind*, Jane (*i.e.* Mrs. Williams) and I are off together, and talk morality and pluck violets by the way. I look forward to many duets with this lady and Hunt. She has a very pretty voice, and a taste and ear for music which is almost miraculous. The harp is her favourite instrument; but we have none, and a very bad piano; however, as it is, we pass very pleasant evenings, though I can hardly bear to hear her sing "Donne l'amore"; it transports me so entirely back to your little parlour at Hampstead—and I see the [Pg 333] piano, the bookcase, the prints, the casts—and hear Mary's *far-ha-ha-a*!

We are in great uncertainty as to where we shall spend the summer. There is a beautiful bay about fifty miles off, and as we have resolved on the sea, Shelley bought a boat. We wished very much to go there; perhaps we shall still, but as yet we can find but one house; but as we are a colony "which moves altogether or not at all," we have not yet made up our minds. The apartments which we have prepared for you in Lord Byron's house will be very warm for the summer; and indeed for the two hottest months I should think that you had better go into the country. Villas about here are tolerably cheap, and they are perfect paradises. Perhaps, as it was with me, Italy will not strike you as so divine at first; but each day it becomes dearer and more delightful; the sun, the flowers, the air, all is more sweet and more balmy than in the *Ultima Thule* that you inhabit.

M. W. S.

The journal for the next few weeks has nothing eventful to record. The preceding letter to Mrs. Hunt gives a simple and pleasing picture of their daily life. Perhaps Mary had never been quite so happy before; she wrote to the Hunts that she thought she grew younger. Both she and Shelley were occasionally ailing, and Shelley's letters show that his spirits suffered depression at times, still, in this respect as well as in health, he was better than he had been in any former spring. The proximity of Byron and his circle was not, however, favourable to inspiration or to literary composition. Byron's temperament acted as a damper to enthusiasm in others, and Shelley, though his estimate of Byron's genius was very high, was perpetually[Pg 334] jarred and crossed by his worldliness and his moral shallowness and vulgarity. He invariably, acted, however, as Byron's true and disinterested friend; and Byron was fully aware of the value of his friendship and of his literary help and criticism.

Trelawny, to whom Byron had taken kindly enough, estimated the difference in the moral worth of the two poets with singular justice.

"I believed in many things then, and believe in some now," he wrote, more than five and thirty years afterwards: "I could not sympathise with Byron, who believed in nothing."

His friendship for Byron, nevertheless, was to be loyal and lasting. But his favourite resort in these Pisan days was the "hospitable and cheerful abode of the Shelleys."

"There," he says, "I found those sympathies and sentiments which the Pilgrim denounced as illusions, believed in as the only realities."

At Byron's social gatherings—riding-parties or dinner-parties—he made a point of getting Shelley if he could; and Shelley was very compliant, although the society of which Byron was the nucleus was neither congenial nor interesting to him, and he always took the first good opportunity of escaping. Daily intercourse of this kind tended gradually to estrange rather than unite the two poets: by accentuating differences it brought into evidence that gulf between their[Pg 335] natures which, in spite of the one touch of kinship that certainly existed, was equally impassable by one and by the other. Besides, the subject of Clare and Allegra, never far below the surface, would occasionally come up, and this was a sore point on both sides. As has already been said, Byron appreciated Shelley, though he did not sympathise with him. In after days he bore public testimony to the purity and unselfishness of Shelley's character and to the upright and disinterested motives which actuated him in all he did. But his respect for Shelley was not so strong as his antipathy to Clare, and Shelley's feeling towards her was regarded by him with a cynical sneer which he had no care to hide, and of which its object could not always be unconscious. It is not wonderful that at times there swept across Shelley's mind, like a black cloud, the conviction that neither a sense of honour nor justice restrained Byron from the basest insinuations. And then again this suspicion would pass away as too dreadful to be entertained.

Meanwhile Clare, in the pursuit of her newly-adopted profession, was thinking of going to Vienna, and she longed for a sight of her child first. She had been unusually long, or she fancied so, without news of Allegra, and she was growing desperately anxious,—with only too good cause, as the event showed. She wrote to Byron, [Pg 336]entreating him to arrange for a visit or an interview. Byron took no notice of her letters. The Shelleys dared not annoy him unnecessarily on the subject, as he had been heard to threaten if they did so to immure Allegra in some secret convent where no one could get at her or even hear of her. Clare, working herself up into a state of half-frenzied excitement, sent them letter after letter, suggesting and urging wild plans (which Shelley was to realise) for carrying off the child by armed force; indeed, one of her schemes seems to have been to take advantage of the projected interview, if granted, for putting this design into execution. Some such proposed breach of faith must have been the occasion of Shelley's answering her—

I know not what to think of the state of your mind, or what to fear for you. Your late plan about Allegra seems to me in its present form pregnant with irremediable infamy to all the actors in it except yourself.

He did not think that in her present excited mental condition she was fit to go to Vienna, and he entreated her to postpone the idea. His advice, often repeated in different words, was, that she should not lose herself in distant and uncertain plans, but "systematise and simplify" her motions, at least for the present, and, if she felt in the least disposed, that she should come and stay with them—

If you like, come and look for houses with me in our boat; it might distract your mind.

[Pg 337]He and Mary had resolved to quit Pisa as soon as the weather made it desirable to do so; but their plans and their anxieties were alike suspended by a temporary excitement of which Mary's account is given in the following letter—

MRS. SHELLEY TO MRS. GISBORNE.

PISA, *6th April 1822*.

MY DEAR MRS. GISBORNE—Not many days after I had written to you concerning the fate which ever pursues us at spring-tide, a circumstance happened which showed that we were not forgotten this year. Although, indeed, now that it is all over, I begin to fear that the King of

Gods and men will not consider it a sufficiently heavy visitation, although for a time it threatened to be frightful enough. Two Sundays ago, Lord Byron, Shelley, Trelawny, Captain Hay, Count Gamba, and Taafe were returning from their usual evening ride, when, near the Porta della Piazza, they were passed by a soldier who galloped through the midst of them knocking up against Taafe. This nice little gentleman exclaimed, "Shall we endure this man's insolence?" Lord Byron replied, "No! we will bring him to an account," and Shelley (whose blood always boils at any insolence offered by a soldier) added, "As you please!" so they put spurs to their horses (*i.e.* all but Taafe, who remained quietly behind), followed and stopped the man, and, fancying that he was an officer, demanded his name and address, and gave their cards. The man who, I believe, was half drunk, replied only by all the oaths and abuse in which the Italian language is so rich. He ended by saying, "If I liked I could draw my sabre and cut you all to pieces, but as it is, I only arrest you," and he called out to the guards at the gate *arrestategli*. Lord Byron laughed at this, and saying *arrestateci pure*, gave spurs to his horse and rode towards the gate, followed by the rest. Lord Byron and Gamba passed, but before the others could, the soldier got under the gateway, called on[Pg 338] the guard to stop them, and drawing his sabre, began to cut at them. It happened that I and the Countess Guiccioli were in a carriage close behind and saw it all, and you may guess how frightened we were when we saw our cavaliers cut at, they being totally unarmed. Their only safety was, that the field of battle being so confined, they got close under the man, and were able to arrest his arm. Captain Hay was, however, wounded in his face, and Shelley thrown from his horse. I cannot tell you how it all ended, but after cutting and slashing a little, the man sheathed his sword and rode on, while the others got from their horses to assist poor Hay, who was faint from loss of blood. Lord Byron, when he had passed the gate, rode to his own house, got a sword-stick from one of his servants, and was returning to the gate, Lung' Arno, when he met this man, who held out his hand saying, *Siete contento?* Lord Byron replied, "No! I must know your name, that I may require satisfaction of you." The soldier said, *Il mio nome è Masi, sono sargente maggiore*, etc. etc. While they were talking, a servant of Lord Byron's came and took hold of the bridle of the sergeant's horse. Lord Byron ordered him to let it go, and immediately the man put his horse to a gallop, but, passing Casa Lanfranchi, one of Lord Byron's servants thought that he had killed his master and was running away; determining that he should not go scot-free, he ran at him with a pitchfork and wounded him. The man rode on a few paces, cried out, *Sono ammazzato*, and fell, was carried to the hospital, the Misericordia bell ringing. We were all assembled at Casa Lanfranchi, nursing our wounded man, and poor Teresa, from the excess of her fright, was worse than any, when what was our consternation when we heard that the man's wound was considered mortal! Luckily none but ourselves knew who had given the wound; it was said by the wise Pisani, to have been one of Lord Byron's servants, set on by his padrone, and they pitched upon a poor fellow merely because *aveva lo sguardo fiero, quanto un assassino*. For some days Masi continued in great danger, but he is now recovering. As long as it was thought he would die, the Government did nothing; but now[Pg 339]that he is nearly well, they have imprisoned two men, one of Lord Byron's servants (the one with the *sguardo fiero*), and the other a servant of Teresa's, who was behind our carriage, both perfectly innocent, but they have been kept *in segreto* these ten days, and God knows when they will be let out. What think you of this? Will it serve for our spring adventure? It is blown over now, it is true, but our fate has, in general, been in common with Dame Nature, and March winds and April showers have brought forth May flowers.

You have no notion what a ridiculous figure Taafe cut in all this—he kept far behind during the danger, but the next day he wished to take all the honour to himself, vowed that all Pisa talked of him alone, and coming to Lord Byron said, "My Lord, if you do not dare ride out to-day, I will alone." But the next day he again changed, he was afraid of being turned out of Tuscany, or of being obliged to fight with one of the officers of the sergeant's regiment, of neither of which things there was the slightest danger, so he wrote a declaration to the Governor to say that he had nothing to do with it; so embroiling himself with Lord Byron, he got between Scylla and Charybdis, from which he has not yet extricated himself; for ourselves, we do not fear any ulterior consequences.

10th April.

We received *Hellas* to-day, and the bill of lading. Shelley is well pleased with the former, though there are some mistakes. The only danger would arise from the vengeance of Masi, but the moment he is able to move, he is to be removed to another town; he is a *pessimo soggetto*, being the crony of Soldaini, Rosselmini, and Augustini, Pisan names of evil fame, which, perhaps, you may remember. There is only one consolation in all this, that if it be our fate to suffer, it is more agreeable, and more safe to suffer in company with five or six than alone. Well! after telling you this long story, I must relate our other news. And first, the Greek Ali Pashaw is dead, and his head sent to Constantinople; the reception of it was celebrated there by the massacre of four thousand Greeks.[Pg 340] The latter, however, get on. The Turkish fleet of 25 sail of the line-of-war vessels, and 40 transports, endeavoured to surprise the Greek fleet in its winter quarters; finding them prepared, they bore away for Lante, and pursued by the Greeks, took refuge in the bay of Naupacto. Here they first blockaded them, and obtained a complete victory. All the soldiers on board the transports, in endeavouring to land, were cut to pieces, and the fleet taken or destroyed. I heard something about Hellenists which greatly pleased me. When any one asks of the peasants of the Morea what news there is, and if they have had any victory, they reply: "I do not know, but for us it is η ταν, η επι τας," being their Doric pronunciation of η ταν, η επι της, the speech of the Spartan mother, on presenting his shield to her son; "With this or on this."

I wish, my dear Mrs. Gisborne, that you would send the first part of this letter, addressed to Mr. W. Godwin at Nash's, Esq., Dover Street. I wish him to have an account of the fray, and you will thus save me the trouble of writing it over again, for what with writing and talking about it, I am quite tired. In a late letter of mine to my father, I requested him to send you *Matilda*. I hope that he has complied with my desire, and, in that case, that you will get it copied and send it to me by the first opportunity, perhaps by Hunt, if he comes at all. I do not mention commissions to you, for although wishing much for the things about which I wrote [we have], for the present, no money to spare. We wish very much to hear from you again, and to hear if there are any hopes of your getting on in your plans, what Henry is doing, and how you continue to like England. The months of February and March were with us as hot as an English June. In the first days of April we have had some very cold weather; so that we are obliged to light fires again. Shelley has been much better in health this winter than any other since I have known him, Pisa certainly agrees with him exceedingly well, which is its only merit, in my eyes. I wish fate had bound us to Naples instead. Percy is quite well; he begins to talk, Italian only now, and to call things *bello* and *buono*, but the droll thing is,[Pg 341] that he is right about the genders. A silk *restito* is *bello*, but a new *frusta* is *bella*. He is a fine boy, full of life, and very pretty. Williams is very well, and they are getting on very well. Mrs. Williams is a miracle of economy, and, as Mrs. Godwin used to call it, makes both ends meet with great comfort to herself and others. Medwin is gone to Rome; we have heaps of the gossip of a petty town this winter, being just in the *coterie* where it was all carried on; but now *Grazie a Messer Domenedio*, the English are almost all gone, and we, being left alone, all subjects of discord and clacking cease. You may conceive what a *bisbiglio* our adventure made. The Pisans were all enraged because the *maledetti inglesi* were not punished; yet when the gentlemen returned from their ride the following day (busy fate) an immense crowd was assembled before Casa Lanfranchi, and they all took off their hats to them. Adieu. *State bene e felice*. Best remembrances to Mr. Gisborne, and compliments to Henry, who will remember Hay as one of the Maremma hunters; he is a friend of Lord Byron's.—Yours ever truly,

MARY W. S.

This affair, and the consequent inquiry and examination of witnesses in connection with it took up several days, on one of which Mary and Countess Guiccioli were under examination for five hours.

In the meantime Byron decided to go to Leghorn for his summer boating; whereupon Shelley wrote and definitively proposed to Clare that she should accompany his party to Spezzia, promising her quiet and privacy, and immunity from annoyance, while she bided her time with regard to Allegra. Clare accepted the offer, and joined them at Pisa on the 15th of April in the expectation of starting very shortly. It turned out, [Pg 342] however, that no suitable houses were, after all, to be had on the coast. This was an unexpected disappointment, and on the 23d she and the Williams' went off to Spezzia for another search. They were hardly on their way when letters were received by Shelley and Mary with the grievous news that Allegra had died of typhus fever in the convent of Bagnacavallo.

[Pg 343]

CHAPTER XVI
APRIL-JULY 1882

"Evil news. Not well."

These few words are Mary's record of this frightful blow. She was again in delicate health, suffering from the same depressing symptoms as before Percy's birth, and for a like reason.

No wonder she was made downright ill by the shock, and by the sickening apprehension of the scene to follow when Clare should hear the news.

On the next day but one—the 25th of April—the travellers returned.

Williams says, in his diary for that day—

Meet S., his face bespoke his feelings. C.'s child was dead, and he had the office to break it to her, or rather not to do so; but, fearful of the news reaching her ears, to remove her instantly from this place.

Shelley could not tell Clare at once. Not while they were in Pisa, and with Byron close by. One, unfurnished, house was to be had, the Casa Magni, in the Bay of Lerici. Thither, on the chance of getting it, they must go, and instantly. Mary's[Pg 344] indisposition must be ignored; she must undertake the negotiations for the house. Within twenty-four hours she was off to Spezzia, with Clare and little Percy, escorted by Trelawny; poor Clare quite unconscious of the burden on her friends' minds. Shelley remained behind another day, to pack up the necessary furniture; but, on the 27th, he with the whole Williams family left Pisa for Lerici. Thence, while waiting for the furniture to arrive by sea, he wrote to Mary at Spezzia.

SHELLEY TO MARY.

LERICI, *Sunday, 28th April 1822.*

DEAREST MARY—I am this moment arrived at Lerici, where I am necessarily detained, waiting the furniture, which left Pisa last night at midnight, and as the sea has been calm and the wind fair, I may expect them every moment. It would not do to leave affairs here in an *impiccio*, great as is my anxiety to see you. How are you, my best love? How have you sustained the trials of the journey? Answer me this question, and how my little babe and Clare are. Now to business—

Is the Magni House taken? if not, pray occupy yourself instantly in finishing the affair, even if you are obliged to go to Sarzana, and send a messenger to me to tell me of your success. I, of course, cannot leave Lerici, to which port the boats (for we were obliged to take two) are directed. But *you* can come over in the same boat that brings you this letter, and return in the evening. I hear that Trelawny is still with you. Tell Clare that, as I must probably in a few days return to Pisa for the affair of the lawsuit, I have brought her box with me, thinking she might be in want of some of its contents.

I ought to say that I do not think there is accommodation for you all at this inn; and that, even if there were, you would be better off at Spezzia; but if the Magni House is taken, then[Pg 345] there is no possible reason why you should not take a row over in the boat that will bring this; but do not keep the men long. I am anxious to hear from you on every account.—Ever yours,

S.

Mary's answer was that she had concluded for Casa Magni, but that no other house was to be had in all that neighbourhood. It was in a neglected condition, and not very roomy or convenient; but, such as it was, it had to accommodate the Williams', as well as the Shelleys, and Clare. Considerable difficulty was experienced by Shelley in obtaining leave for the landing of the furniture; this obstacle got over, they at last took possession.

EDWARD WILLIAMS' JOURNAL.

Wednesday, May 1.—Cloudy, with rain. Came to Casa Magni after breakfast, the Shelleys having contrived to give us rooms. Without them, heaven knows what we should have done. Employed all day putting the things away. All comfortably settled by 4. Passed the evening in talking over our folly and our troubles.

The worst trouble, however, was still impending. Finding how crowded and uncomfortable they were likely to be, Clare, after a day or two, decided that it was best for herself and for every one that she should return to Florence, and announced her intention accordingly. Compelled by the circumstances, Shelley then disclosed to her the true state of the case. Her grief was excessive, but was, after the first, succeeded by a calmness unusual in her and surprising to her friends;[Pg 346] a reaction from the fever of suspense and torment in which she had lived for weeks past, and which were even a harder strain on her powers of endurance than the truth, grievous though that was, putting an end to all hope as well as to all fear. For the present she remained at the Villa Magni.

The ground floor of this habitation was appropriated, as is often done in Italy, for stowing the implements and produce of the land, as rent is paid in kind there. In the autumn you find casks of wine, jars of oil, tools, wood, occasionally carts, and, near the sea, boats and fishing-nets. Over this floor were a large saloon and four bedrooms (which had once been whitewashed), and nothing more; there was an out-building for cooking, and a place for the servants to eat and sleep in. The Williams had one room, and Shelley and his wife occupied two more, facing each other.[47]

Facing the sea, and almost over it, a verandah or open terrace ran the whole length of the building; it was over the projecting ground floor, and level with the inhabited story.

The surrounding scenery was magnificent, but wild to the last degree, and there was something unearthly in the perpetual moaning and howling of winds and waves. Poor Mary now began to feel the ill effects of her enforced over-exertions. She became very unwell, suffering from utter prostration of strength and from hysterical affections. Rest, quiet, and freedom from worry were essential to her condition, but none of these could she have, nor even sleep at night. The absence[Pg 347] of comfort and privacy, added to the great difficulty of housekeeping, and the melancholy with which Clare's misfortune had infected the whole party, were all very unfavourable to her.

After staying for three weeks, Clare returned for a short visit to Florence. Shelley's letters to her during her absence afford occasional glimpses, from which it is easy to infer more, into the state of affairs at Casa Magni. Mrs. Williams was "by no means acquiescent in the present system of things." The plan of having all possessions in common does not work well in the kitchen; the respective servants of the two families were always quarrelling and taking each other's things. Jane, who was a good housekeeper, had the defects of her qualities, and "pined for her own house and saucepans." "It is a pity," remarks Shelley, "that any one so pretty and amiable should be so selfish." Not that these matters troubled him much. Such little "squalls" gave way to calm, "in accustomed vicissitude" (to use his own words); and Mrs. Williams had far too much tact to dwell on domestic worries to him. His own nerves were for a time shaken and unstrung, but he recovered, and, after the first, was unusually well. He was in love with the wild, beautiful place, and with the life at sea; for to his boat he escaped whenever any little breezes ruffled the surface of domestic life so that its mirror no longer reflected his own[Pg 348]unwontedly bright spirits. At first he and Williams had only the small flat-bottomed boat in which they had navigated the Arno and Serchio, but in a fortnight there arrived the little schooner which Captain Roberts had built for Shelley at Genoa, and then their content was perfect.

For Mary no such escape from care and discomfort was open; she was too weak to go about much, and it is no wonder that, after the Williams' installation, she merely chronicles, "The rest of May a blank."

Williams' diary partly fills this blank; and it is so graphic in its exceeding simplicity that, though it has been printed before, portions may well be included here.

EXTRACTS FROM WILLIAMS' DIARY.

Thursday, May 2.—Cloudy, with intervals of rain. Went out with Shelley in the boat—fish on the rocks—bad sport. Went in the evening after some wild ducks—saw nothing but sublime scenery, to which the grandeur of a storm greatly contributed.

Friday, May 3.—Fine. The captain of the port despatched a vessel for Shelley's boat. Went to Lerici with S., being obliged to market there; the servant having returned from Sarzana without being able to procure anything.

Sunday, May 5.—Fine. Kept awake the whole night by a heavy swell, which made a noise on the beach like the discharge of heavy artillery. Tried with Shelley to launch the small flat-bottomed boat through the surf; we succeeded in pushing it through, but shipped a sea on attempting to land. Walk to Lerici along the beach, by a winding path on the mountain's side. Delightful evening,—the scenery most sublime.

[Pg 349]*Monday, May 6.*—Fine. Some heavy drops of rain fell to-day, without a cloud being visible. Made a sketch of the western side of the bay. Read a little. Walked with Jane up the mountain.

After tea walking with Shelley on the terrace, and observing the effect of moonshine on the waters, he complained of being unusually nervous, and stopping short, he grasped me violently by the arm, and stared steadfastly on the white surf that broke upon the beach under our feet. Observing him sensibly affected, I demanded of him if he were in pain. But he only answered by saying, "There it is again—there"! He recovered after some time, and declared that he saw, as plainly as he then saw me, a naked child (Allegra) rise from the sea, and clap its hands as in joy, smiling at him. This was a trance that it required some reasoning and philosophy entirely to awaken him from, so forcibly had the vision operated on his mind. Our conversation, which had been at first rather melancholy, led to this; and my confirming his sensations, by confessing that I had felt the same, gave greater activity to his ever-wandering and lively imagination.

Sunday, May 12.—Cloudy and threatening weather. Wrote during the morning. Mr. Maglian called after dinner, and, while walking with him on the terrace, we discovered a strange sail coming round the point of Porto Venere, which proved at length to be Shelley's boat. She had left Genoa on Thursday, but had been driven back by prevailing bad winds, a Mr. Heslop and two English seamen brought her round, and they speak most highly of her performances. She does, indeed, excite my surprise and admiration. Shelley and I walked to Lerici, and made a stretch off the land to try her, and I find she fetches whatever she looks at. In short, we have now a perfect plaything for the summer.

Monday, May 13.—Rain during night in torrents—a heavy gale of wind from S.W., and a surf running heavier than ever; at 4 gale unabated, violent squalls....

... In the evening an electric arch forming in the clouds announces a heavy thunderstorm, if the wind lulls. Distant[Pg 350] thunder—gale increases—a circle of foam surrounds the bay—dark, evening, and tempestuous, with flashes of lightning at intervals, which give us no hope of better weather. The learned in these things say, that it generally lasts three days when once it commences as this has done. We all feel as if we were on board ship—and the roaring of the sea brings this idea to us even in our beds.

Wednesday, May 15.—Fine and fresh breeze in puffs from the land. Jane and Mary consent to take a sail. Run down to Porto Venere and beat back at 1 o'clock. The boat sailed like a witch. After the late gale, the water is covered with purple nautili, or as the sailors call them, Portuguese men-of-war. After dinner Jane accompanied us to the point of the Magra; and the boat beat back in wonderful style.

Wednesday, May 22.—Fine, after a threatening night. After breakfast Shelley and I amused ourselves with trying to make a boat of canvas and reeds, as light and as small as possible. She is to be 8½ feet long, and 4½ broad....

Wednesday, June 12.—Launched the little boat, which answered our wishes and expectations. She is 86 lbs. English weight, and stows easily on board. Sailed in the evening, but were becalmed in the offing, and left there with a long ground swell, which made Jane little better than dead. Hoisted out our little boat and brought her on shore. Her landing attended by the whole village.

Thursday, June 13.—Fine. At 9 saw a vessel between the straits of Porto Venere, like a man-of-war brig. She proved to be the *Bolivar*, with Roberts and Trelawny on board, who are taking her round to Livorno. On meeting them we were saluted by six guns. Sailed together to try the vessels—in speed no chance with her, but I think we keep as good a wind. She is the most beautiful craft I ever saw, and will do more for her size. She costs Lord Byron £750 clear off and ready for sea, with provisions and conveniences of every kind.

In the midst of this happy life one anxiety there[Pg 351] was, however, which pursued Shelley everywhere; and neither on shore nor at sea could he escape from it,—that of Godwin's imminent ruin.

The first of the letters which follow had reached Mary while still at Pisa. The next letter, and that of Mrs. Godwin were, at Shelley's request, intercepted by Mrs. Mason and sent to him. He could not and would not show them to Mary, and wrote at last to Mrs. Godwin, to try and put a stop to them.

GODWIN TO MARY.

SKINNER STREET, *19th April 1822.*

MY DEAREST MARY—The die, so far as I am concerned, seems now to be cast, and all that remains is that I should entreat you to forget that you have a father in existence. Why should your prime of youthful vigour be tarnished and made wretched by what relates to me? I have lived to the full age of man in as much comfort as can reasonably be expected to fall to the lot of a human being. What signifies what becomes of the few wretched years that remain?

For the same reason, I think I ought for the future to drop writing to you. It is impossible that my letters can give you anything but unmingled pain. A few weeks more, and the formalities which still restrain the successful claimant will be over, and my prospects of tranquillity must, as I believe, be eternally closed.—Farewell,

WILLIAM GODWIN.

GODWIN TO MARY.

SKINNER STREET, *3d May 1822.*

DEAR MARY—I wrote to you a fortnight ago, and professed my intention of not writing again. I certainly will not write when the result shall be to give pure, unmitigated pain. It is the questionable shape of what I have to communicate that still thrusts the pen into my hand. This day we are[Pg 352] compelled, by summary process, to leave the house we live in, and to hide our heads in whatever alley will receive us. If we can compound with our creditor, and he seems not unwilling to accept £400 (I have talked with him on the subject), we may emerge again. Our business, if freed from this intolerable burthen, is more than ever worth keeping.

But all this would, perhaps, have failed in inducing me to resume the pen, but for *one extraordinary accident.* Wednesday, 1st May, was the day when the last legal step was taken against me; and Wednesday morning, a few hours before this catastrophe, Willats, the man who, three or four years before, lent Shelley £2000 at two for one, called on me to ask whether Shelley wanted any more money on the same terms. What does this mean? In the contemplation of such a coincidence, I could almost grow superstitious. But, alas! I fear—I fear—I am a drowning man, catching at a straw.—Ever most affectionately, your father,

WILLIAM GODWIN.

Please to direct your letters, till you hear further, to the care of Mr. Monro, No. 60 Skinner Street.

MRS. MASON TO SHELLEY.

May 1822.

I send you in return for Godwin's letter one still worse, because I think it has more the appearance of truth. I was desired to convey it to Mary, but that I should not think right. At the same time, I don't well know how you can conceal all this affair from her; they really seem to want assistance at present, for their being turned out of the house is a serious evil. I rejoice in your good health, to which I have no doubt the boat and the Williams' much contribute, and wish there may be no prospect of its being disturbed.

Mary ought to know what is said of the novel, and how can she know that without all the rest? You will contrive what is best. In the part of the letter which I do send, she (Mrs. Godwin) adds, that at this moment Mr. Godwin does not offer the novel to any bookseller, lest his actual situation might make it be supposed that it would be sold cheap.[Pg 353] Mrs. Godwin also wishes to correspond directly with Mrs. Shelley, but this I shall not permit; she says Godwin's health is much the worse for all this affair.

I was astonished at seeing Clare walk in on Tuesday evening, and I have not a spare bed now in the house, the children having outgrown theirs, and been obliged to occupy that which I had formerly; she proposed going to an inn, but preferred sleeping on a sofa, where I made her as comfortable as I could, which is but little so; however, she is satisfied. I rejoice to see that she has not suffered so much as you expected, and understand now her former feelings better than at first. When there is nothing to hope or fear, it is natural to be calm. I wish she had some determined project, but her plans seem as unsettled as ever, and she does not see half the reasons for separating herself from your society that really exist. I regret to perceive her great repugnance to Paris, which I believe to be the place best adapted to her. If she had but the temptation of good letters of introduction!—but I have no means of obtaining them for her—she intends, I believe, to go to Florence to-morrow, and to return to your habitation in a week, but talks of not staying the whole summer. I regret the loss of Mary's good health and spirits, but hope it is only the consequence of her present situation, and, therefore, merely temporary, but I dread Clare's being in the same house for a month or two, and wish the Williams' were half a mile from you. I must write a few lines to Mary, but will say nothing of having heard from Mrs. Godwin; you will tell her what you think right, but you know my opinion, that things which cannot be concealed are better told at once. I should suppose a bankruptcy would be best, but the Godwins do not seem to think so. If all the world valued obscure tranquillity as much as I do, it would be a happier, though possibly much duller, world than it is, but the loss of wealth is quite an epidemic disease in England, and it disturbs their rest more than the[48] ... I should have a thousand things to[Pg 354] say, but that I have a thousand other things to do, and you give me hope of conversing with you before long.—Ever yours very sincerely,

M. M.

SHELLEY TO MRS. GODWIN.

LERICI, *29th May 1882.*

DEAR MADAM—Mrs. Mason has sent me an extract from your last letter to show to Mary, and I have received that of Mr. Godwin, in which he mentions your having left Skinner Street.

In Mary's present state of health and spirits, much caution is requisite with regard to communications which must agitate her in the highest degree, and the object of my present letter is simply to inform you that I thought it right to exercise this caution on the present occasion. Mary is at present about three months advanced in pregnancy, and the irritability and languor which accompany this state are always distressing, and sometimes alarming. I do not know even how soon I can permit her to receive such communications, or even how soon you or Mr. Godwin would wish they should be conveyed to her, if you could have any idea of the effect. Do not, however, let me be misunderstood. It is not my intention or my wish that the circumstances in which your family is involved should be concealed from her; but that the detail of them should be suspended until they assume a more prosperous character, or at least till letters addressed to her or intended for her perusal on that subject should not convey a supposition that she could do more than she does, thus exasperating the sympathy which she already feels too intensely for her

Father's distress, which she would sacrifice all she possesses to remedy, but the remedy of which is beyond her power. She imagined that her novel might be turned to immediate advantage for him. I am greatly interested in the fate of this production, which appears to me to possess a high degree of merit, and I regret that it is not Mr. Godwin's intention to publish it immediately. I am sure that Mary would be delighted to amend anything that her Father thought imperfect in it, though I confess that if his objection relates to the [Pg 355]character of Beatrice, *I* shall lament the deference which would be shown by the sacrifice of any portion of it to feelings and ideas which are but for a day. I wish Mr. Godwin would write to her on that subject; he might advert to the letter (for it is only the last one) which I have suppressed, or not, as he thought proper.

I have written to Mr. Smith to solicit the loan of £400, which, if I can obtain in that manner, is very much at Mr. Godwin's service. The views which I now entertain of my affairs forbid me to enter into any further reversionary transactions; nor do I think Mr. Godwin would be a gainer by the contrary determination; as it would be next to impossible to effectuate any such bargain at this distance, nor could I burthen my income, which is only sufficient to meet its various claims, and the system of life in which it seems necessary I should live.

We hear you hear Jane's (Clare's) news from Mrs. Mason. Since the late melancholy event she has become far more tranquil; nor should I have anything to desire with regard to her, did not the uncertainty of my own life and prospects render it prudent for her to attempt to establish some sort of independence as a security against an event which would deprive her of that which she at present enjoys. She is well in health, and usually resides at Florence, where she has formed a little society for herself among the Italians, with whom she is a great favourite. She was here for a week or two; and although she has at present returned to Florence, we expect her on a visit to us for the summer months. In the winter, unless some of her various plans succeed, for she may be called *la fille aux mille projets*, she will return to Florence. Mr. Godwin may depend upon receiving immediate notice of the result of my application to Mr. Smith. I hope soon to have an account of your situation and prospects, and remain, dear Madam, yours very sincerely,

P. B. SHELLEY.

Mrs. Godwin.

We will speak another time, of what is deeply interesting both to Mary and to myself, of my dear William.

[Pg 356]The knowledge of all this on Shelley's mind,—the consciousness that he was hiding it from Mary, and that she was probably more than half aware of his doing so, gave him a feeling of constraint in his daily intercourse with her. To talk with her, even about her father, was difficult, for he could neither help nor hide his feeling of irritation and indignation at the way in which Godwin persecuted his daughter after the efforts she had made in his behalf, and for which he had hardly thanked her.

It would have to come, the explanation; but for the present, as Shelley wrote to Clare, he was content to put off the evil day. Towards the end of the month Mary's health had somewhat improved, and the letter she then wrote to Mrs. Gisborne gives a connected account of all the past incidents.

MARY SHELLEY TO MRS. GISBORNE.

CASA MAGNI, Presso a LERICI,
2d June 1822.

MY DEAR MRS. GISBORNE—We received a letter from Mr. Gisborne the other day, which promised one from you. It is not yet come, and although I think that you are two or three in my debt, yet I am good enough to write to you again, and thus to increase your debt. Nor will I allow you, with one letter, to take advantage of the Insolvent Act, and thus to free yourself from all claims at once. When I last wrote, I said that I hoped our spring visitation had come and was gone, but this year we were not quit so easily. However, before I mention anything else, I will finish the story of the *zuffa* as far as it is yet gone. I think that in my last I left the sergeant recovering; one of Lord Byron's and one of the[Pg 357] Guiccioli's servants in prison on suspicion, though both were innocent. The judge or advocate, called a Cancelliere, sent from Florence to determine the affair, dislikes the Pisans and, having *poca paga*, expected a present from Milordo, and so favoured our part of the affair, was very civil, and came to our houses to take depositions against the law. For the sake of the lesson, Hogg should have been there to learn to cross-question. The Cancelliere, a talkative buffoon of a Florentine, with "mille scuse per l'incomodo," asked, "Dove fu lei la sera del 24 marzo? Andai a spasso in carozza, fuori della Porta della Piaggia." A little clerk, seated beside him, with a great pile of papers before him, now dipped his pen in his ink-horn, and looked expectant, while the Cancelliere, turning his eyes up to the ceiling, repeated, "Io fui a spasso," etc. This scene lasted two, four, six, hours, as it happened. In the space of two months the depositions of fifteen people were taken, and finding Tita (Lord Byron's servant) perfectly innocent, the Cancelliere ordered him to be liberated, but the Pisan police took fright at his beard. They called him "il barbone," and, although it was declared that on his exit from prison he should be shaved, they could not tranquillise their mighty minds, but banished him. We, in the meantime, were come to this place, so he has taken refuge with us. He is an excellent fellow, faithful, courageous, and daring. How could it happen that the Pisans should be frightened at such a *mirabile mostro* of an Italian, especially as the day he was let out of *segreto*, and was a *largee* in prison, he gave a feast to all his fellow-prisoners, hiring chandeliers and plate! But poor Antonio, the Guiccioli's servant, the meekest-hearted fellow in the world, is kept in *segreto*; not found guilty, but punished as such,—*e chi sa* when he will be let out?—so rests the affair.

About a month ago Clare came to visit us at Pisa, and went with the Williams' to find a house in the Gulf of Spezzia, when, during her absence, the disastrous news came of the death of Allegra. She died of a typhus fever, which had been raging in the Romagna; but no one wrote to[Pg 358] say it was there. She had no friends except the nuns of the Convent, who were kind to her, I believe; but you know Italians. If half of the Convent had died of the plague, they would never have written to have had her removed, and so the poor child fell a sacrifice. Lord Byron felt the loss at first bitterly; he also felt remorse, for he felt that he had acted against everybody's counsels and wishes, and death had stamped with truth the many and often-urged prophecies of Clare, that the air of the Romagna, joined to the ignorance of the Italians, would prove fatal to her. Shelley wished to conceal the fatal news from her as long as possible, so when she returned from Spezzia he resolved to remove thither without delay, with so little delay that he packed me off with Clare and Percy the very next day. She wished to return to Florence, but he persuaded her to accompany me; the next day he packed up our goods and chattels, for a furnished house was not to be found in this part of the world, and, like a torrent hurrying everything in its course, he persuaded the Williams' to do the same. They came here; but one house was to be found for us all; it is beautifully situated on the sea-shore, under the woody hills,—but such a place as this is! The poverty of the people is beyond anything, yet they do not appear unhappy, but go on in dirty content, or contented dirt, while we find it hard work to purvey miles around for a few eatables. We were in wretched discomfort at first, but now are in a kind of disorderly order, living from day to day as we can. After the first day or two Clare insisted on returning to Florence, so Shelley was obliged to disclose the truth. You may judge of what was her first burst of grief and despair; however she reconciled herself to her fate sooner than we expected; and although, of course, until she form new ties, she will always grieve, yet she is now tranquil—more tranquil than when prophesying her disaster; she was for ever forming plans for getting her child from a place she judged but too truly would be fatal to her. She has now returned to Florence, and I do not know whether she will join us again. Our colony is much smaller than we expected, which we consider a benefit.[Pg 359] Lord Byron remains with his train at Montenero. Trelawny is to be the commander of his vessel, and of course will be at Leghorn. He is at present at Genoa, awaiting the finishing of this boat. Shelley's boat is a beautiful creature; Henry would admire her greatly; though only 24 feet by 8 feet she is a perfect little ship, and looks twice her size. She had one fault, she was to have been built in partnership with Williams and Trelawny. Trelawny chose the name of the *Don Juan*, and we acceded; but when Shelley took her entirely on himself we changed the name to the *Ariel*. Lord Byron chose to take fire at this, and determined that she should be called after the Poem; wrote to Roberts to have the name painted on the mainsail, and she arrived thus disfigured. For days and nights, full twenty-one, did Shelley and Edward ponder on her anabaptism, and the washing out the primeval stain. Turpentine, spirits of wine, buccata, all were tried, and it became dappled and no more. At length the piece had to be taken out and reefs put, so that the sail does not look worse. I do not know what Lord Byron will say, but Lord and Poet as he is, he could not be allowed to make a coal barge of our boat. As only one house was to be found habitable in this gulf, the Williams' have taken up their abode with us, and their servants and mine quarrel like cats and dogs; and besides, you may imagine how ill a large family agrees with my laziness, when accounts and domestic concerns come to be talked of. *Ma pazienza*. After all the place does not suit me; the people are *rozzi*, and speak a detestable dialect, and yet it is better than any other Italian sea-shore north of Naples. The air is excellent, and you may guess how much better we like it than Leghorn, when, besides, we should have been involved in English society—a thing we longed to get rid of at Pisa. Mr. Gisborne talks of your going to a distant country; pray write to me in time before this takes place, as I want a box from England first, but cannot now exactly name its contents. I am sorry to hear you do not get on, but perhaps Henry will, and make up for all. Percy is well, and Shelley singularly so; this incessant boating does him a great deal of[Pg 360] good. I have been very unwell for some time past, but am better now. I have not even heard of the arrival of my novel; but I suppose for his own sake, Papa will dispose of it to the best advantage. If you see it advertised, pray tell me, also its publisher, etc.

We have heard from Hunt the day he was to sail, and anxiously and daily now await his arrival. Shelley will go over to Leghorn to him, and I also, if I can so manage it. We shall be at Pisa next winter, I believe, fate so decrees. Of course you have heard that the lawsuit went against my Father. This was the summit and crown of our spring misfortunes, but he writes in so few words, and in such a manner, that any information that I could get, through any one, would be a great benefit to me. Adieu. Pray write now, and at length. Remember both Shelley and me to Hogg. Did you get *Matilda* from Papa?—Yours ever,

MARY W. SHELLEY.

Continue to direct to Pisa.

Clare returned to the Casa Magni on the 6th of July. The weather had now become intensely hot, and Mary was again prostrated by it. Alarming symptoms appeared, and after a wretched week of ill health, these came to a crisis in a dangerous miscarriage. She was destitute of medical aid or appliances, and, weakened as she already was, they feared for her life. She had lain ill for several hours before some ice could be procured, and Shelley then took upon himself the responsibility of its immediate use; the event proved him right; and when at last a doctor came, he found her doing well. Her strength, however, was reduced to the lowest ebb; her spirits also; and within a[Pg 361] week of this misfortune her recovery was retarded by a dreadful nervous shock she received through Shelley's walking in his sleep.[49]

While Mary was enduring a time of physical and mental suffering beyond what can be told, and such as no man can wholly understand, Shelley, for his part, was enjoying unwonted health and good spirits. And such creatures are we all that unwonted health in ourself is even a stronger power for happiness than is the sickness of another for depression.

He was sorry for Mary's gloom, but he could not lighten it, and he was persistently content in spite of it. This has led to the supposition that there was, at this time, a serious want of sympathy between Shelley and Mary. His only want, he said in an often-quoted letter, was the presence of those who could feel, and understand him, and he added, "Whether from proximity, and the continuity of domestic intercourse, Mary does not."

It would have been almost miraculous had it been otherwise. Perhaps nothing in the world is harder than for a person suffering from exhausting illness, and from the extreme of nervous and mental depression, to enter into the mood of temporary elation of another person whose spirits, as a rule, are uneven, and in need of constant [Pg 362]support from others. But the context of this very letter of Shelley's shows clearly enough that he meant nothing desperate, no shipwreck of the heart; for, as the people who could "feel, and understand him," he instances his correspondents, Mr. and Mrs. Gisborne, saying that his satisfaction would be complete if only *they* were of the party; although, were his wishes not limited by his hopes, Hogg would also be included. He would have liked a little intellectual stimulus and comradeship. As it was, he was well satisfied with an intercourse of which "words were not the instruments."

I like Jane more and more, and I find Williams the most amiable of companions.

Jane's guitar and her sweet singing were a new and perpetual delight to him, and she herself supplied him with just as much suggestion of an unrealised ideal as was necessary to keep his imagination alive. She, on her side, understood him and knew how to manage him perfectly; as a great man may be understood by a clever woman who is so far from having an intellectual comprehension of him that she is not distressed by the consciousness of its imperfection or its absence, but succeeds by dint of delicate social intuition, guided by just so much sense of humour as saves her from exaggeration, or from blunders; and who understands her great man on his human[Pg 363] side so much better than the poor creature understands himself, as to wind him at will, easily, gracefully, and insensibly, round her little finger. And so, without sacrificing a moment's peace of mind, Jane Williams won over Shelley an ascendency which was pleasing to both and convenient to every one. No better instance could be given of her method than the well-known episode of his sudden proposal to her to overturn the boat, and, together, to "solve the great mystery"; inimitably told by Trelawny. And so the month of June sped away.

"I have a boat here," wrote Shelley to John Gisborne, ... "it cost me £80, and reduced me to some difficulty in point of money. However, it is swift and beautiful, and appears quite a vessel. Williams is captain, and we glide along this delightful bay, in the evening wind, under the summer moon, until earth appears another world. Jane brings her guitar, and if the past and the future could be obliterated, the present would content me so well that I could say with Faust to the present moment, 'Remain; thou art so beautiful.'"

And now, like Faust, having said this, like Faust's, his hour had come.

He heard from Genoa of the Leigh Hunts' arrival, so far, on their journey, and wrote at once to Hunt a letter of warmest welcome to Italy, promising to start for Leghorn the instant he should hear of the Hunts' vessel having sailed for that port.

[Pg 364] Poor Mary, who sends you a thousand loves, has been seriously ill, having suffered a most debilitating miscarriage. She is still too unwell to rise from the sofa, and must take great care of herself for some time, or she would come with us to Leghorn. Lord Byron is in *villeggiatura* near Leghorn, and you will meet besides with a Mr. Trelawny, a wild, but kindhearted seaman.

The Hunts sailed; and, on the 1st of July, Shelley and Williams, with Charles Vivian, the sailor-lad who looked after their boat, started in the *Ariel* for Leghorn, where they arrived safely. Thence Shelley, with Leigh Hunt, proceeded to Pisa. It had not been their intention to stay long, but Shelley found much to detain him. Matters with respect to Byron and the projected magazine wore a most unsatisfactory appearance; Byron's eagerness had cooled, and his reception of the Hunts was chilling in the extreme. Poor Mrs. Hunt was very seriously ill, and the letter which Mary received from her husband was mainly to explain his prolonged absence. She had let him go from her side with the greatest unwillingness; she was haunted by the gloomiest forebodings and a sense of unexplained misery which they all ascribed to her illness, and her letters were written in a tone of depression which made Shelley anxious on her account, and Edward Williams on that of his wife, who, he feared, might be unhappy during his absence from her.

[Pg 365] But Jane wrote brightly, and gave an improved account of Mary.

SHELLEY TO MARY.

PISA, *4th July 1822.*

MY DEAREST MARY—I have received both your letters, and shall attend to the instructions they convey. I did not think of buying the *Bolivar*; Lord Byron wishes to sell her, but I imagine would prefer ready money. I have as yet made no inquiries about houses near Pugnano—I have had no moment of time to spare from Hunt's affairs. I am detained unwillingly here, and you will probably see Williams in the boat before me, but that will be decided to-morrow.

Things are in the worst possible situation with respect to poor Hunt. I find Marianne in a desperate state of health, and on our arrival at Pisa sent for Vaccà. He decides that her case is hopeless, and, although it will be lingering, must end fatally. This decision he thought proper to communicate to Hunt, indicating at the same time with great judgment and precision the treatment necessary to be observed for availing himself of the chance of his being deceived. This intelligence has extinguished the last spark of poor Hunt's spirits, low enough before. The children are well and much improved. Lord Byron is at this moment on the point of leaving Tuscany. The Gambas have been exiled, and he declares his intention of following their fortunes. His first idea was to sail to America, which was changed to Switzerland, then to Genoa, and last to Lucca. Everybody is in despair, and everything in confusion. Trelawny was on the point of sailing to Genoa for the purpose of transporting the *Bolivar* overland to the Lake of Geneva, and had already whispered in my ear his desire that I should not influence Lord Byron against this terrestrial navigation. He next received *orders* to weigh anchor and set sail for Lerici. He is now without instructions, moody and disappointed. But it is the worse for poor Hunt, unless the present storm should blow over. He places his [Pg 366] whole dependence upon the scheme of the journal, for which every arrangement has been made. Lord Byron must, of course, furnish the requisite funds at present, as I cannot; but he seems inclined to depart without the necessary explanations and arrangements due to such a situation as Hunt's. These, in spite of delicacy, I must procure; he offers him the copyright of the *Vision of Judgment* for the first number. This offer, if sincere, is *more* than enough to set up the journal, and, if sincere, will set everything right.

How are you, my best Mary? Write especially how is your health, and how your spirits are, and whether you are not more reconciled to staying at Lerici, at least during the summer. You have no idea how I am hurried and occupied; I have not a moment's leisure, but will write by next post. Ever, dearest Mary, yours affectionately,

S.

I have found the translation of the *Symposium*.

SHELLEY TO JANE WILLIAMS.

PISA, *4th July 1822.*

You will probably see Williams before I can disentangle myself from the affairs with which I am now surrounded. I return to Leghorn to-night, and shall urge him to sail with the first fair wind without expecting me. I have thus the pleasure of contributing to your happiness when deprived of every other, and of leaving you no other subject of regret but the absence of one scarcely worth regretting. I fear you are solitary and melancholy at the Villa Magni, and, in the intervals of the greater and more serious distress in which I am compelled to sympathise here, I figure to myself the countenance which has been the source of such consolation to me, shadowed by a veil of sorrow.

How soon those hours passed, and how slowly they return, to pass so soon again, and perhaps for ever, in which we have lived together so intimately, so happily! Adieu, my dearest friend. I only write these lines for the pleasure of tracing what will meet your eyes. Mary will tell you all the news.

S.

FROM JANE WILLIAMS TO SHELLEY.

6th July.

MY DEAREST FRIEND—Your few melancholy lines have indeed cast your own visionary veil over a countenance that was animated with the hope of seeing you return with far different tidings. We heard yesterday that you had left Leghorn in company with the *Bolivar*, and would assuredly be here in the morning at 5 o'clock; therefore I got up, and from the terrace saw (or I dreamt it) the *Bolivar* opposite in the offing. She hoisted more sail, and went through the Straits. What can this mean? Hope and uncertainty have made such a chaos in my mind that I know not what to think. My own Neddino does not deign to lighten my darkness by a single word. Surely I shall see him to-night. Perhaps, too, you are with him. Well, *pazienza*!

Mary, I am happy to tell you, goes on well; she talks of going to Pisa, and indeed your poor friends seem to require all her assistance. For me, alas! I can only offer sympathy, and my fervent wishes that a brighter cloud may soon dispel the present gloom. I hope much from the air of Pisa for Mrs. Hunt.

Lord B.'s departure gives me pleasure, for whatever may be the present difficulties and disappointments, they are small to what you would have suffered had he remained with you. This I say in the spirit of prophecy, so gather consolation from it.

I have only time left to scrawl you a hasty adieu, and am affectionately yours,

J. W.

Why do you talk of never enjoying moments like the past? Are you going to join your friend Plato, or do you expect I shall do so soon? *Buona notte.*

Mary was slowly getting better, and hoping to feel brighter by the time Shelley came back. On the 7th of July she wrote a few lines in her journal, summing up the month during which she had left it untouched.

Sunday, July 7.—I am ill most of this time. Ill, and then convalescent. Roberts and Trelawny arrive with the *Bolivar*. On Monday, 16th June, Trelawny goes on to Leghorn with her. Roberts remains here until 1st July, when the Hunts being arrived, Shelley goes in the boat with him and Edward to Leghorn. They are still there. Read *Jacopo Ortis*, second volume of *Geographica Fisica*, etc. etc.

Next day, Monday the 8th, when the voyagers were expected to return, it was so stormy all day at Lerici that their having sailed was considered out of the question, and their non-arrival excited no surprise in Mary or Jane. So many possibilities and probabilities might detain them at Leghorn or Pisa, that their wives did not get anxious for three or four days; and even then what the two women dreaded was not calamity at sea, but illness or disagreeable business on shore. On Thursday, however, getting no letters, they did become uneasy, and, but for the rough weather, Jane Williams would have started in a row-boat for Leghorn. On Friday they watched with feverish anxiety for the post; there was but one letter, and it turned them to stone. It was to Shelley, from Leigh Hunt, begging him to write and say how he had got home in the bad weather of the previous Monday. And then it dawned upon them—a dawn of darkness. There was no news; there would be no news any more.

One minute had untied the knot, and solved the great mystery. The *Ariel* had gone down in the storm, with all hands on board.

And for four days past, though they had not known it, Mary Shelley and Jane Williams had been widows.

END OF VOL. I

Printed by R. & R. CLARK, *Edinburgh.*

AT ALL BOOKSELLERS.
WORD PORTRAITS OF FAMOUS WRITERS.
EDITED BY MABEL E. WOTTON.
In large crown 8vo. 7s. 6d.

'"The world has always been fond of personal details respecting men who have been celebrated." These were the words of Lord Beaconsfield, and with them he prefixed his description of the personal appearance of Isaac d'Israeli.... The above work contains an account of the face, figure, dress, voice, and manner of our best known writers, ranging from Geoffrey Chaucer to Mrs. Henry Wood—drawn in all cases, when it is possible, by their contemporaries. British writers only are named, and amongst them no living author.'—FROM THE PREFACE.

CONTENTS.

Joseph Addison.
Harrison Ainsworth.
Jane Austen.
Francis, Lord Bacon.
Joanna Baillie.
Benjamin, Lord Beaconsfield.
Jeremy Bentham.
Richard Bentley.
James Boswell.
Charlotte Brontë.
Henry, Lord Brougham.
Elizabeth Barrett Browning.
John Bunyan.
Edmund Burke.
Robert Burns.
Samuel Butler.
George, Lord Byron.
Thomas Campbell.
Thomas Carlyle.
Thomas Chatterton.
Geoffrey Chaucer.
Philip, Lord Chesterfield.
William Cobbett.
Hartley Coleridge.
Samuel Taylor Coleridge.
William Collins.
William Cowper
George Crabbe.
Daniel De Foe.
Charles Dickens.
Isaac D'Israeli.
John Dryden.
Mary Anne Evans (George Eliot).
Henry Fielding.
John Gay.
Edward Gibbon.
William Godwin.
Oliver Goldsmith.
David Gray.
Thomas Gray.
Henry Hallam.
William Hazlitt.
Felicia Hemans.
James Hogg.
Thomas Hood.
Theodore Hook.
David Hume.
Leigh Hunt.
Elizabeth Inchbald.
Francis, Lord Jeffrey.
Douglas Jerrold.
Samuel Johnson.
Ben Jonson.
John Keats.

Walter Savage Landor.
Charles Lever.
Matthew Gregory Lewis.
John Gibson Lockhart.
Sir Richard Lovelace.
Edward, Lord Lytton.
Thomas Babington Macaulay.
William Maginn.
Francis Mahony (Father Prout).
Frederick Marryat.
Harriet Martineau.
Frederick Denison Maurice.
John Milton.
Mary Russell Mitford.
Lady Mary Wortley Montagu.
Thomas Moore.
Hannah More.
Sir Thomas More.
Caroline Norton.
Thomas Otway.
Samuel Pepys.
Alexander Pope.
Bryan Waller Procter.
Thomas de Quincey.
Ann Radcliffe.
Sir Walter Raleigh.
Charles Reade.
Samuel Richardson.
Samuel Rogers.
Dante Gabriel Rossetti.
Richard Savage.
Sir Walter Scott.
William Shakespeare.
Mary Wollstonecraft Shelley.
Percy Bysshe Shelley.
Richard Brinsley Sheridan.
Sir Philip Sidney.
Horace Smith.
Sydney Smith.
Tobias Smollett.
Robert Southey.
Edmund Spenser.
Arthur Penrhyn Stanley.
Sir Richard Steele.
Laurence Sterne.
Sir John Suckling.
Jonathan Swift.
William Makepeace Thackeray.
James Thomson.
Anthony Trollope.
Edmund Waller.
Horace Walpole.
Izaac Walton.
John Wilson.

John Keble.
Charles Kingsley.
Charles Lamb.
Letitia Elizabeth Landon.

Ellen Wood (Mrs. Henry Wood).
William Wordsworth.
Sir Henry Wotton.

RICHARD BENTLEY & SON, NEW BURLINGTON STREET,
Publishers in Ordinary to Her Majesty the Queen.

Footnotes:

[1] "Address to the Irish People."

[2] Possibly this may refer to Count Schlaberndorf, an expatriated Prussian subject, who was imprisoned in Paris during the Reign of Terror, and escaped, but subsequently returned, and lived there in retirement, almost in concealment. He was a cynic, an eccentric, yet a patriot withal. He was divorced from his wife, and Shelley had probably got hold of a wrong version of his story.

[3] Byron.

[4] *Ibid.*

[5]
Thy dewy looks sink in my breast;
Thy gentle words stir poison there;
Thou hast disturbed the only rest
That was the portion of despair!
Subdued to Duty's hard control,
I could have borne my wayward lot:
The chains that bind this ruined soul
Had cankered then, but crushed it not.

[6] See his letter to Baxter, quoted before.

[7] *Journal of a Six Weeks' Tour.*

[8] *Journal of a Six Weeks' Tour.*

[9] *Journal of a Six Weeks' Tour.*

[10] The bailiffs.

[11] She was staying temporarily at Skinner Street.

[12] Referring to Fanny's letter, enclosed.

[13] Peacock's mother.

[14] A friend of Harriet Shelley's.

[15] It is presumed that these were for Clara, in answer to an advertisement for a situation as companion.

[16] Godwin's friend and amanuensis.

[17] Which, unfortunately, may not be published.

[18] From this time Miss Clairmont is always mentioned as Clare, or Claire, except by the Godwins, who adhered to the original "Jane."

[19] Byron.

[20] Word obliterated.

[21] Matthew Gregory Lewis, known as "Monk" Lewis.

[22] Hogg.

[23] *Revolt of Islam*, Dedication.

[24] *Revolt of Islam*, Dedication.

[25] The work referred to would seem to be Shelley's Oxford pamphlet.

[26] Baxter's son.

[27] Mr. Booth.

[28] What this accusation was does not appear.

[29] Alba.

[30] Shelley's solicitor.

[31] The nursemaid.

[32] Mrs. Hunt.

[33] See Godwin's letter to Baxter, chap. iii.

[34] Preface to *Prometheus Unbound.*

[35] Page 205.

[36] In *Frankenstein.*

[37] *Notes to Shelley's Poems*, by Mrs. Shelley.
[38] Letter to Mr. Gisborne, of June 18, 1822.
[39] Letter of Shelley's to Mr. Gisborne. (The passage, in the original, has no personal reference to Byron.)
[40] Announcing the stoppage of Shelley's income.
[41] "The Boat on the Serchio."
[42] *Notes to Shelley's Poems*, by Mary Shelley.
[43] Godwin's *Answer to Malthus*.
[44] This initial has been printed C. Mrs. Shelley's letter leaves no doubt that Elise's is the illness referred to.
[45] Trelawny's "Recollections."
[46] Williams' journal for this last day runs—
February 18.—Jane unwell. S. turns physician. Called on Lord B., who talks of getting up *Othello*. Laid a wager with S. that Lord B. quits Italy before six months. Jane put on a Hindostanee dress and passed the evening with Mary, who had also the Turkish costume.
[47] Trelawny's "Recollections."
[48] Word illegible.
[49] Recounted at length in a subsequent letter, to be quoted later on.

Printed in Great Britain
by Amazon